REFORM AND REACTION: CITY POLITICS IN TOLEDO

NEW FRONTIERS IN AMERICAN POLITICS SERIES

L. Harmon Zeigler, Jr., General Editor
University of Oregon

CONGRESS IN CRISIS: POLITICS AND CONGRESSIONAL REFORM
Roger H. Davidson, David M. Kovenock (Dartmouth College)
Michael K. O'Leary (Syracuse University)

REFORM AND REACTION: CITY POLITICS IN TOLEDO
Jean L. Stinchcombe (University of Michigan)

FORTHCOMING VOLUMES:

STATE POLITICS: LOBBYIST-LEGISLATIVE INTERACTION
L. Harmon Zeigler, Jr., (University of Oregon)

BUREAUCRATIC COMMUNICATIONS
Benjamin Walter (Vanderbilt University)

AN AMERICAN POLITICAL DILEMMA: COMMUNITY EDUCATIONAL POLITICS
Robert Agger (University of Oregon)
Marshall Goldstein (University of Hawaii)

Wadsworth Publishing Company, Inc., Belmont, California

REFORM AND REACTION: CITY POLITICS IN TOLEDO

JEAN L. STINCHCOMBE
University of Michigan

Wadsworth Publishing Company, Inc., Belmont, California

L. C. Cat. Card No.: 68–20741

Printed in the United States of America

NEW FRONTIERS IN AMERICAN POLITICS SERIES

Political science is a changing discipline, but the changes that are taking place are not very different from those that took place in other social sciences a good many years ago. Briefly, political scientists are becoming interested in empirical (some would say ''causal'') theory and are seeking the appropriate methodologies that will enable them to develop reliable descriptions of recurring patterns in political life. The nature of the articles that are published in professional journals and monographs, which are no longer the exclusive property of university presses, attest to the general improvement of the discipline. Scholars are beginning to be a little self-conscious about using the term ''behavior'' as though it designated a specific and unique ''branch'' of political science.

Graduate education in political science is reflective of this trend. Most departments of political science require that their students acquire a level of sophistication in statistics and research design that would have been considered extreme as late as ten years ago. Thus, a majority of graduate students, rather than a minority as was formerly the case, begin their teaching careers with an appreciation for the importance of a systematic study of political life.

However, one must question the extent to which undergraduate students are exposed to political science research—as it is being conducted today. After all, very few undergraduate students, even if they are political science majors, go to graduate school; and the proportion of political science students who are aware of new developments in research technique or new explorations of "old" substantive areas is probably unfortunately small. Although each year sees the appearance of more texts that rely heavily upon recently published material, one frequently hears the argument that much of the current research is over the heads of undergraduates and must be distilled and compressed to be useful.

It is the assumption of this series that a fruitful way to introduce students to political science research is to let them read it for themselves. They can see the problem faced by the researcher, judge the validity or logic of the methods, evaluate the extent to which evidence is supportive of the conclusions, and formulate some idea of the nature of social research. There is no reason why the pedagogical assumptions of undergraduate instruction should differ from those of the graduate program. If there are facts of political and social life worth knowing, all students should be made aware of them.

L. Harmon Zeigler, Jr.
Series Editor

University of Oregon

CONTENTS

TABLES AND FIGURES

ACKNOWLEDGMENTS

Many people have been of help in this study. Particular thanks are due to M. Kent Jennings, who provided valuable suggestions and ideas from the inception of the study (as a possible dissertation subject) to publication. Arthur W. Bromage, Robert S. Friedman, and William A. Gamson also caused me to ponder problems in research and writing which might otherwise have escaped my attention.

I would also like to thank the community leaders and other citizens of Toledo, who were promised anonymity; the time, information, and assistance they gave me were invaluable.

Finally, I am grateful to Linda and Gordon Wilcox and Suzanne and Charles Mayer for their interest and contributions, and to my husband, William Stinchcombe, for his help throughout the study. Thanks, also, to my parents, Mr. and Mrs. Eldridge Lovelace, and my brother, Richard Lovelace, for their interest and assistance.

The Woodrow Wilson National Fellowship Foundation provided generous financial support for this research.

J. L. S.

University of Michigan

For Bill

1 INTRODUCTION: LITERATURE AND RESEARCH PURPOSES

This study of community politics and decision-making in Toledo, Ohio, places emphasis on the relation between formal governmental institutions and informal patterns of political participation and influence in the community. In particular, an effort is made to assess the impact of the council-manager form of government, nonpartisanship, and at-large elections on various facets of politics and decision-making in an industrial city of 390,000.

What are the characteristics and consequences of such institutions in one of the relatively few large cities to have these governmental forms?[1] To what extent do governmental institutions affect community leadership and action, the local political structure, and the participation and influence of various groups in the community? These concerns have their origins in traditional and contemporary political science, for political scientists have had a long-standing interest in the study of governmental institutions as important determinants of public decisions. However, this interest in institutions has become, in the view of some critics, an excessive preoccupation, which has resulted in a neglect of other influences affecting public policy and shaping the nature of the institutions themselves. Studies

---

[1] Four cities over 500,000 have the council-manager plan. They are Dallas, San Antonio, San Diego, and Cincinnati. Twelve cities from 250,000 to 500,000 also have it: Kansas City, Phoenix, Oakland, Fort Worth, Long Beach, Oklahoma City, Rochester, Toledo, Norfolk, Miami, Dayton, and Wichita.

1

of institutions which fail to describe the political processes within them and the relation of governmental institutions to a particular social and economic context are correctly considered sterile and insignificant. Yet efforts to study political behavior without including governmental institutions are equally misleading.

The Study of Local Government

Traditional approaches. Before 1945, political science was, to a great degree, devoted to a normative rather than an empirical consideration of institutions of local government. Many political scientists were closely identified with the municipal reform movement. Reformers believed that increased efficiency, honesty, and democracy at the local level could be assured by such provisions as the initiative, recall, and referendum; the direct primary; the nonpartisan ballot; off-year, at-large elections; and the council-manager form of government.

Political scientists studying local government often shared the reform conviction that institutional and legal arrangements determine the kind of political system which prevails in a community. Much of the literature of the first half of this century presented unsubstantiated declarations about the beneficial effects of nonpartisanship in producing independent voting, the irrelevancy of parties at the local level, and the association of good business practices with the council-manager form of government. Political scientists reflected the reform belief that running a city is largely a matter of efficient management of service functions rather than one of issues, politics, and conflict. Writers such as Frank G. Bates, Robert C. Brooks, Richard S. Childs, and Ellen D. Ellis presented a message about local government rather than an empirically based discussion.[2] Textbooks, as well as specialized works, were long committed to orthodox prescriptions about municipal government.[3]

---

[2] Frank G. Bates, ''Nonpartisan Government,'' *American Political Science Review*, IX (May 1915), 313–315; Richard S. Childs, *Civic Victories* (New York: Harper and Row, 1952); Ellen D. Ellis, ''National Parties and Local Politics,'' *American Political Science Review*, XXIX (February 1935), 60–67; Robert C. Brooks, *Political Parties and Electoral Problems* (New York: Harper and Row, 1923).

[3] For a comment on textbooks in municipal government, see Lawrence J. R. Herson, ''The Lost World of Municipal Government,'' *American Political Science Review*, LI (June 1957), 330–345.

In recent years the polemical approach has given way to a great variety of empirical studies on community decision-making. These studies are basically concerned with the distribution of power and the location of leadership in a community. They attempt to isolate actual and potential decision-makers; they examine why and how certain decisions are made and the consequences of this process of decision-making for the political system.

The initial impetus for the study of community decision-making came from Floyd Hunter's *Community Power Structure*, published in 1953.[4] Hunter, a sociologist, stimulated a new interest in the local community and the development of new perspectives for studying it. He turned attention from formal and moral considerations to the fundamental questions of who makes community decisions, whose interests are served, and whose interests are injured. Hunter attempted to determine who had power and how it was used to make decisions and resolve conflicts. After asking officials in four community organizations to name top community leaders, Hunter studied the leadership designations and interactions of these people. He concluded that power is concentrated in a small, cohesive elite of business leaders and that political structure is subservient to the predominant economic leaders of a community.

Soon after publication of *Community Power Structure*, Hunter's methodology and variations of it were applied in other cities;[5] and new literature on the local community rapidly appeared, largely within the field of sociology. Finally, after several years, the concept of the community power structure aroused the interest of political scientists. They used Floyd Hunter's methodology and conclusions as a stalking horse in their attempt to define their approach to community decision-making. They suspected the sociologists' assumption that a reputation for power is a measure of the actual distribution of power. They suggested that the technique of studying leaders ranked as the most influential presupposes rather than demonstrates the existence of an elite. Wolfinger, Polsby,

[4] Chapel Hill: University of North Carolina Press.

[5] See, for example, Donald W. Olmsted, "Organizational Leadership and Social Structure in a Small City," *American Sociological Review*, XIX (June 1954), 273–281; Peter H. Rossi, "Community Decision-Making," *Administrative Science Quarterly*, I (March 1957), 415–443; William V. D'Antonio and Eugene C. Erickson, "The Reputational Technique as a Measure of Community Power," *American Sociological Review*, XXVII (June 1962), 362–376; and Delbert C. Miller, "Decision-Making Cliques in Community Power Structures: A Comparative Study of an American and an English City," *American Journal of Sociology*, LIV (November 1958), 229–310.

Kaufman and Jones, and other political scientists contended that the identification of reputational leaders is an inadequate description of a political system: Such an approach studies power indirectly at best, assumes a static distribution of power, and fails to discriminate between actual and potential power. They argued that rather than reputational rankings and hearsay evidence, actual activity in particular decisions and concrete data pertaining to decisions and events should constitute the basis for research in community affairs.[6]

The outstanding community study in political science and the source for the pluralist or decisional approach is Robert A. Dahl's *Who Governs?*[7] Dahl's study of New Haven, unlike Hunter's discussion of Atlanta, is concerned with change over time and within the system.[8] Dahl is impressed with the variety within the political system, the fragmentation of influence, and the multiple possibilities for mobilizing this influence. By studying historical changes in the city and its officeholders, examining decisions in several issue areas, and analyzing patterns in voting results and community participation, Dahl demonstrated the variability of influence in New Haven. Scopes of power were found to be largely specialized rather than general. Community leadership took the form of changing patterns, such as rival sovereignties, spheres of influence, or an executive-centered coalition. Instead of a cohesive ruling elite, Dahl found a "slack system," in which dispersed resources could be exploited and pyramided in many ways.

In spite of the virtually universal praise accorded it, *Who Governs?*, as well as the pluralist creed defined by Nelson Polsby and Raymond Wolfinger, can be criticized on several grounds. Peter

[6] See Herbert Kaufman and Victor Jones, "The Mystery of Power," *Public Administration Review*, XIV (Summer 1954), 205–212; Nelson Polsby, "The Sociology of Community Power: A Reassessment," *Social Forces*, XXXVII (March 1959), 232–236; and Raymond Wolfinger, "Reputation and Reality in the Study of Community Power," *American Sociological Review*, XXV (October 1960), 636–644. For a strong statement in behalf of the reputational approach, see William A. Gamson, "Reputation and Resources in Community Politics," *American Journal of Sociology*, LXXII (September 1966), 121–131.

[7] New Haven, Conn.: Yale University Press, 1961.

[8] Other studies employing the reputational technique do not share the ahistorical character of *Community Power Structure*, however. See Robert Schulze, "The Bifurcation of Power in a Satellite City," Morris Janowitz, ed., *Community Political Systems* (New York: The Free Press, 1961), pp. 19–81.

Bachrach and Morton Baratz contend that while the pluralists' criticisms of elitists are sound, the pluralists have assumed that power is fully embodied in concrete decisions or activity bearing on these decisions. This assumption places the emphasis on initiating, deciding, and vetoing rather than on the less apparent repression of issues or limitation of the scope of community action.[9]

The reputational and decisional approaches of *Community Power Structure* and *Who Governs?* also share defects largely neglected in the methodological controversy. Both Hunter and Dahl concentrate on the leadership pattern within the community as a whole rather than on the extent of the contribution of different groups and organizations to this pattern. Because of this emphasis, Dahl fails to analyze the effects of political parties on community power. Yet the presence of a strong party system may have a significant impact on the patterns of influence which he is describing.[10] Similarly, Hunter fails to account for the community role of political alliances and Negro organizations, which other studies have shown to be important in Atlanta.[11]

Governmental institutions and their effects in defining the rules and rituals of local politics are not described in either *Community Power Structure* or *Who Governs?* Dahl examines the representation of ethnic groups in city government, but he does not consider the possible effects of the electoral system on this process. Nor does he discuss the ability and impact of governmental institutions in mobilizing influence or pyramiding resources. Dahl focuses on New Haven's mayor, Richard Lee, as an admirable leader and political builder, but he fails to consider the effect of the governmental institutions of New Haven—a mayor-council plan with partisan elections. Further, he fails to recognize that many cities of New Haven's size have a council-manager form of government with nonpartisan elections.[12]

[9] Peter Bachrach and Morton Baratz, ''The Two Faces of Power,'' *American Political Science Review*, LVI (September 1962), 947–953.

[10] For a discussion of this, see Hugh Douglas Price's review of *Who Governs?*, *Yale Law Review*, LXI (July 1962), 1589–1596.

[11] See M. Kent Jennings and Harmon Zeigler, ''Class, Party, and Race in Four Types of Elections: The Case of Atlanta,'' *Journal of Politics*, XXVIII (June 1966), 391–407.

[12] This fact was noted by Price, in his review of *Who Governs?* (see *n.* 10). At the time of the 1960 Census New Haven had a population of 152,048. Only 37 per cent of the cities between 100,000 and 250,000 in population have the

The advantages and defects of the reputational and decisional approaches have generated a number of studies adopting a middle course. Robert Schulze, Kent Jennings, Robert Presthus, Linton Freeman, and others have shown the value of combining techniques.[13] Historical evidence, case studies, election analysis, and other techniques used in earlier research can provide complementary perspectives on community decision-making.

Contemporary approaches. Recent empirical studies have used a variety of techniques to examine the role of major groups and organizations in the community. Robert Schulze, Delbert Miller, and Kent Jennings have considered business leaders as economic dominants.[14] Charles Adrian and Gladys Kammerer have examined the community role of city managers.[15] Political leadership in two contrasting communities has been investigated by Robert T. Daland and Lincoln Smith.[16] William H. Form, Warren Sauer, and James McKee have considered the reputed influence of organized labor in several cities; and James Q. Wilson has produced the outstanding study of Negro leadership in the context of city politics.[17] These studies have provided a valuable balance to the emphasis on the "top leaders" in a community. Also, in their analysis of the role of important components of the community, these studies provide a

---

mayor-council plan. See John H. Kessel, "Governmental Structure and Political Environment: A Statistical Note about American Cities," *American Political Science Review*, LVI (September 1962), 615–620.

[13] Schulze, "The Bifurcation of Power in a Satellite City"; M. Kent Jennings, *Community Influentials: The Elites of Atlanta* (New York: The Free Press, 1964); Linton Freeman, *et al.*, "Locating Leaders in Local Communities," *American Sociological Review*, XXVIII (October 1963), 791–798; and Robert Presthus, *Men at the Top* (New York: Oxford University Press, 1964).

[14] Schulze, "The Bifurcation of Power"; Jennings, *Community Influentials: The Elites of Atlanta*; Delbert Miller, "The Seattle Business Leader," *Pacific Northwest Business*, XV (February 1956), 5–12.

[15] Charles R. Adrian, "Leadership and Decision-Making in Manager Cities: A Study of Three Communities," *Public Administration Review*, XVIII (Summer 1958), 208–213; and Gladys Kammerer, "Role Diversity in City Managers," *Administrative Science Quarterly*, VIII (March 1964), 421–442.

[16] Robert T. Daland, *Dixie City: A Portrait of Political Leadership* (Tuscaloosa: University of Alabama, Bureau of Public Administration, 1956); Lincoln Smith, "Political Leadership in a New England Community," *Review of Politics*, XVII (July 1955), 392–409.

[17] William H. Form and Warren L. Sauer, "Organized Labor's Image of Community Power Structure," *Social Forces*, XXVIII (May 1960), 332–341; James B. McKee, "Status and Power in the Industrial Community: A Comment on Drucker's Thesis," *American Journal of Sociology*, LVIII (January 1953), 364–370; James Q. Wilson, *Negro Politics* (New York: The Free Press, 1960).

useful vantage point for studying community decision-making and for checking the observations about power structures drawn from other approaches.

Other recent research has focused on the relation between governmental institutions and community power, politics, and policies and has presented empirical consideration of questions originally raised by reform political scientists. Efforts to assess the impact of institutions on patterns of influence, group participation, party politics, and community policies indicate a convergence of traditional political science and contemporary interest in the community power structure.

An excellent example of this perspective is *Four Cities* by Oliver Williams and Charles Adrian.[18] Williams and Adrian utilize case studies, interview data, and election analysis in this comparative study of four middle-sized Michigan cities. They concentrate on the relation between community characteristics, policies, and the role of the local government as a caretaker, civic booster, arbiter of interests, or provider of life's amenities. Specific questions about nonpartisanship, at-large or ward elections, and the role of mayor, council, and manager are examined in each city; various propositions about these governmental institutions and their effects on leadership, politics, and policies are tested.

A number of articles also examine the interrelation of governmental institutions and various facets of community politics and power. J. Leiper Freeman, for example, has studied the impact of election laws and other variables in local politics in "Bay City," Massachusetts.[19] In contrast to the tenets of reform doctrine, he found election laws less significant for the local party system than the social structure and the character of the national party organizations. Charles Gilbert attempted to evaluate the consequences of nonpartisanship for party politics, community policies, and presidential voting in a number of cities and found it difficult to ascertain any effects.[20] Eugene Lee, on the other hand, in a study of six nonpartisan California cities, concluded that partisanship would be

[18] Philadelphia: University of Pennsylvania Press, 1963.

[19] J. Leiper Freeman, "Local Party Systems: Theoretical Considerations and a Case Analysis," *American Journal of Sociology*, LXIV (November 1958), 282–289.

[20] Charles E. Gilbert, "Some Aspects of Nonpartisan Elections in Large Cities," *Midwest Journal of Political Science*, VI (November 1962), 345–362, and "National Political Alignments and the Politics of Large Cities," *Political Science Quarterly*, LXXIX (March 1964), 25–51.

a welcome means of broadening the political structure.[21] Phillips Cutright found decided differences in party organization and activity in a partisan and a nonpartisan community.[22] In an analysis of St. Louis politics, Robert Salisbury concluded that the governmental structure of the city and county has a significant effect on the alignment of parties and interests.[23] Thus a variety of evidence is mounting on questions which rarely received empirical analysis in the past.

Purpose and Approach of This Study

The research in this book draws on the contributions of the approaches discussed above. From traditional political science comes the concern with the impact of governmental institutions and the reform movement. The interest in the distribution of power and leadership can be traced to the community-power-structure studies initiated by Floyd Hunter. Robert A. Dahl demonstrated the importance of the historical dimension and the analysis of decisions. The utility of studying a political process by examining the role of groups within it also shaped the research design.[24] Finally, the recent concern with the interrelation of governmental institutions, political structure, policy decisions, and community values is central to the objectives of this study.[25]

This book examines the impact of reform institutions— nonpartisanship, at-large elections, and the council-manager form of government—on local election results, political organization, and

[21] Eugene C. Lee, *The Politics of Nonpartisanship* (Berkeley: University of California Press, 1960).

[22] Phillips Cutright, "Activities of Precinct Committeemen in Partisan and Nonpartisan Communities," *Western Political Quarterly*, XVII (March 1964), 93–108.

[23] Robert H. Salisbury, "St. Louis Politics: Relationships Among Interests, Parties, and Governmental Structure," *Western Political Quarterly*, XIII (June 1960), 498–507.

[24] The value of the group approach has been seen in the study of national politics. See Arthur Bentley, *The Process of Government* (San Antonio, Texas: Principia Press of Trinity University, 1949), and David Truman, *The Governmental Process* (New York: Alfred A. Knopf, 1951).

[25] In addition to Williams and Adrian, another example of this orientation is Edward C. Banfield and James Q. Wilson, *City Politics* (Cambridge, Mass.: Harvard University Press and M.I.T. Press, 1963).

leadership in the city of Toledo; it also studies the effect of a large industrial city on certain reform ideals, such as the local election without parties, the nonpolitical city manager, and the businesslike city government. How do reform institutions actually function in Toledo? How has their operation been shaped by other developments of the past 30 years, such as the growth of organized labor, the increasing Negro population, and Toledo's swing into the Democratic column in state and national elections? Conversely, how has the reform tradition affected the potency of these developments at the local level and in state and national politics as well?

Specifically, this research considers the effect of governmental institutions on the participation and influence of various groups in the community. Particular attention is devoted to community power, which is approached indirectly through an examination of the role of leaders from six important components of the urban community: organized labor, political parties, the press, major firms, and Negro organizations. How do leaders from these groups evaluate the impact of reform institutions on the interest and participation of their organizations in the community, on the involvement of other groups, and on the nature of leadership and politics in the community? How do these appraisals compare with the opinions of the mayor and the city councilmen? How are the city councilmen recruited and elected, and what is their role in the political system? This approach will yield certain observations on patterns of influence and leadership in Toledo and the relation of these patterns to governmental institutions.

The objectives of this study are based on the assumption that city government is a political process. Politics, as Edward C. Banfield and James Q. Wilson have written, arises out of conflict and consists of the activities by which conflict is conducted and regulated.[26] Thus, since the operations of local government reflect the differences of opinion and interest which exist among the diverse groups and organizations in cities, this research assumes that political parties can have a vital role in articulating these conflicts, resolving issues, and achieving a degree of unity among contending groups within a given city government.[27] From these general assumptions about city politics, I shall investigate seven hypotheses:

---

[26] Banfield and Wilson, *City Politics*, p. 7.

[27] For a discussion of the role of political parties in representing interests and creating cohesion in local politics and government, see Theodore J. Lowi,

1. Reform institutions allow the maintenance of a pattern of influence not congruent with Toledo's underlying social and economic characteristics or with its political behavior in state and national politics.

2. Nonpartisanship, at-large elections, and the council-manager form of government have depressing effects on local party organization and activity and thus on the distribution of influence and political leadership in the community. The absence of strong parties reduces the possibility of strong public leadership and closes a major avenue of influence for lower-income and minority groups.[28]

3. Lacking the support of a powerful and continuing party organization or the leadership of a strong, elective executive and party leader, city councilmen are in a relatively weakened position, dependent on personal followings and unable to take decisive action; the result is an absence of leadership in city government.

4. The compatibility of reform institutions with middle-class civic ideals encourages the participation of business leaders, particularly those in companies having local ownership or local headquarters; but business ideals and influences are not countered by a strong partisan structure or an elective executive. Thus, a relative compatibility of civic and business leadership develops, and business enjoys a congenial and unthreatened existence.[29]

5. The influence of union leaders and organizations is reduced by nonpartisanship, at-large elections, and the council-manager form of government. The off-year and at-large election, the nonpartisan ballot, and the absence of an elective mayor and active party organizations make it difficult for union leaders to achieve high membership interest and turn-out in elections. In addition, the

At the Pleasure of the Mayor (New York: The Free Press, 1964); Edward C. Banfield, *Political Influence* (New York: The Free Press, 1961); and Robert K. Merton, ''The Latent Functions of the Machine,'' *Social Theory and Social Structure* (New York: The Free Press, 1957), pp. 71–81.

[28] The depressing effects of nonpartisanship on party organization are suggested by Charles Adrian, ''Some General Characteristics of Nonpartisan Elections,'' *American Political Science Review*, XLVI (September 1952), 766–776.

[29] Samuel P. Hays has emphasized the historical tie between business leaders and the reform movement. See his ''The Politics of Reform in Municipal Government in the Progressive Era,'' *Pacific Northwest Quarterly*, LV (October 1964), 157–169.

reform context and ethos may cause labor leaders and politicians to mute their goals and their union identification.[30]

6. Nonpartisanship, at-large elections, and the council-manager form of government reduce the political activity and influence of Negroes. In the absence of ward elections and strong party organizations, Negro political organization is negligible. Instead, middle-class Negro leaders of essentially middle-class organizations hold nominal influence without actual power.[31]

7. The decentralization of power fostered by the reform movement enhances the influence of the local newspaper and its officials in the community.[32]

[30] Banfield and Wilson, *City Politics*, pp. 277–293.

[31] Wilson, *Negro Politics;* and Lee, *Politics of Nonpartisanship*, pp. 172–185.

[32] Banfield and Wilson, *City Politics*, pp. 323–325.

2 METHODOLOGY AND RESEARCH SETTING

This research is a case study of a single community—Toledo, Ohio. Present generalizations about city politics are derived from a growing, but still small collection of evidence—witness the relatively few cities which Banfield and Wilson discuss in their interpretation of city politics.[1] Studies of a small number of cities have given rise to theories and interpretations not yet substantiated. Many types of communities and questions remain unexamined. Additional studies can add to the information available on city politics as well as propose and test hypotheses relevant to other communities. The purpose of this research is to examine a particular community with attention to certain questions of general significance.

The focus of this research is on a subject which has received relatively little empirical attention in political science—the impact of the reform movement and its institutions. Toledo is a particularly appropriate city for such a study. An early stronghold of reform in the days of "Golden Rule" Jones, Toledo is now a large, industrial, Democratically-inclined city. It is relatively unusual to find council-manager government, at-large elections, and nonpartisanship in such a setting. Thus Toledo provides a remarkably interesting, suitable, and accessible locale for investigating the hypotheses listed in the previous chapter.

---

[1] Edward C. Banfield and James Q. Wilson, *City Politics* (Cambridge, Mass.: Harvard University Press and M.I.T. Press, 1963).

The Methodology

The methodology of this research is derived from the judgments of Chapter 1, which suggested the value of different perspectives on a community political system. This study utilizes several approaches to the study of community decision-making. Certain features of both Hunter's and Dahl's methods are employed. The technique of asking individuals in key positions or organizations to designate the "top leaders" in the city is not used as a method for identifying community leaders or studying local decision-making, although questions concerning reputed leaders in the community and in various groups are included in the research design. Several cases of decision-making are reviewed, but these do not provide the central method for studying the community.

The research concentrates on the community role of leaders in organized labor, Negro groups, political parties, major firms, the press, and the city council. It is through an analysis of these major actors in the community that an effort is made to assess the relation between governmental institutions and the distribution of influence. Thus the point of departure for studying Toledo is the role of six major categories of participants rather than a reconstruction of key decisions or the identification of attributed influentials.

These six groups were selected for study for a number of reasons. Each is an important component of the urban community, and a study of their interaction helps to characterize the political system. Moreover, in a period in which the role of interest groups in national government has received much attention,[2] it is instructive to examine the role of such groups at the local level. Finally, each of the six groups provides a convenient means for testing certain hypotheses about the effects of reform institutions on the role of lower-income and minority groups, on party organization, and on civic and political leadership. Thus the community role of labor unions and Negro organizations is important in a consideration of the local influence of minority and lower-income groups. Similarly, political parties are of concern because they are significant avenues of influence for lower-income and minority groups, as well as

---

[2] See, for example, Bertram Gross, *The Legislative Process: A Study in Social Combat* (New York: Thomas Y. Crowell Co., 1953).

sources of public leadership at all levels of government. Also, political parties are a crucial group to examine in an appraisal of the reputed and actual consequences of the apolitical ethos of the reform movement. Nor would it be possible to omit the elective arm of the local government, the city council, in a study of institutions in the local political system. Major firms had to be included in order to test the effects of the reform movement from another direction; they provided a means for investigating the proposition that reform institutions encourage the participation of business leaders and enhance the influence of middle- and upper-income groups. Similarly, the influence of the press is often said to increase under reform politics. Thus, an examination of the local newspaper is necessary to determine the validity of this assumption in Toledo.

To begin research on these groups and questions required considerable background on Toledo. I read the meager written sources and conducted 15 preliminary interviews to develop a familiarity with the city. The preliminary interviews consisted of informal conversations with leaders in the Chamber of Commerce, *The Blade*, organized labor, Negro organizations, and political parties. These conversations were useful in clarifying the concerns of my study and in introducing me to many facets of community politics in Toledo.

The excellent coverage of local politics in *The Blade*, the evening paper, was also helpful in acquainting me with the community. I spent a number of weeks reading back issues of *The Blade* since 1950. This provided a valuable background on issues and personalities and on trends in voting and party organization.

Selection of case studies. With the benefit of information drawn from *The Blade* and preliminary interviews, I selected four cases of decision-making for study: the unsuccessful efforts to introduce the strong mayor plan in 1957 and 1959; the passage of a fair housing ordinance in 1961; Toledo's urban renewal program as seen in the Chase Park project, 1955–1965; and the mayoralty election of 1965. The charter battles and the fair housing conflict were among the most controversial of recent years. Urban renewal, too, has been a source of recurrent controversy for more than a decade. The 1965 mayoralty election marked the first time in thirty years that the mayor of Toledo was directly elected. These case studies include many of the significant community concerns of 1955–1965.

After a thorough preliminary study of the issues, groups, and community selected for examination, I wrote an 87-question questionnaire, one section of which was devoted to the groups and issues selected for study. Most of the questions were open-ended, geared to the select group of community leaders I planned to interview. The emphasis was on cognitive and descriptive information. The questionnaire was designed to reveal the perceptions and appraisals of respondents on the participation and influence of various groups; on trends in the involvement of these groups; and on the effects of reform institutions on group participation, leadership, and political organization. Between January and June 1965, I conducted 75 interviews, lasting from one to three and one-half hours.[3] In the chapters which follow, all quotations given without source are from these interviews.

Selection of interviewees. Respondents were chosen largely on the basis of their positions of leadership in organizations within the six categories. A list of city councilmen and officials holding executive positions in organized labor, Negro groups, political parties, the press, and major firms was compiled. Also included on this list were several leaders who had recently retired from positions of leadership and several who were described in my preliminary interviews as influential and/or good informants. The vast majority of respondents selected hold or have held positions of leadership.

During a six-month period I was able to interview officials in every category.[4] Thus, in the case of organized labor, interviews were conducted with top officials in the United Auto Workers, the Teamsters, the Building Trades Council, the Port Council, the United Glass Workers, and the Toledo Area AFL-CIO Council. Negro leaders in the Toledo chapters of the NAACP and CORE, the Federated Council, the Interdenominational Ministerial Alliance, and public positions were interviewed. I had appointments with the presidents or, in a few cases, the vice-presidents of the 14 largest employers and the three major banks in the city. The mayor, all city councilmen, the city manager, and the urban renewal director were

---

[3] Eight additional informal interviews were conducted in the fall of 1966 to confirm and amplify information gained in the original interviews and to check the significance of developments after the completion of my research.

[4] Refusals were limited to two business leaders, two Negro leaders, and one labor leader. Because of the large number of interviews conducted, it is extremely doubtful that these few omissions would have affected the evidence and interpretations presented.

interviewed.[5] I talked with party leaders including the chairmen of the executive committees for both parties, other executive committee officials, members of the Board of Elections, officeholders in the county as well as the city government, and the Congressman from the Toledo district. At *The Blade* I had discussions with both reporters and key officials.

I also succeeded in interviewing several retired business leaders and a prominent retired UAW official. Conferences with a number of former mayors and councilmen were included for historical perspective. I interviewed several respondents who had special information about a particular group or who had personal knowledge about one or more of the four cases of decision-making.

Toledo—The Setting

The setting, as well as the methodology of this research, requires a brief explanation. It is helpful to have the basic features of Toledo in mind before beginning an account of its political system. Toledo is located in northwestern Ohio at the mouth of the Maumee River on the western shore of Lake Erie. The city, the fourth largest in Ohio and the county seat of Lucas County, borders on the Ohio-Michigan line, 57 miles south of Detroit and 107 miles west of Cleveland. The 1960 Census gave the population of Toledo as 318,003. Estimates of the 1965 population vary between 392,500 and 393,300, with annexations accounting for most of the increase since 1960.[6] Civic boosters take pride in Toledo's six-year rise from the 39th to the 31st largest city in the United States. With the exception of increases through annexations, the population has been relatively stable over the last 30 years, however.[7] The Toledo Standard Metropolitan Statistical Area, which was expanded in 1963 to include Wood County to the south and Monroe in Michigan in addition to Lucas County, has a population of 630,647. On the basis

[5] The councilmen referred to here are those serving on the 1963–1965 city council. The 1965 election produced only two new councilmen.

[6] Information on 1965 estimates comes from *The Blade*, January 2, 1966, Section H, p. 2. Population increases by annexations are as follows: 1960, 5,718; 1961, 8,820; 1963, 21,954.

[7] In 1900, Toledo's population was 131,822. Since that time percentage changes in population have been as follows: 1910, 27.8 per cent increase; 1920, 44.3 per cent increase; 1930, 19.6 per cent increase; 1940, 2.9 per cent decline; 1950, 7.5 per cent increase; 1960, 4.7 per cent increase.

of 1960 figures, Toledo serves as the core city for the 44th largest metropolitan area in the country.

The economy. Economically, Toledo is an industrial and commercial city. It is a center for the manufacture of glass products and automobile parts and accessories. Three major glass firms— Owens-Illinois, Inc., Libbey-Owens-Ford Glass Company, and Owens-Corning Fiberglas Corporation—have their national headquarters in Toledo. A fourth glass company, the Johns Manville Fiber Glass Corporation, has its division headquarters in Toledo. Glass products manufactured by these companies include bottles, jars, plate glass, insulating glass, mirror glass, windshields, tableware, TV bulbs, glass-enforced plastic, scientific and medical equipment, and glass textile yarns.

Other major companies with Toledo headquarters are the Champion Spark Plug Company, the Toledo Scale Corporation, Dana Corporation, and the DeVilbiss Company. Such companies as Dura Corporation, Kaiser Jeep, AP Parts, Eltra Corporation, Textileather Division of General Tire and Rubber, and General Motors have large installations in Toledo. Automobile supplies produced in Toledo include windshields, universal joints, transmissions, hydraulic torque converters, spark plugs, window regulators, die casting, electrostatic coating equipment, batteries, and ignition systems. Other manufactured goods include canvas products, scales, electrical machinery, and plastics.

Toledo is also one of the largest oil-refining centers in the Midwest. The Pure, Gulf, Standard, and Sun oil companies have refineries in Toledo which process over 8,000,000 gallons of crude oil daily. Geographical location, eleven railroads, and an excellent Great Lakes port make commerce and transportation important in Toledo's economy. The railroad network is claimed to be the third largest in the United States.[8] Rail transport through Toledo consists of the shipment of coal and iron ore, grain, steel, and automobile supplies. The growth of the Port of Toledo since the opening of the St. Lawrence Seaway has made the city an expanding center for the shipment of heavy cargo, including coal, ore, steel, petroleum, grain, and automobile supplies. The Port of Toledo is now the ninth largest in the United States and the only Foreign Trade Zone on the Great Lakes.[9]

[8] "This Is Toledo," Toledo Area Chamber of Commerce Publication, 1964.

[9] Toledo-Lucas County Port Authority, "Port Newsletter," March–April 1965.

The industrial character of the Toledo area is evident in the breakdown of employment in the standard metropolitan statistical area: 38 per cent of those employed are in manufacturing; 22 per cent in wholesale and retail trade; 13 per cent in service establishments; eight per cent in transportation and utilities; five per cent in construction; and 14 per cent in others.[10] For the city itself the percentage employed in manufacturing has been high for many decades (see Figure 2.1).

FIGURE 2.1

Per Cent Employed in Manufacturing in Toledo, 1900–1960*

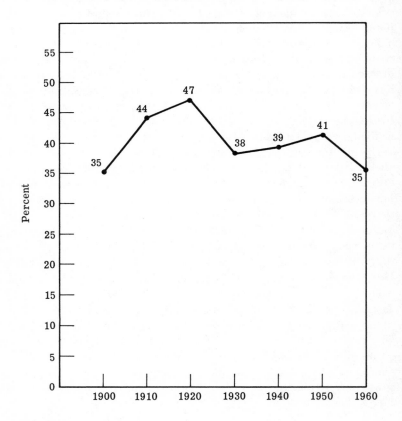

* Data from U.S. Census reports.

[10] These are Toledo Chamber of Commerce calculations for 1964.

In the mid-1960s employment is high in Toledo and the city is reasonably prosperous.[11] Two thirds of all men over 14 are employed in blue collar occupations. Two thirds of Toledo families have an annual income of $5,000 or more; the median family income for 1960 was $7,034. Sixty-nine per cent of all housing units in the city are owner-occupied. Educational attainments in Toledo do not match wage scales. Forty per cent of the population 25 years and over has no more than an eighth-grade education.

Ethnic groups. Since this study will give particular attention to the role of one minority group, it would be well to consider the general ethnic picture. The total foreign stock in the Toledo population in 1960 was 65,240 or slightly more than one fifth of the total population.[12] The German, French, and Irish groups which were important in the settlement and development of Northwest Ohio are no longer significant as ethnic groups, although those of German descent represented five per cent of the total population in 1960.[13] People of Polish birth or descent also constitute five per cent of the city's population.[14] The Polish group is relatively concentrated in two areas of the city, although dispersion is increasing rapidly. Evidence of Polish influence in city politics and elections, especially in the 4th and 14th wards, will be referred to in several parts of this study. Hungarians constitute one per cent of Toledo's population.[15] People of Hungarian birth or descent are concentrated on the East side of the Maumee River and particularly in the 20th ward, where they are 12 per cent of the local population. The Hungarian population is generally associated with the glass industry, particularly the Libbey-Owens-Ford plants in East Toledo and Rossford, while the Polish ethnic group is identified with the automotive industry.

---

[11] In 1965, unemployment in the Toledo area, officially defined by the Federal government as Lucas and Wood counties and Monroe County (Michigan), was 2.8 per cent of the total work force. In 1960 unemployment in the city of Toledo was 4.9 per cent of the total work force. The 1960 figure is from the United States Census. The 1965 figure is from *The Blade*, January 2, 1966, Section H, p. 1.

[12] The term "foreign stock" is used as defined by the Bureau of the Census. Foreign stock consists of the foreign-born population combined with the native population of foreign or mixed parentage.

[13] U.S. Bureau of the Census, *U.S. Censuses of Population and Housing: 1960, Final Report*, PHC (1)–158.

[14] *Ibid.*

[15] *Ibid.*

Negroes are the largest and the most rapidly increasing minority group in the city. At the time of the 1960 Census, Negroes constituted 13 per cent of the city's total population.[16] Between 1940 and 1950 Toledo's Negro population increased by 60 per cent; the decade from 1950 to 1960 saw an increase of 61 per cent. There are 42,863 Negroes in Toledo, most of them concentrated in the sixth and eighth wards in the core of the city, where the white population has drastically declined in the last 20 years. Figure 2.2 indicates the growth of the Negro population in Toledo in this century.

FIGURE 2.2

Negro Population in Toledo, 1900–1960*

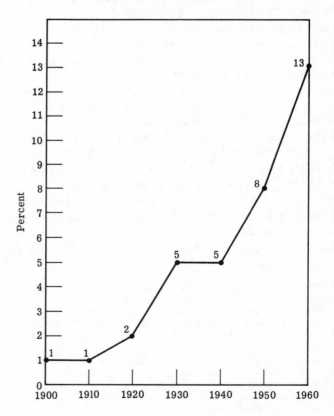

* Data from U.S. Census reports.

[16] *Ibid.*

Religious life. Since religion and church membership are not covered in the United States Census, complete and reliable information on these subjects is lacking. A study of churches and church membership by the National Council of Churches is of some value in filling this gap. In Toledo members of 173 Protestant churches represent 43 per cent of the total church membership of the city; members of 43 Catholic churches represent 53.2 per cent of the total church membership; and members of Jewish temples and synagogues represent 3.5 per cent of the total church membership. Church members as percentages of the total population are as follows: Protestants, 20.5 per cent; Catholics, 25.2 per cent; and Jews, 2 per cent. The limitations of this information are obvious. Since the percentages are based on church membership, they fail to include large numbers of persons who consider themselves Catholic, Protestant, or Jewish without having a specific membership. Furthermore, the understanding of membership and the methods of computing it vary from one church to another, so inconsistencies in reporting may distort the percentages.[17]

Business and labor organizations. Business and labor organizations will be discussed in detail later, so a brief discussion will suffice here. The Toledo Area Chamber of Commerce is an organization of 3,000 members. Downtown business and professional interests are·represented in Downtown Toledo Associates, Incorporated. On the labor front, Toledo is highly unionized. There are an estimated 70,000 union members in the Toledo area; one out of three adults in the Toledo area is a union member.[18] Major unions in Toledo include the United Auto Workers, which is nearly twice as large as any other union, the Teamsters, Electrical Workers, United Glass Workers, Flint Glass Workers, Building Trades, and Maritime Trades.

News media. Toledo is served by several news media. Overshadowing all is *The Blade*, an evening newspaper with excellent news coverage and analysis and potent editorial positions. *The Blade* and its publisher, Paul Block, Jr., are regarded as willing

---

[17] Information on churches and church membership is from the National Council of Churches, ''Churches and Church Membership in the United States: An Enumeration and Analysis by Counties, States, and Regions,'' Series D, No. 2, Denominational Statistics by Metropolitan Areas, 1957.

[18] Information on the estimated total union membership is from local union leaders.

and able to give the kiss of death to wayward politicians and civic leaders. *The Blade* has a daily circulation of 180,833, while the morning paper, *The Times*, which also is published by Paul Block, Jr., has a circulation of 30,956.[19] In addition to *The Blade* and *The Times*, Toledo is served by television stations WSPD-TV, WTOL-TV, and WDHO-TV (an ultra-high frequency station) and several radio stations. Specialized newspapers serving Toledo include the *Ameryka Echo Polish Weekly;* the *Hungarian and American Weekly; The Bronze Raven*, a Negro newspaper; the *Toledo Union Journal*, an AFL-CIO weekly newspaper published under the auspices of the United Auto Workers; and the *Team and Wheel*, the monthly newspaper of the Teamsters.[20]

Institutions of local government. In governmental institutions Toledo has shown a long-standing acceptance of reform prescriptions. Toledo has had nonpartisan city primaries and elections since 1915. In 1934 a charter amendment was passed providing for a nine-member city council elected at large by proportional representation and a city manager selected by the council. Under this arrangement the city council elected one of its members to serve as mayor. In 1949 a charter amendment eliminated proportional representation; a 1963 charter amendment provided for the direct election of the mayor as of November 1965.[21]

Toledo's governmental institutions are rather unusual for a city of its size and character. The council-manager form of government is most often found in cities between 25,000 and 250,000 (see Figure 2.3). Furthermore, the council-manager plan is least common in manufacturing cities. John H. Kessel has noted a decreasing use of the manager plan by medium-sized cities when they are

[19] *The Blade* has a Sunday circulation of 186,074. *The Times* is not published on Sunday. Circulation figures on *The Blade* and *The Times* are from *N. W. Ayer and Son's Directory of Newspapers and Periodicals, 1966*, William F. McCallister, ed. (Philadelphia: N. W. Ayer and Son, Inc., 1966), p. 863.

[20] The *Toledo Union Journal* has a circulation of 26,150. *The Bronze Raven's* circulation is 6,000. These figures are from *N. W. Ayer and Son's Directory, 1966*, p. 863. The *Team and Wheel*, not included in *Ayer and Son's Directory*, has a circulation of 18,500. This figure is cited in Teamsters Local 20, *Record of the Second Triennial Stewards Convention, January 15 and 16, 1966*, p. 29. Circulation figures on the Polish and Hungarian weeklies are not available.

[21] Under the 1963 charter amendment, the Vice Mayor continues to be elected by city council, in accordance with 1935 charter provisions.

The governmental arrangements of Lucas County are in contrast to those of Toledo. Lucas County is governed by a three-member commission elected at large on a partisan ballot.

FIGURE 2.3

Governmental Form and Community Size*

1,000,000 and over	100%	N = 5
500,000 - 1,000,000	26.7% / 73.7%	N = 15
250,000 - 500,000	43.3% / 40.0% / 16.7%	N = 30
100,000 - 250,000	48.8% / 37.5% / 13.8%	N = 80
50,000 - 100,000	50.5% / 35.3% / 14.2%	N = 190
25,000 - 50,000	52.8% / 34.0% / 13.1%	N = 388
10,000 - 25,000	40.3% / 49.7% / 10.0%	N = 1005
5,000 - 10,000	28.1% / 66.7% / 5.2%	N = 1257

Commission

Mayor-Council

Manager

* Data from John H. Kessel, ''Governmental Structure and Political Environment: A Statistical Note about American Cities,'' *American Political Science Review*, LVI (September 1962), 615.

arranged by predominant economic types in this order: personal service; retail; finance; professional; public administration; wholesale; transport; diversified; and manufacturing.[22] In addition, the

[22] John H. Kessel, ''Governmental Structure and Political Environment: A Statistical Note about American Cities,'' *American Political Science Review*, LVI (September 1962), 615–620.

FIGURE 2.4

Democratic Percentage in Presidential Elections, 1876–1964*

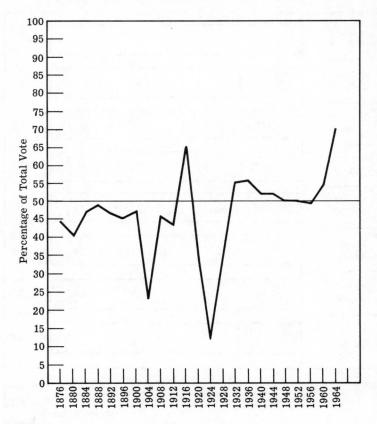

* Data from Lucas County Board of Elections, *Election Abstracts.*

council-manager plan is most frequently used by cities with high growth rates rather than stable populations.[23] Toledo, as a large manufacturing city with a stable population, is an exception to general patterns found for the council-manager plan.

Politically, the 1932 presidential election marked Toledo's decisive break with a Republican past. In presidential elections since 1932, Toledo has been consistently Democratic, with the exception of the 1956 election in which Dwight Eisenhower had a one per cent edge over Adlai Stevenson. The changing fortunes of the political parties in presidential elections are seen in Figure 2.4. Democratic senatorial, congressional, and gubernatorial candidates have drawn comfortable margins of victory in Toledo in the '50s and '60s. Republican candidates in nonpartisan city elections have fared better than their counterparts in state and national politics. Later discussions will examine this phenomenon in detail.

[23] *Ibid.*

3 THE REFORM MOVEMENT IN TOLEDO

For nearly a century the municipal reform movement has been a distinctive influence in American cities. Although the issues have varied from city to city and decade to decade, the movement as a whole has had several enduring goals.[1] It has sought to make city government more honest, more efficient, and in some sense more democratic. These goals reflect what Wilson and Banfield have described as the Anglo-Saxon Protestant middle-class political ethos, a view emphasizing morality and individual obligation in politics. The reform ethos assumed the existence of a public interest which should triumph over competing private interests. The prevailing political ethos, according to reformers, condoned special interests, boodling, and bosses at the expense of the good of the city as a whole. Reformers envisioned a political system in which the voters would have the opportunity to arrive at their own political convictions. They believed that the public, when freed from the corrupting influence of political parties and special interests, would elect highly qualified officeholders to determine city policies. The execution of these policies would in turn be left to professional administrators.

[1] This interpretation follows Edward C. Banfield and James Q. Wilson, *City Politics* (Cambridge, Mass.: Harvard University Press and M.I.T. Press, 1963), Chapter XI.

Goals of the Reformers

To realize their ideals, reformers advocated certain measures designed to release the public-spirited influences in the community.[2] The municipal reform program included the initiative, referendum, and recall to break the hold of professional politicians; proportional representation and the direct primary to achieve a more responsive political system; nonpartisan, off-year elections to divorce local politics from the irrelevant and debilitating partisanship of national and state government; at-large elections to emphasize the importance of the city as a whole rather than the divisive, selfish interests of its parts; and the council-manager form of government to provide competent management of public services.

Reform recommendations were not completely consistent with each other. Proportional representation, for example, was not compatible with representing the interest of the whole rather than competing groups.[3] The referendum did not facilitate decision-making by qualified officeholders and technicians. Nor did all reformers agree on what measures would best assure good government at the local level. Inconsistencies and disagreements did not impede Toledo's experimentation with reform, however. During the 20th century, Toledo tried all the major proposals of reform from the nonpartisan ballot and at-large elections to proportional representation and the council-manager plan. In addition to reflecting virtually all phases and issues of reform, Toledo contributed several distinctive personalities and ideas to the movement. This chapter will sketch the story.

The reform movement in Toledo started at the turn of the century. At this time, progressivism, a quest for political, social, and economic reform, extended to every level of government. At the

[2] The reform program is summarized in the Model City Chapters of the National Municipal League. See also the National Municipal League, *Getting the National Parties Out of Municipal Elections* (July 1953, mimeographed); and National Municipal League, *A Guide for Charter Commissions,* third edition, 1957.

[3] For a discussion of the effects of proportional representation on group representation in city government, see Ralph A. Straetz, *PR Politics in Cincinnati* (New York: New York University Press, 1958).

local level, progressivism directed attention to the defects of city life and government in a period of rapid urban growth. In Los Angeles, Chicago, New York, and other cities, groups organized to discuss solutions to problems such as the political boss, the party machine, corruption, crime, and monopoly. In 1894 the National Municipal League was organized.[4] Nonpartisan reform clubs, municipal ownership leagues, and direct legislation leagues were found in many cities by 1900.[5] The articles of Lincoln Steffens, Ben Lindsey, George Kernan, and others and the election of reform mayors in Cleveland, Detroit, and Toledo further dramatized the progressive concern with cities.

The reform mayors were Hazen S. Pingree of Detroit, Tom Johnson of Cleveland, and Samuel M. Jones of Toledo. Toledo, at the time of Jones's election in 1897, was a city of not quite 100,000. It was a rapidly growing commercial and transportation center, with an increasing immigrant population. Politically, the Republican Party was dominant in presidential elections. But the local Republican organization was divided between a faction loyal to Marcus Alonzo Hanna and a faction supporting Joseph B. Foraker. Although a Democrat had nearly defeated the Republican candidate for mayor in 1895, the local Democratic Party was badly divided by the money issue raised in the presidential campaign of 1896. These conditions opened the way to the distinctive political philosophy and practices of Samuel M. Jones.

Golden Rule Jones and His Significance

Samuel M. "Golden Rule" Jones of Toledo, who attempted to put Christian precepts into practice in city government, was easily the most eccentric of the reform mayors. A Welsh immigrant, Jones had had a successful career in the oil fields of Pennsylvania and Ohio before coming to Toledo to open a factory for the production of oil pumping equipment which he had invented. Jones's social

---

[4] The origins and development of the National Municipal League are discussed by Frank Mann Stewart, *A Half Century of Reform: The History of the National Municipal League* (Berkeley: University of California Press, 1950).

[5] George E. Mowry, *The Era of Theodore Roosevelt and the Birth of Modern America* (New York: Harper and Row, 1958), p. 61.

conscience is said to have been awakened by the experience of opening his factory, the Acme Sucker Rod Company, in the depression year of 1894. Distressed by the sight of willing and able men without employment, Jones began to consider social problems. He was shocked at the wages and working conditions of factory life. "I studied social conditions," he said, "and these led me to feel very keenly the degradation of my fellow men."[6]

In developing a social philosophy, Jones turned to the works of Whitman, Emerson, and Tolstoi. He also admired George Davis Herron's version of the social gospel and the essay, "The Philosophy of the Lord's Prayer," in which Herron argued that if God is the Father, then all men must be treated as brothers. Jones came to envision a cooperative society in which all men would be brothers rather than competitors. Jones's ideal was Whitman's "land of comrades," a harmonious society in which every individual could develop fully.[7]

Golden Rule Jones entered politics in the spring of 1897, when the Republican city convention was deadlocked by conflicting factions of Hanna, Foraker, and reform Republicans. The Hanna faction of the party offered Jones's name to the convention in a desperate effort to snatch victory from its opponents. Professional Republican politicians, fearing that Jones lacked party loyalty, then arranged to deprive the candidate of influence in party committees. This did not disturb Jones, who saw himself as a man above parties and politics. Instead of devoting himself to partisan electioneering, Jones conducted a campaign for a set of principles calling for a more humane society.[8] He was elected mayor by 534 votes, with 21,430 ballots cast.

After his election, Jones continued to deviate from past political practices. He refused to award city jobs to Republican party workers or contributors, saying that he never dismissed an employee as long as the man was doing his job. As mayor, Jones expounded on other interests and enthusiasms which the Republican Party, the

---

[6] Quoted by Russell Nye, *Midwestern Progressive Politics* (East Lansing: Michigan State College Press, 1951), p. 187.

[7] Robert H. Bremner, "Civic Revival in Ohio: Samuel M. Jones," *The American Journal of Economics and Sociology*, XIII (January 1949), 151–162.

[8] Harvey S. Ford, "The Life and Times of Golden Rule Jones," unpublished Ph.D. dissertation, Department of History, University of Michigan, 1953, p. 76.

clergy, and a large segment of local business found unappealing. He advocated municipal ownership of all utilities, including electricity, telephone, telegraph, railroads, and gas. He favored a more democratic local government through home rule, the initiative, referendum, and recall, and the demise of political parties. Jones sympathized with unions in the strikes of the period. ''Competition,'' he said, ''is the knife that is letting the life blood of the nation.''[9]

Most shocking to conservative elements in the community was Jones's attitude toward vice, crime, and law enforcement. Golden Rule Jones instructed policemen to carry light canes instead of clubs. When sitting as police magistrate, he dismissed drunks and thieves with lectures on morality. A man carrying a gun without a permit was ordered to smash it in public with a sledge. An assault case was lectured on the power of love and the futility of force. Jones declined to close the saloons, which brought him the censure of the Ministers' Union of Toledo. When ministers appealed to him to drive prostitutes out of town, he asked, ''to where?'' As an alternative, the mayor proposed that ministers join him in taking prostitutes into their homes for rehabilitation. Jones believed that prostitution, drunkenness, and crime were the consequences of a basically evil system rather than individual weakness or wickedness. Restrictive laws and punishments would do nothing to eradicate the problems or their sources. Such questions could be resolved only through the creation of a more humane society which would eliminate poverty, ignorance, and privilege and allow men to live in brotherhood.

In 1899, when Republican party leaders refused to renominate Jones, he ran for reelection as an independent candidate. In spite of the heated opposition of *The Blade,* both parties, and local businessmen and ministers, Jones won 70 per cent of the votes cast. He insisted that the election was not a personal triumph, but evidence of a popular repudiation of political parties. With this conviction in mind, Jones offered himself as a nonpartisan candidate for governor in 1900. He was defeated, partly as a result of Senator Mark Hanna's intervention in the campaign. Nevertheless, Jones drew the largest vote that a third party gubernatorial candidate had ever received in Ohio.[10]

[9] Ford, p. 182.

[10] Jones received 106,721 votes. By the time of Jones's venture into state politics, the Hanna faction had consolidated control of the local Republican organization.

By 1900 Jones was moving away from the Republican Party and toward a tacit alliance with the Democratic Party and the Democratic editor of the Toledo *Bee*, N. D. Cochran. In 1900 he endorsed William Jennings Bryan for the presidency. The following year Jones received the Democratic endorsement for mayor, although he insisted that he was a nonpartisan candidate and never publicly acknowledged the endorsement. In the 1901 campaign and in his last campaign in 1903, Jones addressed himself to the "poison of partyism," denouncing all political organizations with equal fervor.

During his years as mayor, Golden Rule Jones introduced a number of reforms in Toledo. He placed the police and fire departments under civil service; introduced the eight-hour day for employees in the city waterworks and public safety department; and established a minimum wage for city laborers. Jones also initiated a program to develop children's playgrounds and a system of public parks.[11] Free public baths were constructed and free kindergartens introduced in the public school system.

Golden Rule Jones was less successful in attaining larger goals such as home rule, public ownership of utilities, and the initiative, referendum, and recall.[12] His political style was in the realm of exhortation rather than specific legislation or achievements. His approach and his personality are evident in Lincoln Steffens's description of a visit with the Golden Rule Mayor:

> Sam Jones took me home, sat me down, and humorously, wonderingly, for hours read aloud to me Walt Whitman and the New Testament. Never a word about the State or the Nation, nothing about the city, even, or politics. The poet and the prophet were his policy leaders. He was practicing what they preached, literally, religiously, gleefully.[13]

Jones's distinctive contribution to progressivism and to the municipal reform movement was his insistence on nonpartisanship. He believed that a political party is by its very nature representative of only part of the people. A party inevitably becomes a link in the

[11] See James H. Rodalbaugh, "Samuel Jones, Evangel of Equality," *Quarterly Bulletin of the Historical Society of Northwest Ohio*, XXVIII (Winter 1943), 15.

[12] See the evaluation by Harvey S. Ford, "Recent Election May Have Ended Nonpartisanism Here," *The Blade*, November 18, 1951, Section 2, p. 3.

[13] Lincoln Steffens, *Autobiography* (New York: Harcourt, Brace, & World, 1958), pp. 470–471.

system of privilege which deprives people of their freedom. In 1900 Jones said:

> I believe that partyism is destructive of the nobler impulses of the soul; that it enslaves millions of men who are born to be free; that they can never be politically free while they "belong" to something outside of themselves; that it makes hypocrites, pretenders, and haters of men in whom the divine impulse is planted. Too long, far too long have we been dupes and slaves. We are men, we are brothers, not haters; we are patriots, not partisans. Let us so live and so act, always remembering that patriotism and partyism cannot abide together for "No man can serve two masters."[14]

Jones believed that parties and partisanship, which were already disappearing from the local scene, were also destined to vanish from national and state elections. "Political parties," he said, "are played out in America."[15] The entire political system would eventually be purged of the poison.

Although Mayor Jones had a deep belief in democracy, he was more interested in its moral dimension than in its actual operation. He never proposed any alternative to political parties other than an exhortation to brotherhood. Jones's refusal to permit his followers to organize as a political party meant that he never commanded significant support in the city council and other city offices. Consequently, he was able to accomplish relatively little. In his campaigns and in his public statements, Jones always placed his greatest emphasis on moral truths rather than specific political issues or political reforms. "Love," he said, "is the only regenerative force."[16]

Sam Jones contended that he was not a reformer. This was true to the extent that he did not place his greatest reliance on institutional changes. It is unlikely, for example, that Jones would have favored the nonpartisan ballot as a means to rid the political system of parties.[17] Nor did he think that municipal ownership of electric

---

[14] Samuel M. Jones, *Annual Statement of the Finances of Toledo Together with the Mayor's Message for the Year Ending April 1, 1900* (Toledo: City of Toledo Publication, 1900), p. 38.

[15] Quoted in Ford, ''The Life and Times of Golden Rule Jones,'' p. 738.

[16] Quoted in Nye, *Midwestern Progressive Politics*, p. 188.

[17] This is the interpretation of Ford, ''The Life and Times of Golden Rule Jones,'' p. 739.

plants or the street railway system would bring a harmonious society. Jones believed that politics cannot improve radically until personal ideals and conduct are raised to a higher plane. The reform that Jones envisioned was more total than that contemplated by most municipal reformers. Jones placed his faith in a social and individual regeneration which would make Toledo and all of society a community of love and human solidarity in which "each citizen would be a member of a family that owned everything and took care of each other."[18]

After the death of Golden Rule Jones in 1904, the reform movement in Toledo entered a new phase. Toward the end of his life, Jones had vetoed a franchise extension sought by the overcapitalized street railway company. When the street car question revived after Jones's death, his followers faced a crisis. They saw that only through political organization would it be possible to repel the renewed efforts of utilities, parties, and other opponents of good government.

Brand Whitlock Carries On

Brand Whitlock, a close associate of Jones, disagreed with Jones's argument that all political parties must be renounced. He contended that a nonpartisan local government requires a nonpartisan local political party to advance the goals of reform. After Jones's death Whitlock and other independents organized a grass roots nonpartisan party with delegates from every precinct and ward. The party held conventions and nominated candidates for a full slate of city and county offices. The Independent Party dedicated itself to the principles of nonpartisanship; home rule; the initiative, referendum, and recall; and strict municipal control over utilities. Party principles held that local government was to be separated from state and national politics and that candidates should await rather than seek nominations for public office.[19]

In 1905 Brand Whitlock was elected mayor and the Independents took control of city council. Whitlock, former secretary to Governor

[18] Quoted in Nye, *Midwestern Progressive Politics*, p. 189.
[19] Wendell F. Johnson, *Toledo's Nonpartisan Movement* (Toledo, Ohio: H. J. Chittenden Co. Press, 1922), pp. 19–33.

Altgeld of Illinois and an author of popular novels, had no great love of politics or of Toledo.[20] He shared many of Jones's views without having his predecessor's evangelical mentality. Whitlock thought of the city as a working model for larger democracies in state and national government. The community, as a natural rather than an artificial institution, should provide the locale for the full development of democratic self-government. In Whitlock's opinion, "the failures and shames of the American city have not been the failures and shames of democracy, but they have been the failures and shames incident of a lack of democracy."[21]

Whitlock urged that national parties be excluded from local issues because "the man who is responsible for the ills of our cities is the man who in municipal elections always votes the straight party ticket." Such a voter, Whitlock argued, sacrifices his individuality so that the party no longer exists for the principles, but the principles for the party. Bosses arise and people condone them for the sake of the party. Consequently, politics gains a bad name, crime and robbery become prevalent, and "beyond all this is a withering away of the character, the wasting of strength, the disintegration of personality."[22]

As mayor, Whitlock devoted himself to the same goals that Jones had advocated. Like Jones, Whitlock favored home rule and municipal regulation of utilities. He also shared Jones's view of crime and law enforcement, believing that society had sadly failed to understand the causes of crime or the ways to prevent it. During his four terms as mayor, Whitlock continued the humanitarian, reform atmosphere of Mayor Jones. Whitlock, however, lacked Jones's confident faith in the possibility of sweeping individual and social reform. Throughout his years as mayor and later, Whitlock was subject to periods of disillusionment about the prospects of improving the political system even slightly.[23]

Both Whitlock and Jones had profound commitment to the participation of the individual citizen in economic and political affairs. Their ideal was an individualistic, laissez-faire society in which

---

[20] See Whitlock's autobiographical account, *Forty Years of It* (New York: D. Appleton and Company, 1925).

[21] Quoted in Samuel M. Jones, III; "Brand Whitlock and the Independent Party," *Northwest Ohio Quarterly*, XXXI (Winter 1959), 98.

[22] Jones, p. 99.

[23] Whitlock, *Forty Years of It.*

each citizen would have the opportunity to determine his own destiny. In the early 20th century, Jones, Whitlock, and other progressives saw this ideal threatened by the development of big business, monopoly, party machines, and labor unions. Large organizations were clotting society into powerful aggregates which cut off the opportunity and influence of the individual.[24] In the cities, control was passing into the hands of a few who could use this control to amass still greater power and wealth.[25]

The objective of Jones and Whitlock was to break down the concentrated power of political parties, utilities, and big business. Nonpartisanship, the initiative, referendum, and recall would restore self-government to the individual citizens of the city. The individual citizen, when freed from the domination of special interests and the corrupt few, was a moral and rational person who would rule for the good of the community. As Whitlock expressed it: "The people are at heart sound and good. Those found grafting do not represent the people. They are representing, of course, some privileged corporation or interest, and the way to get rid of graft is to get rid of the privileged corporations."[26] The ideal of municipal reform was individual participation and responsibility untainted by self-interest.

Jones and Whitlock hoped to return the community to individual citizens with a minimum of organization and governmental action. Jones's deep distrust of organization is evident in his refusal to permit his followers to form a political party. Although Jones and Whitlock wanted to improve the lot of labor, they feared that unions could become a dangerously divisive influence. They believed in a reform which would free the community of even well-

[24] See the interpretation of Richard Hofstadter, *The Age of Reform* (New York: Vintage Books, 1960), Chapter VI, "The Struggle Over Organization," pp. 215–272.

[25] This argument follows Mowry, *The Era of Theodore Roosevelt*, and Hofstadter, *The Age of Reform*. For a different interpretation, see Samuel P. Hays, "The Politics of Reform in Municipal Government in the Progressive Era," *Pacific Northwest Quarterly*, LV (October 1964), 157–169. Hays argues that municipal reform was advanced by upper-class business leaders who wished to centralize and rationalize political decision-making. Although the interest in rationality and efficiency was a definite part of reform, Hays has difficulty explaining how such reform measures as the initiative and referendum, proportional representation, and the absence of an elective executive facilitated modernized, centralized decision-making.

[26] Brand Whitlock, "As to Grafters," *Cosmopolitan*, XLIX (July 1910), 143.

intentioned special interest groups, allowing for complete individual self-determination.

Neither Jones nor Whitlock thought that reform required a significant measure of governmental action or regulation. Although Whitlock favored municipal regulation of utilities, he found it difficult to reconcile public ownership of utilities with his belief in free enterprise. He decided to work for public ownership as a means of control only "if the people vote it that way."[27] Jones and Whitlock wanted to improve the urban environment, but they did not propose specific governmental action or legislation for this end. In the changed atmosphere of reform, the consciences of individuals would be awakened and they would again have the desire and the ability to take action. Few changes in governmental machinery would be necessary.

The nonpartisanship of Jones and Whitlock can be understood as one feature of a reform ideal which stood for the practices and conditions of an earlier period, a time before the growth of large, industrial cities, before large scale immigration, the development of big businesss and political machines, and the beginnings of organized labor. Nonpartisanship was one of the means to create a community in which each individual could have equal opportunity, equal access, and equal influence. Although the ideal and the means for achieving it were poorly suited to the highly organized urban society of the 20th century, they became part of the political heritage of Toledo.

During Whitlock's years as mayor, reform ideals had the support of the Independent Party, which was finally organized after the death of Golden Rule Jones. The Independent Party enjoyed success in city politics between 1905 and 1913, although it was consistently defeated when it tried to extend its influence into county and state government. The Democratic Party during this period dwindled to such insignificance that the Democratic candidate for mayor in 1911 ran fourth behind the Socialist candidate. The Republican Party, although strongly opposed to Jones and Whitlock, was badly divided. Many Independents, with the notable exception of Whitlock, who was a Democrat in national politics, were Republican defectors. The Republican Party made several futile efforts to appease its wayward factions and to rebuild its strength in city

---

[27] Jones, "Brand Whitlock and the Independent Party," p. 97.

politics. Despite efforts at internal reform, the Republican Party failed to regain its power. Defeats during this period caused the Republican Party to become increasingly disorganized until 1913, when Whitlock's retirement as mayor opened a new era in city politics.[28]

Whitlock's refusal to run for reelection in 1913 led to fatal divisions in the Independent Party, which found itself unable to agree on a candidate for mayor. Rival independent candidates and slates entered the race. A wave of anti-Catholic and anticrime sentiment also benefited the Republican candidate, who received an overwhelming victory.[29]

At the time of its eclipse, the Independent Party had achieved certain goals. In 1912 the Ohio constitution had been amended to provide for municipal home rule. A commission elected under the new home rule provisions of the state constitution drafted a new municipal charter requiring all public utility franchises to be submitted to popular vote and providing for nonpartisan municipal primaries and elections.[30] Thus the nonpartisanship originally based on the personalities of Jones and Whitlock was legislated into the city charter of 1914, which is still the basic law of Toledo.[31]

Politics under the City Charter of 1914

In the first two municipal elections after the adoption of the new charter, partisan activity was inconsequential. Both Democrats and Republicans remained aloof in the 1915 and 1917 elections. In 1919 the Democrats sponsored a candidate for mayor, who came in a

---

[28] He was appointed ambassador to Belgium in 1913 by President Wilson.

[29] Randolph C. Downes, ''The Toledo Political-Religious Municipal Election of 1913 and the Death of the Independent Party,'' *Northwest Ohio Quarterly*, XXX (Summer 1958), 137–163.

[30] Department of Political Science, University of Toledo, *The Background of City Government and Politics in Toledo* (University of Toledo, 1955, mimeographed), p. 15.

[31] The city charter of 1914 also provided for the initiative, referendum, and recall. The recall provision was repealed in November 1934, but the initiative and referendum provisions remain in the charter.

weak third behind the Socialist candidate. The winner, incumbent Cornell Schreiber, had been one of the unsuccessful Independent candidates in 1913. Although Schreiber had fallen heir to part of Brand Whitlock's following, he was not to sustain even this fragment of the Independent movement for long.[32] The disinterest of the national parties, particularly the Republican Party, in local elections proved to be short-lived.

The Republican Party and its leader, Walter F. Brown, emerged from the 1920 elections in a strengthened position. Brown had served as Warren Harding's floor manager in the Republican convention and had contributed to the success of Republican campaigns at the national, state, and county levels.[33] In 1921 Brown took charge of the municipal campaign in Toledo in an effort to regain city offices and rejuvenate the local party organization. Under Brown's leadership, the Republican Party entered a full ticket of candidates for city offices and campaigned vigorously for their election. The Republican candidate for mayor, Judge Bernard Brough, also received tacit support from the local Democratic leader. In spite of these assets, Brough won the election with only 42 per cent of the vote.[34] After serving two terms, Brough was succeeded by another Republican, Fred J. Mery, whose administration was considered weaker and more partisan than that of his predecessor. Mery's abrupt dismissal of his Service Director, William T. Jackson, provoked public demand for a charter commission, which was elected in 1927.

The dominant issue in the 1927 municipal election was the charge of "organization control" in local politics, expressed in the campaign slogan of "Down with the Brown Machine." William T. Jackson, the deposed Service Director and a maverick Republican, won the election over the party candidate, at once rebuffing the regular Republicans and demonstrating the continued affinity of Toledo voters for maverick politicians. Initial satisfaction with the Jackson administration perhaps influenced the public reaction to

[32] Donovan Emch, "The City Manager Government of Toledo, Ohio, Part I," unpublished manuscript prepared for the Committee on Public Administration of the Social Science Research Council, 1938, p. 51.

[33] Harvey S. Ford, "Walter Folger Brown," *Northwest Ohio Quarterly*, XXVI (Summer 1954), 200–210.

[34] Emch, "The City Manager Government of Toledo, Ohio, Part I," pp. 51–54.

the charter commission's proposal that Toledo adopt the city manager form of government. In 1928, and again in 1931, four different manager proposals were defeated.[35] These votes did not assure the future of the Jackson administration, which suffered the fate of depression officeholders in 1931. In that year another maverick Republican, Addison C. Thacher, won 70 per cent of the votes cast.

Thacher's administration prepared the way for eventual passage of the council-manager form of government. At this time Toledo suffered from bank failures, high unemployment, heavy debts, virtual bankruptcy, and other acute depression-related urban problems. City services were sharply curtailed or suspended. Mayor Thacher's conduct in office and his administration of relief, in particular, were considered questionable. An investigation of the city relief system revealed many irregularities.[36] Although a grand jury inquiry produced no indictments, there was an aura of corruption.

In 1933 Solon T. Klotz, the perennial Socialist candidate of the 1920s, received the unofficial endorsement of the Republican Party as a rebuke to Mayor Thacher, who had attempted to challenge Walter F. Brown's leadership in the party. Klotz received 38 per cent of the vote, defeating Thacher by 2,619 votes. The Toledo *News-Bee* and other papers were soon highly critical of Mayor Klotz's leadership qualities, and conflicts raged between department heads who were attempting to seize the helm in the absence of direction by the mayor.[37] The ineptitude of the mayor and the financial crisis which found the city defaulting on its bonds and paying salaries in script led to a reconsideration of charter revision. In the opinion of some former Independents, Toledo needed a complete change from the old mayor-council system.

---

[35] The 1928 proposals were for (1) a city manager and a small council elected at large by proportional representation—this proposal received the support of 41 per cent of those voting; (2) a city manager and a council of eleven, ten elected by wards and one elected at large—this proposal received the support of 32 per cent of those voting.

The 1931 proposals were for (1) a city manager and a council of nine, five elected by districts and four elected at large—37.5 per cent of those voting supported this proposal; (2) a city manager and a council of 21 elected by wards—this proposal received the support of 26.5 per cent of those voting.

[36] Emch, ''The City Manager Government of Toledo,'' p. 63.

[37] Emch, p. 66.

Pressure for the Council-Manager System

In the fall of 1933, *The Blade* started a series of six articles on the council-manager plan of government, especially as practiced in Cincinnati. Although *The Blade* had opposed the council-manager proposals in 1928 and 1931, it now appeared to be sympathetic to such a move. The Toledo *News-Bee* had consistently advocated a small city council elected by proportional representation and a city manager appointed by the council.

At the same time that *The Blade* was featuring the manager form, Charles F. Weiler, a leader in the Independent Movement, organized a citizens' commission to draft a charter amendment. The Citizens' Charter Committee included many who had participated in the earlier reform period. Among the members were Percy Jones, son of Golden Rule Jones, Wendell Johnson, student of the Jones-Whitlock period, O. Garfield Jones, Joseph Yager, and others who hoped that charter reform would make it possible for Toledo to have a truly efficient, nonpartisan, and democratic local government. In the judgment of committee members, the nonpartisan ballot alone had not produced the qualified officeholders and competent city government which Toledo needed.

The Citizens' Charter Committee used Cincinnati as a model in drafting an amendment providing for a city manager and a nine-member city council elected at large by proportional representation. The amendment proposed that the mayor and the vice-mayor be chosen by the city council instead of by direct election. It called for the abolition of the mayor's veto powers, making the mayor a ceremonial rather than an actual executive. The proposed charter amendment granted the city manager extensive administrative powers.[38]

In planning a strategy to achieve acceptance of the proposal, the Citizens' Charter Committee decided to place the amendment on the ballot by initiative petition. Such a campaign would provide an opportunity to interest and educate the voters. Members of the Committee also hoped that this would discourage submission of

[38] For a detailed discussion of the provisions of the charter amendment, see Emch, pp. 132–136.

alternative plans, which had confused the manager issue in both 1928 and 1931. Dr. O. Garfield Jones, chairman of the petitions committee, appealed to the alumni and students of the University of Toledo for aid.[39] A city-wide organization, consisting mostly of University of Toledo students, canvassed the city and obtained the necessary signatures.

The campaign for the city manager proposal was sluggish. Very few organizations or papers opposed the charter amendment. Although organized labor was generally unsympathetic to the manager plan, it did not offer significant opposition. The Central Labor Union (A.F. of L.) objected to the amendment on the basis of its provision for at-large rather than ward elections.[40] The UAW, which was struggling to establish itself as a federal union in the A.F. of L., was not yet in a position to consider such questions as municipal charter amendments.

The manager proposal received the support of community organizations and leaders, with only a few exceptions. An East Toledo club and paper registered their fear that at-large elections would mean a loss of representation for the East side. Walter F. Brown, Republican party chairman, criticized proportional representation as "bewildering, fortuitous, and un-American." On the affirmative side were *The Blade, The Times,* and the Toledo *News-Bee,* all of which gave the amendment enthusiastic editorial support. The manager proposal was also endorsed by the League of Women Voters; the American Association of University Women; the South Side Chamber of Commerce; the Associated Taxpayers of Lucas County, Inc.; and the Lions Club. Additional support came from the Toledo Area Chamber of Commerce and the clergy.[41]

On November 6, 1934, 54.5 per cent of those voting favored the charter amendment providing for the council-manager form of government, a marked contrast with earlier efforts. Donovan Emch of the University of Toledo concluded that the most important reasons for passage of the amendment included the editorial support of the press, the poor record of Mayors Klotz and Thacher, the financial crisis of the depression, and the absence of organized opposition.

[39] Dr. Jones was also chairman of the Political Science Department at the University of Toledo.

[40] Emch, ''The City Manager Government of Toledo,'' p. 147.

[41] Emch, pp. 142, 148.

Formation and activities of the City Manager League. Shortly
after the November election, members of the Citizens' Committee
met to consider plans for a permanent organization to support the
council-manager form of government. In January 1935, the City
Manager League of Toledo was incorporated for the purpose of
"making the city charter an effective instrument for good government and to foster and defend efficient and nonpartisan local government."[42] The preamble of the League constitution stated:

> Believing that the continuous and constructive concern of citi-
> zens is the price of good government, we form this League and
> dedicate ourselves to the task of securing an efficient administra-
> tion of the affairs of Toledo. We unite to fulfill the purpose of the
> City Charter of Toledo by endeavoring to provide our city with
> management inspired by adequate municipal vision, guided by
> practical knowledge and experience, and committed to the ideal of
> local government without partisanship or patronage.[43]

The League's first involvement in politics came in May 1935,
when it fought off an attempt to repeal the manager plan before it
went into effect. The repeal effort, which was supported by the Klotz
administration and the City and County Employees' Union, proposed retention of the old system of an elective executive with a
council of 22 members elected by wards. The City Manager League
conducted a registration drive, a strenuous campaign in the wards
and precincts, and an appeal through the mass media. The repeal
effort was defeated by a 60 per cent vote, but in September 1937,
the City Manager League had another round with the forces of
opposition. The 1937 proposal provided for a city manager and a
council of 22 members elected by wards. The League found its
efforts vindicated on election day when this amendment was defeated by a 66 per cent vote.

The City Manager League also dominated the municipal elections
of 1935 and 1937. The League made its first endorsements in 1935,
when it supported nine candidates for the council. The candidates
in turn pledged themselves to the city manager form of government, nonpartisanship, honesty, and efficiency. In the campaign the
City Manager League maintained a headquarters which provided

---

[42] Quoted in Ford, "Recent Elections May Have Ended Nonpartisanism
Here," p. 3.

[43] Emch, "The City Manager Government of Toledo," p. 161.

literature, advertising, broadcasting, campaign workers, and $500.00 to each candidate for campaign expenses. Five of the endorsed candidates were elected out of a field of 58. In the 1937 municipal election, eight of the nine candidates endorsed by the League were elected from a total of 19 running.

The City Manager League, during this period of maximum activity from 1934 to 1937, had a mailing list of 4,000 and a membership of 1,500.[44] In these years of influence, both political parties were quiescent. The League avoided direct attacks on either party and endorsed both Democrats and Republicans for city council. Nevertheless, observers noted a certain affinity between the City Manager League and the Republican Party. Many of the founders and members of the League were Republicans. The Republican Party accommodated the League by making no endorsements in either 1935 or 1937. The Democratic Party emerged in 1937 only to endorse five Democrats and four Republicans. In 1939 partisan interest revived slightly and the League suffered a serious setback as only four of its nine candidates were elected. For the first time League candidates did not control city council.

In 1940 the City Manager League went out of existence as an incorporated entity, although it has reappeared on several occasions, particularly in the late '50s, as an informal organization. Out of the experience and the membership of the City Manager League developed the Greater Toledo Municipal League. The Municipal League, founded in Toledo in 1935 by many of those active in the City Manager League, is a tax-exempt, research organization committed to the tenets of reform. Unlike the City Manager League, the Municipal League has not involved itself in electoral activity.

Resurgence of partisan politics. During the war, politics in Toledo was subdued. The comfortable Republican majority in city council was not threatened until 1945, when the Democrats elected four councilmen. The increased partisanship of the 1945 election caused *The Blade* to comment on the "deterioration of theoretical nonpartisanship since the death of the City Manager League."[45] Theoretical nonpartisanship had been linked with Republican predominance in Toledo. For many reform leaders, candidates, and voters, Republicanism in national politics took the form of nonpar-

[44] Emch, p. 186.
[45] Quoted in Ford, "Recent Election May Have Ended Nonpartisanism Here," p. 3.

tisanship in local elections. The Roosevelt elections ended Republican predominance and altered the conditions for local nonpartisanship. Democratic victories in presidential and state elections gradually affected the nature of local politics. By 1945, Democratic candidates were more combative and more interested in asserting their partisanship. Republicans also found themselves in changing circumstances. They could no longer expect election as a consequence of the traditional partisan or nonpartisan inclination of Toledo voters. A greater effort by the party organization was required.

The growth of the UAW also altered the local political scene to the advantage of the Democrats and in the direction of increased partisanship in the postwar period. The organizing drives of the late '30s and '40s, the rapid growth during the war years, and the leadership of Richard T. Gosser made the UAW a political influence in Toledo by the middle '40s.[46] In the early '40s the UAW had organized a political arm, the United Labor Committee, which screened candidates and made endorsements. The UAW, with its numbers and its political organization, added an important new component to the Democratic Party in Toledo. Thus postwar politics took place in a context which was significantly changed, yet still deeply influenced by the reform tradition.

The legacy of reform was seen in a half-hearted attempt to abandon the council-manager form of government in 1946. A charter amendment providing for a return to an elective chief executive with a city council of 22 elected by wards failed to arouse an active effort by organized labor or the political parties. The City Manager League remained dormant. Although the manager plan had perhaps met with less than complete enthusiasm in the past decade, it had the benefit of the reform tradition and inertia. Fifty-four per cent of those voting favored retaining the manager plan.

In 1947 party politics was ascendent as the Democrats won their first majority under council-manager government. The Democrats used their five-to-four majority to elect the mayor and the vice-mayor by a party vote. The new council, headed by Mayor Michael V. DiSalle, later Governor of Ohio (1958–1962) and Vice Mayor Thomas Burke of the UAW, called for the resignation of the city manager. They replaced him with a more congenial choice who

<hr/>

[46] Richard Gosser was elected Regional Director UAW Region 2-B in 1942; in 1947 he was elected an international vice-president on the Reuther ticket.

FIGURE 3.1

Democratic Percentage in Different Types of Elections, 1952–1965*

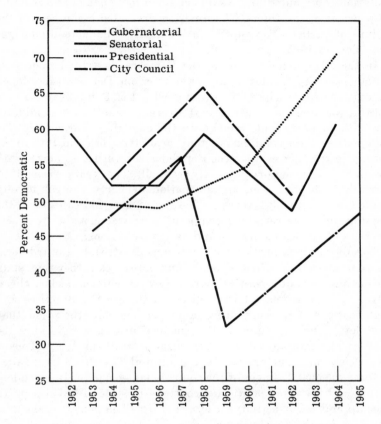

* Data from Lucas County Board of Elections, *Election Abstracts.*

frankly admitted that party affiliation would have a bearing on his selection of administrative officers.[47]

In 1949 the Democratic Party launched a vigorous campaign for the repeal of proportional representation. The voters responded by passing an amendment providing for a nine-member council elected

[47] Ford, ''Recent Election May Have Ended Nonpartisanism Here.''

at large after a primary to reduce the total number of candidates to 18. Fatigue with the complexity and slowness of proportional representation contributed to the support given to a change approved by 66 per cent of the voters. This revision presented a contrast to the failure of earlier efforts to repeal or modify the council-manager provisions of 1935.

In the 1949 council election, the Democrats retained their five-to-four majority, but lost their power after one Democrat developed an unexpected proclivity for voting with the Republicans. Party politics was dominant in the 1951 election as only two candidates ran without party endorsement. In the changing character of Toledo politics, these candidates found themselves 16th and 18th in the voting. In the 1951 election the Republicans returned to power with an eight-to-one majority in city council. The years from 1953 through 1965 have seen an alternation of party control in city council, as Figure 3.1 reveals. The figure also indicates that the Republicans have remained competitive or victorious at the local level despite reversals in state and national elections.

The days when parties took a hands-off attitude toward local elections are now long past. Today candidates seek rather than shun the endorsement of a political party. Few councilmen declare themselves to be men apart from politics. Although the practices and organizations of reform politics no longer dominate the scene, they have left a definite imprint. Reform institutions, now lacking the support of a militant citizens' organization, still survive in Toledo. The Democratic Party, organized labor, and *The Blade* have failed to force the abandonment of the council-manager plan. Independent voting and maverick politicians continue in spite of obvious partisanship and party activity in local politics. The next two chapters will examine these phenomena.

4 POLITICAL PARTIES: THE DEMOCRATIC PARTY

The role of political parties has important consequences for a local political system. Differences resulting from party organization and activity are evident in comparisons of politics in Los Angeles and Chicago or Detroit and New York.[1] Parties may be an important means of centralizing political influence and recruiting and electing officeholders or they may be bystanders in the local electoral and policy process. Reformers hoped to make them bystanders. Yet even among nonpartisan cities there is considerable variety in party organization and activity.[2] The reform movement has generally failed to substitute individual participation for party politics.[3] In some cities, however, reform institutions have affected parties and the political system as a whole.

[1] For a comparison of these cities, see Edward C. Banfield and James Q. Wilson, *City Politics* (Cambridge, Mass.: Harvard University Press and M.I.T. Press, 1963), pp. 110–111; Edward C. Banfield, *Political Influence* (New York: The Free Press, 1961); Wallace S. Sayre and Herbert Kaufman, *Governing New York City* (New York: Russell Sage Foundation, 1960); and David Greenstone, *A Report on the Politics of Detroit* (Cambridge, Mass.: Joint Center for Urban Studies, 1960, mimeographed).

[2] Charles R. Adrian, ''A Typology for Nonpartisan Elections,'' *Western Political Quarterly*, XII (June 1959), 449–458.

[3] For the effects of nonpartisanship in a number of large cities, see Charles E. Gilbert, ''Some Aspects of Nonpartisan Elections in Large Cities,'' *Midwest Journal of Political Science*, VI (November 1962), 345–362.

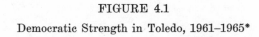

FIGURE 4.1

Democratic Strength in Toledo, 1961–1965*

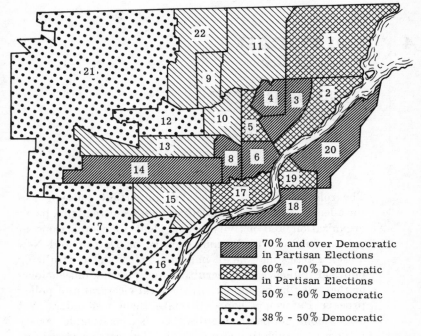

70% and over Democratic
in Partisan Elections

60% - 70% Democratic
in Partisan Elections

50% - 60% Democratic

38% - 50% Democratic

* Democratic strength is measured by a ward's average Democratic vote in partisan elections of the period, 1961–1965. Data from Lucas County Board of Elections, *Election Abstracts.*

In Toledo the Democratic and the Republican parties have had weak organizations since the advent of reform. During the past five decades, both party organizations have gone through several cycles of disintegration and partial revival. The decline of the parties was most acute in the 1930s and 1950s, when neither party could successfully challenge the City Manager League. The '40s and '60s can be seen, in comparison, as decades of relative partisan resurgence. The '40s saw the rebirth of party politics under the city manager form of government and a Democratic predominance in presidential elections. In the following decade, charter battles over the manager plan and the renewed potency of reform groups had a divisive and debilitating effect on both parties. In the '60s both parties have shown signs of revival. The Republican Party has made certain innovations to protect its existence in a Democratic environment. The Democratic Party has indicated an interest in developing an organization capable of adding city government to its record of electoral success. In both the Democratic and the Republican Party there is a segment interested in improving the party organization. In neither case is this segment in a controlling position in party affairs.

Although the Democratic Party has been the weaker of the two parties in organization, it has been bolstered by the favorable political trends resulting from the Roosevelt realignment of the '30s. Since the New Deal, the Democratic Party in Toledo and elsewhere has found its strength in a coalition of organized labor and minority and lower-income groups. In Toledo the Democratic Party draws strong support in the wards where there are high percentages of Negroes, Poles, and Hungarians. Thus the party has a core of consistent strength in the 4th and 14th (Polish), 6th and 8th (Negro), and 20th (Hungarian) wards. The Democratic Party also receives strong support in the other lower-income, predominantly blue-collar wards of the city, the 3rd, 17th, 18th, and 19th wards. Figure 4.1 depicts Democratic strength in partisan elections from 1961 to 1965.

John Patrick Kelly, Democratic Party Chairman

The Democratic party chairman, John Patrick Kelly, is in the tradition of the big-city Irish politician. In assuming the party leadership in 1945, Kelly followed a long line of Irish chairmen. He has continued the style of the oldtime city boss, while lacking the organization to turn out the vote. Kelly had been especially popular in low-income and foreign-born wards in city and county elections of the 1930s.[4] Even today the party chairman is said by his admirers to be the classic political leader to whom the rank and file can and do turn when their families are short on food or coal, when men are out of work, or when children are in trouble.[5] Although this characterization probably has a greater basis in sentiment than in present

[4] *The Blade*, January 25, 1966, p. 12.
[5] *The Blade*, February 1, 1959, Section 2, p. 1.

practices, Kelly is devoted to the traditions, organization, and candidates of the Democratic Party.

As he approaches 70, Kelly finds his power increasingly dependent on the support of other men of his generation. In resisting the challenge of younger Democrats, he can rely on the support of 22 ward chairmen and numerous precinct committeemen who have been elected to these positions with his backing. These longtime local functionaries are closely identified with Kelly and represent a powerful contingent on the Democratic Central Committee and the 72-member Executive Committee which it elects.[6] Thus Kelly has fortified his position by favors and friendships with older party officials and workers who are a substantial and probably a preponderant group in the party structure.

The Kelly group can be described as organization Democrats who are uninterested in political activity. Although they are highly concerned with the party organization and with their stake in it, they do not see the party as a device for strenuous campaign activities. The party, as the Kelly Democrats know it, is a comfortable circle of friendships and associations.[7] The crucial question to older Democrats is not to improve the party's showing in elections but to maintain their own positions of power in the party. Innovations are considered disruptive and threatening.

The Democratic Party, in the opinion of some senior members, is already at maximum effectiveness. One Kelly supporter on the Executive Committee found it "impossible to imagine how the Democratic Party could become more active." The Democrats, in spite of apparent setbacks such as the defeats of 1961, 1963, and 1965, are always, in Kelly's words, in their "best year yet."[8] The assessment of every election yields a favorable forecast. The senior leadership of the Democratic Party does not feel a responsibility to maintain a vigorous political organization in and between campaigns or to participate in unsettling postelection appraisals or reforms.

---

[6] The Executive Committee includes all ward chairmen and the presidents of area Democratic clubs, women's Democratic clubs, and the Young Democrats. There are 18 at-large members—six from labor, six from industry, six from the public.

[7] For a discussion of clubhouse politics and the conflict of the traditional political style with new demands, see Theodore J. Lowi, *At the Pleasure of the Mayor* (New York: The Free Press, 1964), Chapters VIII and IX.

[8] The Democrats elected one councilman in 1961, three councilmen in 1963, and three councilmen in 1965.

Older Democrats defer to the younger men and party officeholders on issues. The associations of a lifetime rather than political
issues or electoral activity are of prime importance to the older
leaders. For this reason, Kelly Democrats sometimes express a kin-
ship with the oldtime leaders of the Republican Party. Both recognize that a situation which would jeopardize the older leaders of one
party would quickly imperil the older leaders of the opposition
party. Their mutual interest in stability is perhaps more significant
than the desire for electoral victories.

Discontent with Kelly's leadership began to increase in the late
1950s, when young Democratic officeholders and their supporters
became restive about their exclusion from positions of influence in
the party.[9] A former Democratic councilman complained that the
party was ruled by a clique which was hostile even to officeholders.
Another complained that "the Democratic Party had gotten to be a
pretty closed club by the late '50s." Other Democratic officeholders
were dissatisfied with the party's failure to provide them with
guidance on state and local issues. In one Democrat's unhappy
recollection:

> I was a complete novice when I was first elected to city council.
> I went to the party leaders to discuss city problems and they
> couldn't have been less interested. The party tie seemed to end the
> day after the election.

Prominent young Democrats were also displeased with the party's apathetic attitude on candidate endorsements. In the judgment
of several popular Democratic officeholders, the party had made no
effort to recruit and endorse attractive candidates:

> X———— and X———— came to the party and said
> "we're Democrats" and they ran as Democrats. One wasn't quali-
> fied for public office and one couldn't win an election. The party
> must go and get good men if it is to build up organization and
> leadership.

Another Democrat objected to the determination of party slates by
"the personal whim of a few men."

Several officeholders were unhappy to discover that victory in an
election and dedication to the job did not mean party support in the

---

[9] The conflict of old line politicians and the younger generation of ambitious
officeholders is not uncommon in city politics. See Banfield and Wilson, *City
Politics*, p. 120.

next contest. One Toledo Democrat in state government found that
the party took a hands-off position in a primary race even though
his opponent had formerly been an Independent candidate and
officeholder. Another Democrat expressed resentment at the reluc-
tance with which the party endorsed him despite his proven popularity at the polls. Local Democrats were especially critical of the
party's failure to endorse candidates for council in the primary
elections prior to 1965. This omission was considered responsible for
the dispersal of the Democratic vote in the primary and the shortage of strong candidates for the general election.

The Young Turk Movement

What became known as the "Young Turk" movement arose in
earnest in 1959, when the Democratic Party's effort to introduce the
strong mayor plan was defeated by the City Manager League, and
when two apostate Democrats were elected to city council. After the
1959 election, there was discussion of party reorganization and
Kelly's removal. But when action was finally taken, Kelly emerged
as chairman of the reorganization committee, which he then pro-
ceeded to appoint.

In 1961, the Young Turks, under the leadership of Congressman
Thomas Ludlow Ashley and County Commission President Ned
Skeldon, renewed their effort to reform the party. In a bitter
Executive Committee battle, Ashley and Skeldon pushed through
reforms designed to broaden the party structure. Four new committees were established to dilute the power of the party chairman and
his contingent on the Executive Committee and to draw more young
Democrats into the party organization. The new committees on
organization, finance, candidate selection and endorsement, and policy testified to Skeldon's and Ashley's influence. But the reorganization was not accomplished without serious costs and limitations.
Senior Democrats were angered by the effort to dislodge them.
Furthermore, the new committees were established on Kelly's
terms. The referral of committee decisions to the Executive Committee meant that Kelly's power remained secure.

Nevertheless, the party leadership was changed by the 1961 conflict. In the years after 1961 neither the senior Democrats nor the
Young Turks were willing to risk a challenge to the other. In the
summer of 1965, one young Democrat explained:

> We can't tangle with them now. We probably couldn't swing it in the Executive Committee with 99 per cent of the ward chairmen and precinct committeemen being Kelly men. As long as Kelly allows us to be active, we won't dispute him or force a showdown.

Those sympathetic to Kelly are at pains to deny any disharmony in the party: "There is no bad feeling. Kelly has the ward organization and the younger men are working on new programs."

The accommodation resulting from the 1961 reorganization allowed the congressman and the president of the Board of County Commissioners to exercise increased influence. One observer commented: "Now the party includes Kelly, Lud [the congressman], and Ned [the president of the Board of County Commissioners]." Ashley and Skeldon used their enlarged role to introduce a number of innovations in party activities. The 1964 campaign provided the testing ground for new campaign and fund-raising practices. A vigorous registration drive was conducted with the cooperation of organized labor. The party initiated a $100-a-plate dinner and "Dollars for Democrats Days" to bolster its finances. Local and state candidates were screened by the committee on candidate selection and endorsement.

Skeldon and Ashley also established a block worker program to invigorate the party's efforts in the wards for the 1964 election. One prominent Democrat active in the 1964 campaign recalled: "Kelly didn't interfere when we used the committee on organization and our 2500 block workers to bypass the old wooden soldiers [in the wards] who were dead and didn't know it." The block workers distributed literature, canvassed the wards, indexed voters and Democratic partisans, and assisted voters to get to the polls. In some cases they worked closely with ward chairmen and precinct committeemen. But the block worker program as a whole represented an effort to develop a separate and more energetic ward organization.

The Municipal Election of 1965 and Its Significance

The 1964 victories were not followed by the usual dormant period between campaigns. Plans were immediately underway for a major effort in the 1965 municipal election in which Toledo was to elect its mayor for the first time in 30 years. The Democratic candidate for mayor, Ned Skeldon, was given the support of an expanded fund-raising program, an enlarged corps of block workers, and a new party headquarters with a full-time staff. In another significant departure from past practices, Skeldon entered the October primary with a slate of eight endorsed candidates for city council. For the first time the Democratic Party endorsed and supported a complete ticket of candidates in the municipal primary.

As the 1965 election approached, there were currents of restrained animosity between Kelly Democrats and the Young Turks. These animosities, although largely concealed from public view, affected the 1965 campaign. Older Democrats recalled Skeldon's efforts to reduce their power in the party. They resented the system of committees by which Skeldon and Ashley had attempted to circumvent Kelly. Senior party leaders interpreted Skeldon's block worker program as an insult to what they might have contributed to the campaign. Furthermore, Kelly Democrats realized that Skeldon was expected to assume party leadership if elected mayor. Thus party loyalties were divided. Many ward and precinct officials could not bring themselves to campaign for Skeldon or to express disappointment at his defeat. On election night John P. Kelly commented:

> It was a good vote today. Democrats voted. Look how some Democrats ran. I guess the electorate just didn't buy Ned's program. But nobody worked harder to win than Ned did.[10]

New campaign practices had proved insufficient to counteract old dissensions.

The Democratic Supporters

Labor. The Democratic Party is more closely identified with organized labor than with any other segment of the community. Yet leaders in the party and in labor agree that this association has not been a happy one through the years. Although the Democratic Party has relied on organized labor in many campaign efforts, "it was a rather unfriendly alliance of necessity—a kind of strange

---

[10] *The Blade*, November 3, 1965, p. 11. Only three of nine Democrats were elected. Skeldon (D.) received 47,556 votes to 65,615 for John Potter (R.).

sharing of the bed," in the judgment of one prominent Democrat. There was a feeling of mutual distrust between Kelly Democrats and union leaders. Oldtime Democrats suspected organized labor and the United Auto Workers, in particular, of trying to capture the party. One older Democrat emphasized his fear that "the Democratic Party has often been in danger of being swallowed by one group—labor." For others, resentment focused on the personalities of labor leaders or on union proposals to strengthen the party. To the older generation, union leaders represented a militant and insatiable element in the party.

The Young Turk movement has attempted to improve the Democratic Party's ties with AFL-CIO unions, particularly the UAW. Several younger Democrats have maintained close personal relationships with union leaders. Others have received consistent support from the union which Kelly Democrats considered the most insidious, the UAW. Most younger Democrats find the fear of labor control to be unwarranted. One leader in the Young Turk movement explained his views this way: "I believe in labor and the philosophy of labor. Labor's political goals are the same as the Democratic Party's. Both labor and the Democratic Party benefit from the association." A former Democratic councilman recalled:

> The UAW contributed so much to my first campaign that I almost worried about it. But they never asked me for anything or even tried. I don't think it's true that labor tries to control when it participates in the party or in a campaign.

Young Democrats believe that union leaders were justified in resenting their exclusion from positions of influence in a party which willingly employed their services. By treating union leaders with suspicion, Kelly Democrats alienated the party's strongest supporters. The Young Turks have stressed the need for the party to include rather than exclude union leaders. Organizational reforms and the close cooperation of the 1964 campaign helped to remove old irritations for a time. Perhaps more important were Skeldon's close ties with labor (and the United Auto Workers, in particular) and his personal efforts in bringing about an improved relationship. Among some union officials, however, there continued to be a lingering suspicion that Skeldon and Ashley, like Kelly, sought to employ labor's services only when it suited their own purposes. The outcome of the 1965 mayoralty election also caused some disillusionment in the AFL-CIO unions which had endorsed and supported Skeldon.[11] Skeldon's subsequent withdrawal from elective politics further reduced the likelihood of increased labor influence in the Democratic Party and in the community.

The Negroes. The Democratic Party's relations with its Negro supporters have been characterized by indifference rather than strain. Since 1932 the Democratic Party in Toledo has relied on the Negro vote without making any particular effort in the direction of Negro voters. Organizational weakness has been acute in Negro areas such as the 6th and the 8th wards. Democratic leaders of both generations agree that the party organization in these areas has suffered from certain difficulties, but they disagree about the causes. Older Democrats contend that Negroes have rebuffed party efforts: "The Democratic Party has tried to get closer cooperation, but Negroes want to get the results by themselves. They've tried to work too much on their own, outside the party." Another senior Democrat argued that the party's efforts were impeded by "the desire of all Negroes to be Indian chiefs rather than Indians."

The younger generation offers a different interpretation. A prominent Democratic officeholder stated his opinion this way:

> Over the years the senior party organization has not worked on developing organization in the Negro areas. Leadership in Negro wards has been weak, and the party organization has not encouraged it to be otherwise.

Others believe that the party has failed to recruit strong Negro candidates, ward chairmen, and precinct committeemen. A young Democrat active in the party organization commented:

> The Democratic organization is poor in the Negro wards and it hurts us. There are so many Republicans in the Negro leadership that it is important for us to have strong people to work through. But we just don't have them.

The Young Turks have advanced a program to remedy these difficulties. They hoped to extend the block worker program and work with organized labor to recruit Negro candidates and support.

---

[11] The United Labor Committee, the political arm of the AFL-CIO Council, endorsed Skeldon. Skeldon also had the support of the Building Trades Council. The Teamsters supported John W. Potter (R.).

Although a young Negro was included on the Democratic councilmanic ticket in 1965, the Young Turks failed to fulfill most of their objectives. Low voter turn-out and Republican inroads in Negro areas indicate the limitations of imposing a new block worker program on wards long affected by political disorganization.[12] Younger Democrats have not prevailed in developing a stronger political organization in Negro areas. Nevertheless, the Democratic Party has had considerable support from minority groups and from labor even without having an effective organization.

Business and industry. In its relations with the major business interests of the city, however, the Democratic Party has had little support or sympathy. One senior party official explained it this way: "The Democratic Party has had little business support, because business, especially big companies, believes that Democrats are too closely tied to labor." Others emphasize the business leaders' distaste for politics or their disinterest in city problems. In the opinion of one Democratic leader:

> Business executives find the Republican Party more congenial. But even in the GOP, their involvement is limited pretty much to national politics. The top men give community duties to junior executives and junior executives are the worst Republicans. They haven't learned to play both sides.

Although senior party leaders accept the antipathy of business to the Democratic Party as inevitable, some young Democrats are anxious to improve the relationship. One Democratic councilman commenting on his years in office said: "I haven't had many direct dealings with major business people. But if they had wanted something, we would have given it to them. One of our main jobs is to keep these people happy." Several young Democrats are convinced that business leaders could play a much more constructive part in the community if they were to realize the importance of city government. They argue that such activity would be extremely beneficial to urban renewal and other programs as well as serving the interest of Toledo business. The possibility of increased business support for local Democratic candidates has not been fully explored, however. Although prominent executives expressed admira-

---

[12] In the 1965 mayoralty election John W. Potter drew 39 per cent of the vote in the 8th ward. The 6th and 8th wards ranked 20th and 22nd in voting participation in the 1965 election.

tion for Skeldon's leadership in the county, the Democratic Party did not enlist their public support in the 1965 mayoralty election.

In the aftermath of the 1965 election, the alliances and organization of the Democratic Party began to drift. The absence of a Democratic coalition at the local level has been particularly evident in the electoral debacles of recent years. After winning only one council seat in 1961, three in 1963, and three in 1965, the Democratic Party found itself with a dearth of established candidates. In the meantime the Republican Party developed a number of well-known incumbent councilmen who could easily defeat novice Democratic candidates backed by a fractured organization. Internally, the party leadership was weak and divided, with the position of senior Democrats at least temporarily fortified by Skeldon's defeat.

The Democrats and Reform Institutions

Democrats believe that the difficulties of the local party are related to reform institutions as well as to internal problems. On this subject there is little disagreement between the two generations of leaders. Nonpartisanship is believed to have blunted the party's appeal in local elections. In the opinion of one oldtime Democrat:

> The nonpartisan ballot is definitely hard on the party and it hurts the electorate more. It's like teaching a child to play the piano. After you've taught him the keyboard, you don't ask him to play the violin. We emphasize the party label and then give the voter something else in municipal elections.

Another Democratic official observed:

> The nonpartisan ballot affects the party very much, especially among nationality groups, Negroes, and the less educated groups which are predominantly Democratic. These people look for the Democratic label and when it isn't there, they mark familiar names. You can have a strong campaign in a nonpartisan election and still find it impossible to impress on the voters unfamiliar Democratic names.

Democrats contend that nonpartisanship has weakened the party organization and has encouraged independent candidates. In their campaigns such candidates are reluctant to emphasize partisanship and after the election "they are the worst prima donnas of all." In addition to damaging party discipline, nonpartisanship is believed to have favored part-time officeholders with a popular name or personality at the expense of career politicians.

The city-manager form of government is also regarded as detrimental to the Democratic Party and to the community. The election of councilmen at large and the long absence of a directly elected mayor have made it difficult to dramatize city politics. In the judgment of one officeholder: "Without leadership and party responsibility, you can't accomplish much in office. It's all personality, which makes it hard to develop party issues in the next campaign. The voter doesn't see the importance of city government." Another Democrat commented: "The whole thing [nonpartisanship, city-manager form of government] is nicey-nice. It tends to dilute the political system and take politics out of politics, which is great for the Republicans."

In the late 1950s, the Democratic Party made two unsuccessful efforts to free itself from this unfavorable situation. Charter amendments providing for the strong mayor form of government were decisively defeated in 1957 and 1959. In 1964 and 1965, younger Democrats had visions of changing city government without risking another charter battle. They were confident that a directly elected Democratic mayor (Skeldon) with a Democratic council majority could inject new spirit and new power into city government. The election results doomed this possibility.

The Condition of the Party in 1966

In 1966 the Democratic Party included two distinct groups dissimilar in age, outlook, and ideology. On the one side were the older men in their late sixties and seventies, many of whom first became active in the party during the presidency of Woodrow Wilson. To these men the Democratic Party was a fraternal lodge or a clubhouse with the benefits of companionship and in some cases a

part-time occupation. On the other side were the postwar Democrats, who were more attuned to the problems and demands of
contemporary politics. The postwar Democrats differed from the
older generation in associating the Democratic Party with a moderately liberal ideology. They saw the Democratic Party as a means
for carrying out equitable, constructive, and vote-getting programs
at every level of government.

These younger Democrats had not realized their hopes for reshap-
ing the party in Toledo. Skeldon's resounding defeat in the mayoralty election and his decision not to seek reelection to the Board of
County Commissioners in November 1966 shook the leadership of
the Young Turks. And the council defeats had thinned the ranks of
potential supporters.

Thus, as of 1966, the Democratic Party was a feeble organization.
Reforms and innovations introduced in 1961 and 1964 were less
than successful. The ward organization was moribund. The influence of Skeldon and Ashley remained an incomplete and uncertain
development in a party weakened by decades of stagnation. The
possibility of change arose, in late January 1966, when party chairman John P. Kelly announced his intention to resign in May. But
Kelly's decision to retire came at the urging of friends at the
County Court House rather than insurgent Democrats,[13] and the
County Central Committee remained pro-Kelly. Kelly recommended
Morton Neipp, a longtime ally, as his successor, and the Central
Committee, composed of precinct committeemen elected by Demo-
cratic voters every two years, accepted him.[14]

Whether the change of leadership will significantly affect the
party is questionable. Morton Neipp, who headed the 1964 Johnson-Humphrey campaign in Ohio, is more concerned with organization and more acceptable to younger Democrats and to labor than
Kelly. But Neipp will not devote his full time to the party leadership; nor is it certain that he is willing to serve as party chairman
for any length of time. The Democratic Party continues to contain
numerous unresolved problems and divisions.

[13] *The Blade,* January 24, 1966, p. 1, and January 25, 1966, p. 3.

[14] *Ibid.* Neipp is an attorney, radio station executive, real estate investor,
and former state representative. After a conflict among Ohio Democrats, Neipp
assumed the state chairmanship in May 1966, to preserve a semblance of unity
in the state party.

Summary

It appears that the Democratic Party, whatever its leadership, will confront serious problems in local politics. The debilitating effects of the reform movement are not easily reversed. In Toledo the heritage of nonpartisanship, maverick politicians, and independent voting is older than the record of Democratic success which dates back only to the New Deal. As a result of the reform movement, Toledo voters became sympathetic to candidates who disavowed any connection with partisanship and dedicated themselves to principles above parties. Since the 1930s, the Toledo Democratic Party has had successive victories in state and national elections. But the local Democratic organization has remained atrophied and beset by Republicans and reformers. Party leaders have not translated the Democratic strength in the community into an organization capable of defeating municipal reform institutions and their Republican and independent proponents. The ethos and practices of reform politics have been strong enough to withstand the impact of national political allegiances.

The organizational weakness which has permitted the survival of reform institutions in a Democratic city is itself related to the reform movement. Nonpartisanship and the council-manager form of government make it more difficult to rely on the traditional Democratic loyalties of labor, nationality groups, and Negroes. The absence of the party label and a ward-based council have contributed to an amorphous situation. Local governmental institutions have provided no focus, on the ballot, in the wards, or in the city as a whole, for a concerted Democratic effort. Under these conditions local government has presented a challenge to a party consistently successful in other elections.

City government did not seem attractive enough to warrant the necessary Democratic effort. With the county government and victories in state and national elections safely in hand, the Democratic Party lacked the motivation for a major effort in the city. One Democrat commented: "The city with its nonpartisan form of government didn't seem important. There seemed to be relatively little to win there." Other Democrats noted that the county government has the power (in a three member board), partisanship, and patronage to appeal to the party at the local level. In contrast, divided power, nonpartisanship, and an extensive civil service have made the city government less attractive.[15] Older Democrats were inclined to doubt the importance of offices without patronage. Younger Democrats doubted that a city government with power divided between a manager and a nine-headed council could do much for the city or for the career of an ambitious politician.

The Democratic Party has had neither the interest nor the organization to prevail in city politics. The Democratic coalition in Toledo has its basis in national politics rather than local organization. When the social and economic issues of state and national politics are removed, the inadequacies of the local organization are fully evident. City government rarely, if ever, provides such effective partisan material as the 1958 right-to-work proposal, the 1964 Goldwater candidacy, or the 1965 reapportionment plan. Consequently, offices and organization are particularly important at the local level.

For thirty years the council-manager plan in Toledo lacked a single, decisive office to emphasize in a partisan appeal. The absence of a directly elected mayor (and a strong political leader) served to insulate city government and the reform tradition from effective Democratic appeals. The first direct election of the mayor in 1965 failed to alter this situation. But a Democratic mayor, when and if elected, would hold a position of leadership from which to emphasize his work on urban renewal, the war on poverty, and civil rights, thereby linking himself with national Democratic policies. Such a position and emphasis could stimulate greater participation from organized labor and other Democratic groups which have shared the party's relative disinterest in city government.

Furthermore, an elective mayor introduces the political stakes long missing in city politics. In a city of 390,000 an elected mayor can be a dominant local figure and a significant influence in state politics. Such an office provides an attractive opportunity for leadership and political exposure. Under these conditions career politicians will join the usual reformers and part-time lawyers in local elections, as the 1965 election indicates. Some of these considerations may affect the future course of a local Democratic Party long lacking in leadership, organization and candidates.

[15] The Democratic showing in county elections has been consistently higher than the Democratic percentage in city council elections. The percentages for council elections in the past ten years: 1955, 51 per cent; 1957, 56; 1959, 33 (endorsed Democrats); 1961, 38; 1963, 43; 1965, 48. The percentages for county elections: 1956, 56 per cent; 1957, 79; 1960, 55; 1962, 60; 1964, 60.

5 POLITICAL PARTIES: THE REPUBLICAN PARTY

In contrast to the Democratic Party, the Republican Party is a more cohesive organization but with smaller support. The Republican Party has not had a broad appeal to all segments of the community since the 1920s, when Walter F. Brown was party chairman. Under Brown's leadership, the Republican Party had substantial support from ethnic groups, Negroes, and working people. With the advent of Franklin D. Roosevelt and the departure of Brown, this support diminished.[1] The Republican Party became and has continued to be a minority party in Toledo. Nevertheless, the party has held its own locally. Although the Democratic Party has had the advantage of national political trends, the Republican Party has had the benefit of local conditions. Nonpartisanship and the city manager form of government have allowed Republicans to be competitive in a decidedly Democratic city.

The Republican Party enjoys its strongest support in five wards[2]—the 7th, 9th, 12th, 16th, and 21st—which are the five highest in the city in terms of social-economic class.[3]

---

[1] For a discussion of Brown's career, see Harvey S. Ford, "Walter Folger Brown," *Northwest Ohio Quarterly*, XXVI (Summer 1954), 200–210. Brown resigned as Republican Party chairman in 1935.

[2] Areas of Republican strength are evident in Figure 4.1, p. 48.

[3] The measure of social-economic class used in this study was based on three components: the percentage with an eighth grade education or less; the percentage employed in a blue collar occupation; and the

The converse is not true for the Democratic Party, however. Of the five wards which are lowest in social-economic class—the 3rd, 6th, 8th, 17th, and 18th—only the 8th and the 18th are in the top five wards of Democratic support.

The leadership of the Republican Party is divided by a conflict of generations roughly similar to that in the Democratic Party. In both parties, officeholders are dissatisfied with the organization and leadership of oldtime party professionals. In both the Democratic and the Republican parties, the disagreement between generations extends to questions of policy as well as organization. Younger Republicans and Democrats are more liberal than the senior leadership of their parties. They are more concerned with issues and with organization. They see their parties as failing to develop the issues and organization needed for maximum success. They want the kind of activity, effort, and innovation which they think they can provide.

John S. Andrews, Republican Party Chairman

In the Republican Party, officeholders believe that a young (45) party chairman has only limited power, while in the Democratic Party officeholders have long wished to restrict the power of an oldline chairman. The Republican Party Chairman, John S. Andrews is a protégé of Ray Bliss, whom he succeeded as Ohio state chairman when Bliss was named national chairman. Andrews was first associated with Bliss in state campaigns of the early '50s. In 1955 he abandoned business for politics by resigning as an executive assistant to the president of Owens-Corning Fiberglas Corporation to become executive director of the Republican Party in Lucas County. He spent 1960–1961 as director of Bliss's field organization and then returned to Toledo as executive director and assumed the party chairmanship in 1962.[4] After his election as state chairman in

---

percentage with a family income of $5,000 or less. These percentages were averaged and subtracted from 100 to produce a scale of social-economic class in which higher scores indicate higher class.

[4] Information on Andrews' career comes from *The Blade*, January 13, 1965, p. 1.

March 1965, Andrews indicated that he would also retain the local party chairmanship.

Andrews' local organization is closely identified with Ray Bliss's ideas for a competitive Republican Party.[5] Like Bliss, Andrews insists that his concern is with organization, not ideology. His private political philosophy resembles the moderately conservative viewpoint of the Republican national chairman. Andrews fully accepts Bliss's conviction that the Republican Party must regain support from ethnic groups, Negroes, and lower-income voters. Both men consider the party's future dependent upon a revival of Republican strength in the big cities. Because of this, the Republican Party cannot continue to write off traditionally Democratic components of the urban vote. Toledo offered Bliss and Andrews an opportunity to test innovations and strategies in an industrial, Democratic city.

One major innovation was the establishment of a full-time executive directorship with an annual salary of $12,000. The purpose of this position was to overcome the ephemeral nature of the local party organization. Andrews and Bliss are convinced that full-time, professional leadership is essential for party success. One of Andrews' associates summarized the party chairman's views this way: "John knows that you don't sell a bar of soap with one ad or one month's work." Under Andrews as executive director, the Republican Party has had a full-time headquarters and staff.

Andrews' prescription for Republican success combines professional leadership with other considerations. The party chairman believes that an effective Republican organization must have efficient fund-raising procedures, attractive candidates, an active ward organization, and the support of Republican volunteers. In both organization and policies, the party must demonstrate that its appeal is not limited by income, occupation, race, or religion. Andrews has hoped to make the local Republican Party an effective organization with a broadened base of community support.

Although the party chairman is relatively young, his most enthusiastic support comes from prominent senior members of the Executive Committee. Older men sympathetic to Andrews include the former party chairman (1949–1962), a longtime member of the

[5] For Bliss's views on political organization and ideology, see articles in *The New York Times*, January 13, 1965, pp. 1 and 10, and April 1, 1965, p. 27.

Board of Elections, a close associate of Ray Bliss, and a construction and insurance man long active in the party.

Views of Senior Republican Party Leaders

Senior Republicans, like their contemporaries in the Democratic Party, are concerned with organization rather than issues. One older Republican commented: "I'm interested in organization and politics. I don't know much about issues. I don't pay much attention to them. They change a lot and the elected people follow them."

Underlying this detachment from issues is, in some cases, a harsh conservatism. While Andrews insists that the Republican Party must develop a broader following, senior Republicans sharply disparage organized labor, Negroes, and lower-income groups. One, for example, denied that the Republican Party needed to attract the support of any group other than business. Senior Republicans believe that the party has had excellent support from the major companies and other business interests. Organized labor is seen as a sinister agent of the Democratic Party. Many older Republicans express a mixture of resentment and envy about the political activities of labor:

> We have to compete with a party which has the advantage of a wealthy and unscrupulous labor movement, its coffers reeking with money. On election day, out at the Kaiser Plant alone you'll find anywhere between 300 and 500 men electioneering—on company time. It's bad enough for city elections, but for national elections, Christ! You have to fight to get into the polling places.

Officials in Toledo unions are depicted as boorish underworld figures seeking to make all officeholders beholden to them and to promote a massive give-away of public funds.

Senior Republicans are no more sympathetic to Negro organizations and the civil rights movement. The Democratic allegiance of Negro voters is considered as inevitable and unyielding as that of organized labor. In the judgment of one oldline Republican:

> Negroes will always vote Democratic. The Goldwater thing cinched that. Prior to Goldwater, it was F.D.R., the white god to

> Negroes. Now this kind of loyalty can't exist without daily feed-
> ing. The unions are nurturing the Negroes and they're Demo-
> cratic.

A senior Republican official summarized his opinion of organized
labor and the civil rights movement this way:

> The unions want to run and control this country at all levels
> and the civil rights movement is encouraging an anarchy every-
> where which will break the camel's back. A lack of restraint and
> judgment is spreading—with the encouragement of Washington,
> D.C. The whole system could collapse.

Senior Republicans are opposed to the "imitation of Democratic
give-away programs." They believe that the Republican Party
should offer the voter a conservative alternative, but that ideology
should not stand in the way of success. For this reason many older
Republicans opposed the Goldwater candidacy in 1964 and continue
to resist the local influence of those committed to Goldwater conservatism.

Like their counterparts in the Democratic Party, senior Republicans value their party for its associations rather than for its ideology or political activities. They are complacent about the past and
future performance of the party. The local Republican organization, in their opinion, is already at a pinnacle of success. By
establishing the position of executive director, the party has surpassed all other party organizations and eliminated the need for
additional reforms or increased activity. Senior Republicans attrib-
ute this utopian condition to the leadership of their protégé in
organization politics, John Andrews. They are no more interested in
strenuous campaign activities than are their contemporaries in the
Democratic Party. In the opinion of one Republican leader: "Parties can only do so much. Every year we do what we *can* do and this
is dependent on the bank account. I know that Kelly also feels that
there are limits on party activity."

Views of Younger Republicans

Many Republican officeholders do not share the senior leaders'
ideology, optimism, or enthusiasm for Andrews. They consider the
party organization to be self-satisfied and the leadership over-

praised. To them, party activities have represented only a token effort. Young Republican critics believe that highly acclaimed leadership and innovations have in fact failed to break the prevailing lethargy. One officeholder commented that the Republican Party, like the Democratic Party, is an incomplete and inactive organization, filled with oldtimers. Another popular Republican vote-getter complained about the exclusion of officeholders from the Executive Committee and party decisions:

> The Republican Executive Committee and the local party organization are strongly controlled by a few men in their seventies. These men make Andrews' policy decisions for him. The rest of us don't have much to say.

A city councilman was disappointed that older leaders of the party had shown no interest in developing an active grass-roots organization. Another councilman summarized his views this way:

> We need a rejuvenation of political parties in Toledo, especially the Republican Party. I see a slow decline of the Republican Party due to the inactivity of the leadership. There are four or five old men who want to keep control and who pretty much do control Andrews. There are lots of dead people at all levels. There are people who could contribute to the party, but don't.

Younger Republicans have numerous complaints about the party leadership. One officeholder criticized Andrews for failing to mediate differences in the party. Others complained about the party leadership's failure to keep abreast of issues: "They—Andrews and the others—aren't up with events. It doesn't serve much purpose to consult with them." One of the party's most experienced officeholders commented:

> The Republican organization could be of more benefit if it would be active after the campaign and if the leaders would pay more attention to what is going on. Party responsibility should be a two-way street, candidate to party and party to candidate and lasting after the campaign.

Republican critics also repudiate the oldtimers' hostility to labor and Negroes. In their judgment, Andrews has talked about a wider party appeal while practicing the restrictiveness of the older generation. Several young Republicans have established friendly relations with organized labor. One local officeholder remarked: "I wouldn't be here without labor, especially the UAW. I sought labor support and it made my election possible." Several ambitious Republican politicians noted their respect for the UAW and its leaders as well as its endorsements. Instead of decrying the influence of labor, these Republicans take pleasure in having their pictures in the AFL-CIO *Toledo Union Journal.* While some have directed their attention primarily to the United Auto Workers, others have sought a closer relation with the Building Trades and the Teamsters. In the opinion of one young Republican: "Toledo Teamsters are under progressive and responsible leadership. The Republican Party makes a mistake in avoiding the Teamsters." Another Republican politician broadened this criticism to include all of organized labor:

> The Republican Party could come to a much better understanding with labor if it worked at it. There is an almost total lack of communication between the Republican Party and organized labor. Many labor leaders serve on the Democratic Executive Committee, but few on our Executive Committee. We can't continue to expect success in Toledo without labor. And we can't expect the help of labor without helping them. John [Andrews] is just not the type to pursue this. He came out of industry and he deals with the men of industry. He probably wouldn't be inclined or able to talk and work with union men.

Young Republicans are equally critical of the party's effort to recruit Negro support. In their judgment, the Goldwater candidacy and its effects are merely a convenient excuse for the failures of the local organization. One prominent young Republican observed: "The Republican Party has included some Negroes, but the party has failed to promote the participation of Negroes. There has been no broad scope to Republican efforts to gain Negro support." Ambitious Republicans do not share the senior leadership's satisfaction with the support of a small circle of prominent Negro Republicans. They criticize party leaders for failing to work with the large number of Republican Negro leaders to develop increased Negro support for the party.

The Republican Party, in the opinion of young critics, must do more to demonstrate its interest in Negro voters and its dedication to civil rights. Mayor John W. Potter (R.) has taken the lead in showing that he is not to be outdone by local Democrats in commitment to civil rights, support of national and state civil rights legislation, sympathy with Southern demonstrations, familiarity with civil rights songs, and cordiality and consultation with local Negro leaders.

Republican officeholders also dispute the senior leadership's satisfaction with business support. Oldtime Republican leaders are generally pleased with the involvement of business leaders in the party and in the community. Republican officeholders, on the other hand, emphasize the passive role of business executives in both party and community affairs. Young Republicans describe the leaders of the major firms as sitting on the sidelines watching for an issue which might directly affect them. One councilman observed:

> In the community, business leaders are mainly involved in charitable activities, fund drives, and good works. In the party they participate financially. They aren't enthusiastic about politics or mixing in issues. They manage to avoid deep involvement.

Republican officeholders, like their Democratic colleagues, believe that business leaders could and should play a more constructive role in Toledo. In the opinion of many young Republicans, the party leadership has failed to encourage business participation in the party and in the community.

Young Republicans reject the complacency and conservatism of their elders in the party. Politically ambitious Republicans are especially eager to escape any connection with the conservative label. In the opinion of one officeholder, the political parties do not represent a liberal-conservative division, particularly at the local level: "I consider myself fairly liberal. In fact, many Republicans in city politics are more liberal than a number of Democrats." Another Republican politician emphasized his belief that liberalism depends on the individual rather than the party. In explaining his political philosophy, this Republican said: "I personally believe that government must be prepared to meet the economic and social needs that exist today. Conditions have changed and government must change to meet these conditions." An ambitious young Republican summarized his views this way:

> Older Republicans have played into the Democratic claim that the Democratic Party is the so-called party of the people, that the Democratic Party has the interest of all citizens at heart. This image is ridiculous. Hell, I'm as interested in all citizens as any Democrat.

When John Andrews became state chairman in the spring of 1965, dissident Republicans saw the possibility of a change in the local leadership of the party. Some hoped that Andrews' absence from Toledo would make it possible to break the tie between senior Republicans and the party leadership. Others confessed an interest in assuming the executive directorship or the party chairmanship, if Andrews should relinquish these positions. Yet discontented Republicans did not openly challenge the party chairman. In January 1966 Andrews resigned from the local chairmanship because of the pressure of state duties.[6] Ralph Hoover, a longtime Republican and ally of Andrews, was named party chairman. Another Andrews deputy, the local campaign chairman, was named executive director in February 1966. Dissatisfaction within the party remains concealed. Republican leadership is in the hands of men who have worked closely with Andrews and with Mayor Potter. Other Republican officeholders are directing their efforts to their own political advancement rather than to conflicts and problems within the organization.

The victories in 1965, when a Republican mayor and five councilmen were elected, enhanced the reputation of the local organization and deflated interest in party reform. Despite dissensions in the party, the Republicans have held a slight edge over the Democrats in organization and effort. Innovations such as primary endorsements were introduced by the Republican Party,[7] and it has also profited from the disarray of the Democratic opposition. Democratic weakness, in 1965 and before, contributed greatly to the illusion of Republican strength. In addition, Republicans have benefited from a local political tradition which has both favored and frustrated them.

Conflicting Viewpoints about Reform

Republicans have mixed feelings about the reform movement. Leaders in both the older and younger generations believe that

---

[6] *The Blade*, January 12, 1966, p. 1.

[7] The Republican Party introduced primary endorsements in 1959. In 1963 the Democratic Party made its first primary endorsements, but endorsed ten candidates instead of nine. 1965 marked the first time that the Democrats endorsed a slate for the places available.

nonpartisanship and the council-manager form of government are related to Republican success in Toledo. If the Republican Party could be confident of repeating its 1965 success in electing a Republican mayor and a Republican council majority, the city manager plan would look less attractive. The Republican dilemma is that reform institutions are not consistent with the needs of partisanship and organization, but they appear to be a necessity for political survival.

Republican officeholders consider nonpartisanship crucial to their success in city politics, though many would prefer a party ballot and increased partisanship.

> My personal choice is a party ballot. But I happen to be a Republican and in a minority party. If we were to put city council on a partisan ballot, it would be impossible to elect a Republican majority. A party ballot would be better for the two party system, party government, and party responsibility, which I'm interested in. To build a strong state and national party organization you need a strong local organization and a strong local organization requires open partisanship. How can you have a strong party if you say, "vote the man, not the party"? But then you can't have party competition in a city like Toledo if it's impossible for Republicans to get elected.

Another Republican officeholder echoed this appraisal by saying:

> Nonpartisanship is a subterfuge perpetrated on the public. It's ridiculous, because we do have a partisan form of government and we should have. From a political standpoint, I prefer partisanship. But from a practical standpoint, I know that it's better for Republicans to run on the nonpartisan ballot in Toledo.

Senior Republicans are inclined to emphasize the opposite side of the dilemma. They argue that as long as nonpartisanship exists, the party will remain weak. Nonpartisanship compels the party to accept ''maverick politicians, who will go it alone, who will not rely on their party or even support it in many instances.'' Some oldtime Republicans are convinced that nonpartisanship has inflicted equal damage on the discipline and organization of both parties. John Andrews has not found this argument persuasive. One of Andrews' associates commented:

> You have to remember that Toledo is predominantly Democratic. When the Republican label shows, we drive away Toledo

voters. There is no doubt that the Republican Party does a lot better on nonpartisan offices. We can make a good government appeal and show how capable our guy is. Look at the offices in Lucas County. There are 19 offices, including the court house, state legislature, and Congressman, elected with the party ballot. The Republicans hold four of these and the Democrats hold 15 in 1965. There are 57 nonpartisan offices—including judgeships and four city councils and city council clerks. Of 57, the Republicans hold 39. That speaks for itself.

Politically minded Republicans are as strained by the council-manager form of government as they are by nonpartisanship. The pretensions and constraints of the manager system are distasteful to party officeholders and organization Republicans alike. One senior Republican confessed:

I've always wanted a strong mayor system. It would be much more interesting politically. I've opposed it only because I felt that we wouldn't be able to elect Republican mayors. At least under the manager plan, we've had a fair share of Republican mayors and councilmen.

Other oldtimers in the party organization believe that the city manager form of government has generated a system of politics in which the Republican Party is subservient to reform groups: "You're always trying to please the do-gooders, to do the right thing so that they'll stay on your side."

Many officeholders object to the nonpolitical ideals of the manager form of government. They believe that governmental decisions are and should be political decisions rather than the judgments of a detached expert. In the process of decision-making, the mayor "could just as well hire his own engineer instead of keeping up the pretense of the independent professional." A number of Republican councilmen share the Democratic conviction that the manager form has damaged political leadership in Toledo. In the opinion of one Republican councilman:

A strong mayor could stimulate greater interest and provide stronger leadership in city government. I don't believe that a manager does or can hit as hard for his programs as a political executive who could put some drive into the system.

But Republicans are apprehensive about a possible change to the strong mayor plan. The new provision for the direct election of the

mayor is also cause for concern. Many Republicans fear that
changes which strengthen leadership in city government may ulti-
mately destroy the political environment in which Republicans have
been able to win elections. One Republican councilman commented:
"If a strong Democrat like Skeldon were elected mayor, the whole
system would be political. A complete mobilization of political
forces wouldn't be in the interest of Republicans." Many Republicans did not expect a victory in the 1965 mayoralty election. Despite this success, they remain concerned about the future:

> I supported the direct election of the mayor, but underneath I
> was opposed. An elected mayor will be in the middle of politics.
> When the whole thing becomes political—through and
> through—the city manager system and Republicans will have a
> hard time surviving.

Although many Republicans now identify reform institutions
with party survival, the reform tradition has had a divisive effect
on the party. Since the turn of the century, the advocates of reform
have constituted an influential segment of the Republican Party. In
the Jones-Whitlock period, the Republican Party was torn by conflicting desires to destroy or to appease the reform Republicans who
denied them local victories. After efforts at destruction failed, the
course of appeasement began. Republican leaders concluded that
victories were dependent upon the support of a potent splinter
group of reformers. A Republican compulsion to satisfy the Independents and their heirs has continued through this century. When
the City Manager League was at its peak in the 1930s and the late
1950s, the Republican Party subordinated itself to the wishes and
decisions of this group of reform Republicans. In deference to
reformers, the party delayed its endorsements until the City Manager League had made its endorsements. One oldtime party leader
recalled:

> The Republican Party had to be very careful when this City
> Manager League was around. The City Manager League was
> largely Republican and very strong. If the party had made its
> endorsements first, the holier-than-thous in the manager groups
> would have picked up their marbles and gone home.

The strength of an independent organization of reform Republicans contributed to Republican victories, but the continuing de-

pendence of the party on a splinter group of reformers eliminated the possibility of a strong organization. Party candidates were more likely to emphasize their reform qualifications than their Republicanism. The pervasive influence of reform opened the way in both parties to mavericks with little sense of party loyalty. The Republican Party, perhaps because of its closer relation to the reform movement, has had a larger share of maverick politicians.

Ironically, the conditions which have weakened the party organization are responsible for the election of Republican officeholders in a Democratic city. Maverick politicians and good government appeals have greater popularity in Toledo than the label or organization of a party consistently repudiated in state and national elections. A strong party organization and appeal might well be self-destructive, as many Toledo Republicans fear.

Summary

In conclusion, political parties can be considered a casualty of the reform movement in Toledo. Although the reform movement did not succeed in eliminating political parties, it weakened them. The identification of candidates and officeholders with political parties has little real significance. Toledo parties resemble the weak parties of other reform cities such as Cincinnati and Kansas City.[8] A longtime professional in the Republican Party accurately described the situation when he said:

> In a nonpartisan election in Toledo, political affiliations are known, but the parties have little control over officials once elected. In campaigns, the parties do some work and the candidates go it alone the rest of the way. Nonpartisanship doesn't work either way. You end up with neither nonpartisanship nor party government.

[8] For a comparison of the Toledo party system and that of other cities, see Kenneth E. Gray, *A Report on Politics in Kansas City, Missouri* (Cambridge, Mass.: Joint Center for Urban Studies, 1959, mimeographed); Robert L. Morlan, ''The Unorganized Politics of Minneapolis,'' *National Municipal Review* (November 1949), pp. 485–490; Ralph A. Straetz, *PR Politics in Cincinnati* (New York: New York University Press, 1958). For a discussion of a strong party organization, see Edward C. Banfield, *Political Influence* (New York: The Free Press, 1961).

The reform movement urged candidates to be above parties and left a political ethos sympathetic to self-styled politicians rather than party candidates. The personalities and organizations of the reform movement stunted both parties. The Democratic Party has faced governmental institutions which dilute the partisan appeal successful at other levels of government. The Republicans have had to deal with a powerful segment committed to nonpolitical government and hostile to partisanship.

In the diffused system of politics resulting from the reform movement both political parties have suffered,[9] but the effects have been more damaging for the Democrats than for the Republicans. In the Democratic case, both the party organization and the party candidates have suffered. Although the Republican party organization has suffered, its candidates have benefited from the confusion.[10] The direct election of the mayor may eventually alter this situation by producing tighter lines in city government and in party organization and competition. This possibility will be considered in later chapters.

[9] Other studies indicate an association of nonpartisanship and weak party organizations. See, for example, Phillips Cutright, ''Activities of Precinct Committeemen in Partisan and Nonpartisan Communities,'' *Western Political Quarterly*, XVII (March 1964), 93–108.

[10] In a study of four Michigan cities, Oliver P. Williams and Charles R. Adrian found that the nonpartisan ballot blunted party voting and benefited the minority party. Toledo presents a similar pattern. See Oliver P. Williams and Charles R. Adrian, ''The Insulation of Local Politics Under the Nonpartisan Ballot,'' *American Political Science Review*, LIII (December 1959), 1052–1063.

6 THE RECRUITMENT AND ELECTION OF LOCAL OFFICIALS

Practices used in the recruitment and election of local officials in Toledo reveal a political system in which organized electoral efforts are rare. The advocates of municipal reform hoped that nonpartisanship would encourage the emergence of more independent and more qualified candidates. In Toledo the reform movement succeeded in reducing the role of political parties, but business, professional, or labor organizations have not assumed the functions of recruiting and electing local officials on a continuing and organized basis. City politics is characterized by individual efforts rather than organized activity by major groups. This situation has facilitated the election of business and professional men, but it has disadvantages for the city, not all of which could be foreseen by reformers.

The Nature of Toledo City Councils

Toledo city councils have been decidedly middle class in character.[1] Seventy-six per cent of the councilmen serving

[1] City councils from 1953 through 1965 have been selected for close examination in this chapter. A survey of biographical information on earlier councilmen indicates that the period 1953 through 1965 was

TABLE 6.1

Occupations of City Councilmen*

Occupations	To-ledo	Kala-mazoo	Jack-son	Bay City	Muske-gon
Owners and Executives (non-retail)	0%	39%	15%	6%	29%
Owners and Executives (retail, service, and allied)	27	14	15	31	38
Sales (insurance, real estate, and others)	10	8	15	10	21
Professional	52	22	11	19	4
Middle Management	0	0	32	12	0
Labor	11	8	4	23	8
Miscellaneous	0	8	9	0	0
Total	100%	99%	101%	101%	100%

* Each selection is calculated separately, so those reelected are counted more than once. This approach, used by Williams and Adrian, was necessary to compare Toledo figures with the figures on the four Michigan cities. Williams and Adrian offer a convincing justification for computing each selection separately: ''A five-term incumbent can grossly inflate an occupational category given the smallness of the numbers. However, the distortion would be even greater if individuals were counted singly. A five-term banker would then equal a one-term factory worker.'' Williams and Adrian, *Four Cities*, p. 78.

from 1963 to 1966 have been college graduates. A vast majority have been in professional, retail, or service occupations. Thirteen of the 14 councilmen in professional occupations have been lawyers. Nine councilmen have been owners or executives in retail firms such as jewelry companies, drug stores, restaurants, automobile agencies, hardware stores, and advertising agencies. Three have been employed in sales occupations, and three have held leadership or administrative positions in labor unions.[2]

typical. The two new councilmen elected in 1965 were both college graduates; one is a former member of the Board of Education and wife of an attorney, and the other operates a marine supply business.

[2] This discussion is based on the occupational classification used by Oliver P. Williams and Charles R. Adrian, *Four Cities* (Philadelphia: University of Pennsylvania Press, 1963), p. 78. Table 6.1 is also based on this classification. The occupations mentioned involve what Herbert Jacob has defined as a brokerage or bargaining role, in which ''practitioners deal with outsiders and try to reach a mutually satisfying agreement.'' Jacob argues that this role provides training in skills useful in politics. See Herbert Jacob, ''Initial Recruitment of Elected Officials in the United States: A Model,'' *Journal of Politics*, XXIV (November 1962), 703–716.

The particularly high concentration in professional occupations is evident when Toledo is compared with the smaller (50,000–70,000) Michigan cities studied by Oliver Williams and Charles Adrian. Table 6.1 depicts the occupational composition of city councils in Toledo, Kalamazoo, Jackson, Bay City, and Muskegon.[3]

The occupational pattern of Toledo city councils does not reflect systematic recruiting by formal groups of any kind. City politics is characterized by self-starting politicians who rely on their own combination of organization and appeal. In going into politics, local officeholders are influenced by a variety of reasons, including convictions about community problems, business or professional advantages of politics, and the interest and encouragement of friends and relatives.

Recruitment of Officeholders— Motivations and Influences

Sixteen persons with experience on city council, including nine incumbents and seven former councilmen of recent years, were asked to assess the influences which affected their decision to enter politics.[4]

Relatively few local officeholders entered politics as a result of strong partisanship. For most councilmen, party identification was a political necessity rather than a motivating influence. Despite the feeble condition of the parties, local candidates found it desirable to have at least a minimal political affiliation. One Democratic councilman described his relations with his party this way:

> I needed the party endorsement more than the organization. The introduction to ward meetings and clubs is important without a doubt. But this had little or nothing to do with why I went into politics.

[3] I take responsibility for translating Williams and Adrian's pseudonyms for the four cities. The data on Toledo comes from the period 1953–1965; the data on the Michigan cities is from 1948 through 1957.

[4] Interviews were also conducted with officeholders in partisan offices, including the Board of County Commissioners and the United States Congress. In each case, references to partisan officeholders are distinguished from city councilmen.

A prominent Republican expressed a similar sentiment: "The Republican Party is important to me chiefly as a forum from which to be heard. The party is a useful way of contacting the voters." Other councilmen were more indifferent or hostile to their parties. Both parties include self-proclaimed mavericks who are careful to define their independence from the party. One Republican commented: "The party didn't draw me into politics. I presented myself to them. I've always been something of a maverick and the party knows it." A former Democratic councilman was equally insistent on his independence from the party:

> I tend to be a Democrat in national politics. But at the local level, the party doesn't mean as much. The party doesn't have as much of a role in local issues. I'm a maverick when it comes to city politics.

Many councilmen found party support for their initial and later campaigns to be inadequate or unreliable; no councilman was drawn into politics by his party's local programs or achievements. Past and present councilmen were unanimous in finding both the Republican and Democratic parties lacking in local policy interests.

Civic activity was a significant influence in drawing officeholders into local politics. Many members of both parties had been involved in hospital drives, the Toledo Museum of Art, the YMCA, advisory commissions in community recreation and industrial development, and the March of Dimes before seeking elective office. In addition to their participation in community projects, officeholders were active in church affairs and in fraternal, service, professional, and alumni organizations. Before beginning political life, the typical councilman belonged to a church (Roman Catholic for most Democrats; Protestant for most Republicans), the American Legion, the Veterans of Foreign Wars, the American Bar Association, the Chamber of Commerce, Eagles, Moose, Masons or the Knights of Columbus, YMCA or PTA, and the University of Toledo Alumni Association. Memberships in labor unions, the United Labor Committee, the Frederick Douglass Community Association, or the NAACP were exceptional rather than typical.

Some councilmen found that city politics, like civic activity, could be combined with a legal or business career. For many councilmen, the move to elective office indicated no immediate change in motives or goals. One Republican, an attorney and councilman, reported:

> Right after I got out of the Navy I started getting involved in various civic projects. I developed contacts and interests through activity in my church, hospital organizations, and the Chamber. Civic activity led to politics.

Recruitment through civic activity is often associated with strong but generally unspecified convictions about the type of policies and officeholders needed to give Toledo effective, forward-looking government. City council is seen as another arena for the achievement of civic goals rather than as an opportunity for a political career. A Republican councilman commented:

> I became active in the community through volunteer services and church activities. In civic affairs I had developed definite ideas about community problems. These ideas were a factor in my running for city council.

Councilmen recruited through civic activity frequently contrast their convictions about community problems and government with the disinterest of their party in these subjects. One Democratic attorney and former councilman commented:

> I don't think the Democratic Party stands for anything locally. It was a disappointment to me to find that the party takes no particular position on programs and policies. Both parties endorse only things which everyone agrees on.

A combination of civic activity and strong convictions generally means adherence to the tenets of municipal reform, and in some cases, the reform movement provided the impetus for seeking elective office. This was the experience of one former Republican councilman:

> I ran for city council because of my concern for good government. I was active in the City Manager League and had its support. We wanted to do a job for the city. I didn't want it politically.

Some councilmen were influenced by less austere considerations. Although all councilmen emphasized the demanding nature of service on city council, some admitted that it also has advantages. Council meetings and responsibilities consume valuable time, but they also increase the potential clientele of a particular law office, restaurant, insurance agency, or drug store. An attorney analyzed his situation this way:

> Being on city council can be a disadvantage professionally. It complicates your schedule. You're attending city council meetings, speaking to ladies' clubs, or giving interviews to students instead of seeing clients. But as a lawyer, I am very well-known because of my political activity. More people have heard of me. This may not be directly transferable into business, but it helps.

Another attorney on city council offered a more succinct opinion: "Lazy lawyers go into politics." The proprietors of hardware stores, jewelry companies, or automobile agencies can also benefit from the publicity of political activity and the $3,600 councilman's salary, as a few of them confessed.[5] Service on city council can enhance a prosperous business or law practice. For business and professional men, city council can be economically attractive. For others, it may be an impossibility, as the occupational characteristics of Toledo city councils suggest.

Economic and political motives are more likely to coincide for Republicans than for Democrats. The daytime meetings and small salary of city council can be an appealing part-time concern for men who control their own schedules. For union members and officials, city council service is often economically impossible. Nevertheless, an involvement or identification with organized labor was the impetus for political activity in a few cases. One Democratic councilman recalled:

> I got interested in politics in 1958, when I worked against the right-to-work proposal. Unions have done a great deal for this country and this town. After '58 I realized that politics is important in achieving what labor stands for.

Another Democratic councilman explained that the concern over the Landrum-Griffin bill impelled him to enter city politics: "I

[5] The mayor and the vice-mayor receive an additional salary. The vice-mayor receives $2,500 per year in addition to his $3,600 salary as a city councilman. The mayor formerly received $5,500 in addition to his salary as a councilman, making the annual salary of the office $6,100. In late 1963, after the passage of a charter amendment providing for the direct election of the mayor, city council increased the salary for the office of mayor to $11,400. The mayor continues to receive $3,600 as a councilman, making his total annual salary $15,000.

came to the conclusion that organized labor needed to have representation, starting right here at home.''

For others, nationality or (in rare cases) race was an influence in the decision to seek political office. One of the few Negro candidates of either party said: ''I was drafted by the Negro community to run for city council. My motive in getting into politics was to get representation for the Negro community.'' An ethnic tie, most frequently Polish, was an influence in the recruitment of several Democratic councilmen. Activity in the Polish National Alliance and the Union of Poles in America was a precursor of political activity in these cases. Nor was recruitment by nationality limited to the Democratic Party. One Republican commented:

> In going into politics I was carrying on a hybrid tradition, the tradition of Polish Republicans. I was the spiritual heir of Ollie Czelusta [a former mayor of Polish descent], and before I retire I'll have a Polish Republican ready to take my place.

Although avowed political ambition was exceptional among Toledo councilmen, it was a major influence in the recruitment of prominent officeholders in both parties. One Republican recalled his longstanding interest in a political career:

> I first became interested in politics when I ran for fire marshal in the third grade. In high school, college, and law school, I was active in student government. In running for city council, I was unequivocally interested in a political career. Politics is a drive with me.

A prominent Democrat described his entrance into politics:

> When I got out of the service, I went into politics. At first I held appointive office. Then I ran for city council. I wanted to be a professional politician. That's what I am, and I'm proud of it.

The politically ambitious, unlike their colleagues, hoped that politics would be a career rather than a temporary supplement to another occupation. City council was seen as a necessary first step in a progression toward higher offices. The politically minded served only one or two terms on city council before attempting to advance their ambitions by running for the Board of County Commissioners, state legislature, or United States Congress. In the event of failure, they retained their interest in city council.

In most cases, officeholders desiring a political career were also influenced by the political activity or interests of their families. One Democratic incumbent in a partisan office mentioned four generations of political participation in his family. A Republican councilman reported: "I grew up in a political climate. My father always followed politics closely. We always tallied the vote on election night and tried to analyze the trends and results." A family interest in politics was associated with *The Blade* in several cases. Relatives working as reporters or editors for *The Blade* contributed to early political interests and ambitions.

Politically ambitious Democrats and Republicans were not recruited by the leaders of their parties. Instead, aspiring politicians sought to demonstrate their merit to a reluctant party. One Republican commented: "The Republican Party was skeptical about me when I first wanted to run for office, but I gradually won their acceptance." A Democratic officeholder reported a similar experience:

> When I first became involved in the organization, I didn't receive encouragement from the party leaders. In my first campaign they didn't encourage me. In the primary race the next time they took a hands-off position. It took a couple of elections before I really got party support.

For ambitious Democrats, the cool reaction of the party leadership was counteracted by the encouragement of key party officeholders. In the late '40s and early '50s, many politically minded Democrats entered politics with the guidance and support of Mayor Michael V. DiSalle, who had been introduced to politics by John J. Quinlivan, a former Democratic county commissioner and party leader. DiSalle's record as a forceful mayor and his efforts to introduce young men to politics attracted several prominent Democrats to public office. One officeholder recalled that DiSalle had encouraged him to enter politics despite the indifference of the party. Another said:

> My association with DiSalle definitely influenced my interest in political office. I admired DiSalle's political achievements. He is the only mayor to give Toledo strong leadership. He was the singular force which Toledo has lacked.

Skeldon and Ashley are now carrying on this pattern of personal recruitment in seeking and encouraging promising young candi-

dates. Some young Democrats consider Skeldon a decisive influence
in their political ambitions:

> I ran for city council because of Skeldon. He asked me to run
> and I did. He's one of the main reasons I'm running again this
> year [1965]. Under Skeldon the Democratic Party is moving
> away from the old dormant state.

In the Republican Party there is no evidence that the politicians
of one generation recruit protégés from the next. This is a cause for
concern to Republicans such as this officeholder:

> Republicans have got to do more recruiting. In the last couple
> of years, Ned [Skeldon] has gotten a couple of boys who could
> have been Republicans. One was a Republican in college, only a
> few years ago. In fact, he headed up a Toledo University group to
> meet Senator Bricker. The other's more conservative than I am.
> He could be a Republican more easily than I can!

While the Republican Party has a larger source of candidates for
civic activity than does the Democratic, it produces fewer full-time
politicians for both political and economic reasons. In Toledo, Republican candidates have difficulty achieving the county, state, or
national offices which would permit them to make politics a full-
time concern. Furthermore, more Republicans are in professional
occupations which can be successfully combined with politics and
which are reluctantly abandoned on attaining higher office.

Democratic and Republican politicians also have divergent attitudes on partisanship. Politically ambitious Democrats feel that a
strong party allegiance was important in their introduction to
politics and will be especially significant if they are to advance to
higher offices. For their more numerous colleagues who do not
aspire to more than several terms on city council, party identification is less salient. The Republican Party reveals a subdued pattern
in the opposite direction. Republican councilmen interested in
higher office are even more wary of partisanship than their strictly
local colleagues. No Republican interested in elective office risks a
strongly partisan identification, but politically ambitious Republicans are perhaps the most insistent on their independence, personal
qualifications, and individual reasons for seeking political office.

Campaign Practices of Officeholders

Campaign practices of city councilmen are closely related to the various types of recruitment and indicate an amorphous political system in which the individual candidate has primary responsibility for his political début and campaign. Recruitment processes favor those who can initiate political activities as a side-line to business or professional careers. Similarly, the weak or inconsistent electoral efforts of major groups accentuate the importance of the individual's ability to conduct and finance his own campaigns.

In naming the organization most important in his political campaigns, no councilman mentioned his party. For most local politicians the party was as insignificant in campaigns as it had been in their introduction to politics. In interviews with Toledo officeholders, the only emphasis of the campaign role of the party came from two Democrats now holding partisan offices.

Organized labor was considered an important influence in city campaigns by only four local officeholders—three Democrats and one Republican. For one officeholder important support from the United Auto Workers developed after he had left city council and served a term on the Board of County Commissioners. A Democratic councilman who relied on the United Auto Workers in his first campaign found this support lacking in 1963, when the UAW was inactive in city politics. In these cases important labor support was limited to one campaign. Another Democratic councilman received the consistent and complete support of the Teamsters Union, in which he was a business agent. In this case the union sponsored rather than supported a brief political career. Only one Democrat found labor support and the United Auto Workers, in particular, consistently important in several campaigns for city council and later for the Board of County Commissioners. Although most councilmen sought the endorsement of labor, very few of them considered labor support more than a slight or intermittent influence.

Six councilmen cited ethnic and religious groups as having an important role in their political campaigns. For two of those interviewed the Polish connection was salient. One said:

> Nationality has been most important to me. Every time you get
> two or three Polacks together, there's a club. Well, I belong to all

of these clubs. In campaigns the Polish-American Congress is very helpful. Poles will vote the -ski, and there are 10,000 Poles in Toledo.

Others found that church or religious associations provided the most important source of campaign support or assistance. In a few cases veterans' or fraternal organizations received special mention. There were also occasional minor references to high school and college alumni associations and neighborhood and area organizations.

Councilmen in both parties emphasized the importance of civic and reform organizations in their political campaigns. One former Democratic councilman stressed the role of the City Manager League in his political career:

> The City Manager League was very important to me. In my last campaign, I was supported by the City Manager League. I didn't get the endorsement of *The Blade,* the unions, or the Democratic Party, but I was elected anyway.

A former Republican councilman also emphasized the impact of reform sentiment and organizations: "Support in the City Manager League and the Municipal League was important to me. They had wide followings and could make a difference in an election."

Most officeholders did not entrust their political hopes to organizations such as the City Manager League, the Masons, the Polish-American Congress, or the United Auto Workers, however. In virtually all cases, local politicians attempted to incorporate their civic, labor, or ethnic support into a personal organization which would counteract party weakness in the wards and the slight or sporadic interest of community groups in local elections.

The basic campaign strategy of local candidates was to build a strong personal organization and bolster it with whatever support they could attract from their party, community organizations, the press, and the opposite party.[6] One Democrat described his successful 1963 campaign this way:

[6] The personal appeal and organization are often characteristic of areas with weak political parties. See Leo M. Snowiss, "Congressional Recruitment and Representation," *American Political Science Review,* LX (September 1966), 627–640, and Lester Seligman, "Political Recruitment and Party Structure," *American Political Science Review,* LV (March 1961), 77–78.

I had a key committee of 21 of my supporters—relatives, friends from business, college, church. I set up my own system of precinct workers. The party gave me nothing but an endorsement and a bill for $300.00 to cover their campaign costs. The endorsement was valuable in the Democratic areas. I also cultivated the Republican areas. In the election, I ran as a weak Democrat in the Democratic areas and a poor Republican in the Republican areas, so that I had a ribbon of support all over the city.

A Republican councilman described his campaign methods in a similar way:

The most important organization at campaign time is the one I build myself. In my first city council campaign I organized a door to door canvass. Over the years I have built an organization of friends and associates drawn from my practice, my church, civic activities, and my neighborhood. This is a continuing organization and carries over from one election to another. It's more important than what the party may or may not do, than my on and off support from *The Blade* and occasional labor endorsements.

Another Republican was equally convinced of the importance of a strong personal organization:

I could never have been elected without my own organization. I run my campaigns this way—I have two very tall and homely women in charge and things work perfectly. The men aren't always trying to make them and the women campaign workers aren't jealous. . . . I have representatives in all the wards and precincts. This organization will do anything and everything for my election.

Republicans were more likely than Democrats to supplement their personal organization with auxiliary services provided by their party. Several Republicans praised the party's guidance on strategy and advertising and in "developing unity in what Republican candidates talk about." Even so, Republicans were cautious in their use of the party label. In the Democratic Party, local candidates found the party's endorsement more valuable than its organization. Local Democrats did not have complete confidence in the Democratic label or a strictly partisan appeal, however. Both Democrats and Republicans used their personal campaign organizations to emphasize their individual qualifications and characteristics. One Democrat reported:

I emphasized the need to break the existing image of city politics. My organization and literature presented me as a competent young man who could do a job—the kind of individual who should be in city government.

A Republican councilman followed a similar approach:

In all my campaigns my organization has worked to sell a name, experience, competence, responsibility. The approach was "Elect X————— X—————, a good man, a man you can count on. X—————, for courage, competence, and character," as my advertising said.

Democratic candidates for partisan office rely on their political party and organized labor to a much greater extent than their colleagues in city politics. Democrats who succeed in leaving city politics for the offices of county, state, and national government usually do so by increased partisanship and strong labor support rather than by personal organization. Republicans perceive that increased partisanship is likely to defeat rather than fulfill their ambitions for higher office. Even improved personal organization is no more likely to bring success, as several Republicans have found in futile efforts to apply local strategies to partisan campaigns. One of the few Republicans to achieve partisan office in recent years observed that the support of organized labor was more crucial in his election than personal organization or the Republican Party.

Important though it is, the use of personal organizations has become somewhat less prevalent in recent years, even in city politics. With the City Manager League dormant since 1959, the Republican Party is taking a more active part in local elections. Republican candidates in the last three elections have felt a stronger allegiance to the party than their predecessors in the late 1950s who ran with the support of the City Manager League. The absence of the City Manager League in recent local elections has facilitated the development of a more effective party effort. In the 1961 campaign, party leaders drew Republican candidates together on a highly successful antiscandal ticket. A more unified party effort continued in the 1963 election, when the eight Republican incumbents stood on the party record of providing "a sensible, businesslike approach to city government in contrast to the haphazard methods of previous Democratic city councils.'"[7] Six of the eight incumbent Republicans

---

[7] *The Blade*, October 30, 1963, p. 3. The effort to include a ninth Republican, a new candidate, in this appeal was unsuccessful. Instead the one Democratic

were reelected. The platform of competence and responsibility was vindicated again in 1965, when the six Republican councilmen were returned for a third term. Although Republican candidates of recent years have continued to use personal organizations, the party has had an increased role in campaign management and strategy.

The disappearance of an independent reform organization from local elections has also eased the conflict of reform and party Democrats. But the Democratic Party has still not recovered the strength it had before 1959, when the party purged four incumbent Democrats endorsed by the City Manager League.[8] Since 1959 the Democratic organization has endorsed party rather than reform Democrats, but it has failed to elect more than three of these candidates in a council election. In 1965 the Democratic Party attempted to remedy this situation by playing a greater role in the local campaign. The 1965 campaign, like others before it, failed for lack of unity and organization.

Thus a trend toward party campaigns and issues in local elections is still uncertain. Many officeholders regard the possibility of such a development with caution, if not distrust. Some Democrats suggest that Ned Skeldon's overt partisanship contributed to his defeat in the 1965 mayoralty election. Republicans, on the other hand, believe that their success in the 1965 election resulted, in part, from a campaign strategy which cut across party lines.

Summary

As of 1966, Toledo city politicians are rarely produced by organized recruitment and sponsorship. Although their electoral activities are now increasing, political parties have had only a peripheral role in the recruitment and election of councilmen. Leaders in major companies have made no organized effort to sponsor or support council candidates in more than two decades. Nor have top- or middle-management executives in the large firms volunteered for

---

incumbent was frequently identified with the Republican slate. Six Republicans and three Democrats were elected in 1963.

[8] This episode is examined in Chapter 7. These four Democrats were the party's top vote-getters in the 1957 election. Two were elected in 1959 without the party endorsement. One retired in 1961 and one was defeated that year.

service on city council. Organized labor has not attached great importance to sponsoring local candidates from labor or to achieving the election of labor-endorsed candidates. The small number of union representatives on the city councils of the last 15 years as well as the large number of councilmen elected without labor support attest to the relative disinterest of labor in city politics. The involvement of reform organizations in electoral politics has been indirect, as in the case of the Municipal League, or inconsistent, as in the case of the City Manager League.

The many business and professional men in city politics have not had decisive encouragement or backing from organized groups. But they have had the benefit of a peculiarly shapeless and individualistic political system. Business, labor, civic, and Negro organizations have found elections for Toledo's innocuous city government inconsequential and uninteresting affairs. The relative disinterest of major community groups and the political parties in city elections has shifted the burden of campaign responsibility to individual candidates.

Individual campaign responsibility is to the disadvantage of candidates from the lower end of the social-economic scale. Also detrimental to these candidates is the use of the at-large election. Representatives of organized labor and minority groups, who could achieve election in wards or at-large with strong organizational support, face serious obstacles in the personal politics of at-large elections.[9] The at-large election increases campaign costs and enlarges the area from which the candidate must draw support. The concentrated political potential of lower-income and minority groups is diluted by an at-large electoral system.

Both the electoral system and the nature of the city council office are suited to business and professional men. The business or professional man is more likely to be in a position to conduct and finance a $4,000–$5,000 city-wide campaign without significant support from

---

[9] See James Q. Wilson's discussion of the effects of the at-large electoral system on Negro political influence: *Negro Politics* (New York: The Free Press, 1960), pp. 3–21. Raymond Wolfinger touches on the relation of wards and ethnic politics in New Haven, Connecticut, in "The Development and Persistence of Ethnic Voting," *American Political Science Review*, LIX (December 1965), 899. Both Dahl and Wolfinger note that members of ethnic groups were elected to New Haven's ward-based Board of Aldermen years before they achieved nomination or election for a city-wide office. See Robert A. Dahl, *Who Governs?* (New Haven, Conn.: Yale University Press, 1961), pp. 52–62.

his political party or other organizations.[10] The freedom and security of his occupation allow him to consider a part-time position with morning meetings and $3,600 salary.

Furthermore, the political ethos of Toledo is sympathetic to candidates who can claim an independence from party, labor, and (to a lesser degree) big business organizations. A continuing distrust of large organizations and their influence on officeholders is a residue of the reform movement. The at-large, nonpartisan election and the reform ethos militate against a close identification with organized interests. Candidates from organized labor have found their union identification a distinct handicap or an actual barrier to election. The few successful labor politicians have striven to project a muted image acceptable to the middle-class reform ethos.[11] The only Negro to win election to city council emphasized his dedication to good government and his allegiance to the City Manager League.

The self-employed business or professional man avoids identification with the large companies. Although he may have the support of groups oriented to business, such as the City Manager League, the Municipal League, and the Chamber of Commerce, he escapes a damaging connection with what are considered "special interests" in reform doctrine. The weakness of the political parties allows him to maintain a nominal affiliation with either party which gives a wide scope for good government and personal appeals. Thus, governmental institutions, political practices, and the reform ethos combine to produce a system which is highly congenial to part-time politicians from business and the professions.

This pattern of self-starting, part-time politicians has been no guarantee of the high caliber local government visualized by municipal reformers. The reduced role of parties and other organizations has not assured the emergence of outstanding local candidates.[12] It

[10] Most councilmen considered $4,000–$5,000 to be the average campaign expenditure. The lowest campaign expenditure mentioned was $2,000. Some candidates were reputed to have spent as much as $12,000, but did not confirm this.

[11] See Edward C. Banfield and James Q. Wilson's comments on the way in which labor has adapted to nonpartisan city politics in Detroit: *City Politics* (Cambridge, Mass.: Harvard University Press and M.I.T. Press, 1963), p. 288.

[12] Duane Lockard concluded that the introduction of the nonpartisan ballot did not alter the type of local candidates in New London, Connecticut. In New London, underlying political conditions and personalities appeared to have a greater effect on the caliber of local candidates than partisanship or nonpartisanship. Duane Lockard, *The Politics of State and Local Government* (New York: Macmillan Co., 1963), pp. 232–234.

has facilitated the election of officeholders from a narrow occupational group. Although some able councilmen have been recruited and elected under this system, Toledo has suffered from an absence of professional politicians whose life concern is politics rather than law, insurance, or real estate.

7 LEADERSHIP AND REFORM: THE POLITICS OF CHARTER REVISION

The Mayoralty in the Council-Manager System

In Toledo's 30 years of council-manager government, the office of mayor has been a largely ceremonial position occupied (with few exceptions) by amateur politicians and reformers. The reform ideal held that the election of competent councilmen would assure leadership and responsibility without strong executive direction. The mayor was to be a leader among equals on city council. His political power was meant never to curtail the role of his colleagues in legislation or to challenge the authority of the city manager in administration.[1]

For 30 years the Toledo version of the council-manager plan was in complete accord with these precepts. From 1935 through 1965, the mayor was chosen by city council

[1] For a discussion of the theory of the council-manager plan, see Arthur W. Bromage, *Introduction to Municipal Government and Administration* (New York: Appleton-Century-Crofts, Inc., 1957), pp. 295–305. Reform ideals and expectations are clearly stated by Leonard D. White, *The City Manager* (Chicago: University of Chicago Press, 1927), pp. 292–302.

rather than by the electorate.[2] The method of election and the
powers of the office did not elevate the mayor above his fellow
councilmen. The mayor's chief function, according to the charter,
was (and is) to preside at council meetings and serve as head
of the city for ceremonial purposes. In administrative matters,
the mayor found his power restricted by the substantial authority
of the city manager, who was appointed by the council to serve as
"the chief administrative officer of the city."[3] In the executive and
legislative realm, the mayor's power was limited by the equal powers of his eight colleagues on city council. All appointments by the
mayor required the approval of a majority in city council.[4] Nor did
the mayor have formal powers relating to the legislative agenda or
the introduction of proposals. The mayor of Toledo was a presiding
councilman with one vote and no veto.

The results of these arrangements were not, however, what reformers had predicted. In the council of equals, all were equally
wary of leadership and controversial issues and equally concerned
with protecting their individual chances for reelection. The office
established by the 1935 charter could be a position of leadership
only under the impact of a mayor with an astute sense of politics.
There have been few such men. Most Toledo mayors have had
neither the ability nor the inclination to exploit and enlarge the
meager resources of the office. Although several mayors served
consecutive terms, few indicated any interest in the possibilities of
the office or the attractions of a political career. Only one, Michael
V. DiSalle, used the office to achieve a widespread reputation as a
political leader. Only DiSalle went from city to state political
prominence. Most mayors have been content with a ceremonial
position which did not place extraordinary demands on their time
and political ability.[5]

[2] In 1963, a charter amendment provided for the direct election of the mayor
as of 1965. Gladys M. Kammerer has noted that the proponents of the
council-manager plan have long resisted the popular election of the mayor
because of the likelihood of a collision between manager and mayor when the
mayor is directly elected. She considers their resistance well justified. See her
"Role Diversity in City Managers," *Administrative Science Quarterly*, VIII
(March 1964), 421–442.

[3] The city manager rather than the mayor selects department and division
heads, prepares budget estimates and financial reports, and appoints and
removes employees.

[4] The mayor appoints the members of 23 boards and commissions with the
approval of a majority in city council.

[5] Local observers believe that the more effective mayors under the 1935

A majority of Toledo mayors have lacked both political ambition and a strong party allegiance. Between 1936 and 1965 five Republican mayors served for a total of 21 years and four Democratic mayors served for eight years. For 15 of these years, however, the mayor was associated with the reform movement. The first Democratic mayor under the council-manager plan was chosen in 1940 with the support of a reform colleague in the Republican Party. In 1959 a Democratic mayor sided with the City Manager League against his own party and later supported a City Manager League Republican for mayor. In the '50s two reform Republicans were elected mayor by councils with Democratic majorities. Other examples of weak party discipline do not specifically involve the reform movement. A Democrat's unexpected affinity for the Republicans cost his party control of city council in 1951. Eight years later a Republican maverick provided a crucial vote in the election of a Democratic mayor.

Toledo mayors have not been elected because of their political ambition or their partisanship; nor was a record as a vote-getter any assurance of elevation to the office. Mayors were frequently chosen as a result of bargains between the parties or factions within the parties. Two council elections provide excellent examples of this method. In 1959 the council was divided between three Democrats, two City Manager League Democrats, two City Manager League Republicans, and two Republicans. A Democratic mayor was elected with the votes of the three regular Democrats, one Republican defector, and a City Manager League Democrat who received the position of vice-mayor in exchange for his support. In 1961 there was only one Democratic councilman, so electoral bargains were confined to the Republican Party. After one of the Republicans was publicly declared to be the new mayor, a faction of councilmen, county Republicans, and party leaders regrouped to reverse the decision. Through a series of negotiations, a newly elected Republican councilman was selected mayor, partly on the basis of his more unknown (hence, safer) record and his less obvious political ambitions.[6]

----

charter provisions include John Carey (D., 1940–1942); Michael DiSalle (D., 1948–1950); and John Potter (R., 1961–1965). These mayors, particularly DiSalle, are believed to have developed the informal powers of the office to a greater extent than others.

[6] Neither the initial nor the final choice for mayor had been the top vote-getter in the 1961 election.

Toledo, then, has lacked an executive with public support and the power to lead. The leadership gap has not been filled by other councilmen (individually or collectively) or by the city manager. Occasional councilmen have been influential on particular problems, but they, like the mayor, have lacked the authority for sustained, day-to-day leadership on a variety of issues. A typical councilman with an instinct for survival has rarely ventured out of the trenches to provide leadership or engage in political controversy.[7] The absence of executive power has produced a situation in which even reasonably competent officeholders are reluctant or unable to exert leadership.

The Role of the City Manager

The city managers, with one exception, have been equally cautious about taking public positions on issues or assuming leadership. This has not varied with the presence or absence of what are called "professional" city managers.[8] A city manager's tenure, whatever his training or experience, is closely tied to the electoral results. Electoral changes in Toledo are often followed by new city managers. The Democratic victory in 1949 ended a decade of service by one manager. When the Republicans returned to power in 1961 after a decade in the minority, they installed a new manager. The 1957 council, which included eight councilmen endorsed by the City Manager League, retained an abrasively professional manager. During the past 30 years, the average tenure for Toledo managers has been slightly over four years. Since 1957, however, only one manager has served for more than three years, and one held office for only eight months.

[7] This is in accord with Charles R. Adrian's account of councilmen in smaller cities in Michigan. See "Leadership and Decision-Making in Manager Cities: A Study of Three Communities," *Public Administration Review*, XVIII (Summer 1958), 208–213.

[8] Of Toledo's seven city managers, three are classified as professional managers by the Greater Toledo Municipal League. The three professionals, with training in engineering, administration, and law, are often contrasted with "local men." Actually the professionals are neither so pure nor the local men so impure as the distinction suggests. The professional managers include men with experience in party politics and elective office, while some of the local men have educational backgrounds identical with those of the professionals.

The individualistic and leaderless character of city politics has provided an uncertain arena for innovations and initiative by the city manager.[9] Most managers have avoided public controversy or conspicuous leadership in order not to jeopardize the support crucial to their continued service and salary.[10] Also, weak party lines and maverick councilmen have made city managers adept at "counting to five." Thus, the manager has generally been merely a caretaker of the city's administrative machinery.

Only one manager abandoned this mellow approach. He took controversial positions on public issues, publicly attacked councilmen, antagonized organized labor, delivered political addresses during a city campaign, and found himself dismissed shortly after the election.[11]

The Absence of Political Leadership in Toledo

Past and present councilmen are unanimous in deploring the long absence of political leadership in Toledo. For some an emphasis on political leadership was an early conviction; others arrived at this conclusion through experience on city council. One former Republican councilman close to the reform movement reluctantly concluded that the council-manager form of government had caused Toledo to lag behind other cities in growth and services. Another Republican had been a strong advocate of Toledo's form of government before his election to city council:

[9] Edward C. Banfield and James Q. Wilson enumerate five patterns in the relations between the city council and the manager. They describe the fifth type as a situation in which there is considerable local conflict, but no stable majority or factional stalemate. Thus the manager must put together majorities on each issue by persuading individual councilmen to "go along" with him. This is characteristic of Toledo. City managers have responded to this situation by taking refuge in routine tasks. For a discussion of this typology, see *City Politics* (Cambridge, Mass.: Harvard University Press and M.I.T. Press, 1963), pp. 177–180. Gladys M. Kammerer *et al.* also present a useful discussion of influences affecting the tenure and role of city managers in *City Managers in Politics* (Gainesville: University of Florida Press, 1962).

[10] The city manager is paid $25,000 a year.

[11] This city manager, generally considered a professional, served from February 1957 to April 1960. During the greater part of this period, a reform majority held office. The manager himself felt strongly about reform institutions, as later discussions will indicate.

I always gave the arguments for the manager system—straight from the civics textbooks. Now I've changed my mind. Our mayors have been floor leaders for debate and nothing else. What does a city manager do that a chief administrator working for the mayor couldn't do? This way the whole thing is falling apart—it lacks cohesion.

A former Democratic councilman described the problem this way:

Toledo city councils typically have no direction. You try out a program, but then the personalities come out in full bloom. There is no way of keeping councilmen together. The manager's role is like the comptroller of a company: "You can't do it. It costs too much." The city manager's a good housekeeper. If I were looking for a wife, I'd marry him.

Leaders in business, labor, and Negro organizations also recognize the absence of strong political leadership in Toledo, although they are less concerned with the causes, effects, and remedies. Many business leaders have difficulty naming any mayors between Golden Rule Jones and Mayor Potter. They are unimpressed with the mayor's role in community affairs. In the opinion of one corporation president:

Toledo is run well enough. Some of its facilities are good. Some civic drives have been successful. But there's been something missing in Toledo. Everytime a kid is born, a man dies in this town. A dynamic political leader is lacking.

Some Negro leaders also accept this assessment, contending that the mayor is inevitably the lackey of the power structure. Among union leaders there is widespread agreement about the low state of city leadership under the council-manager plan. One United Auto Workers official said:

City councilmen are elected on the basis of their individual characters. They bow to no party responsibility or leadership. They're all on their own. The manager is a quiet Republican politician who has gone into retirement as the city manager of Toledo. All the managers have known who appointed them, so they stay in the background. This arrangement isn't set up to emphasize leadership.

The continuing influence of the reform tradition has made the question of governmental change extremely delicate. Nevertheless, the role of the executive in local government has been one of the

controversial issues of recent years. Thus in the late '50s, efforts to
introduce a strong mayor form of government caused bitter conflicts and a revival of reform organization.

Democratic Advocacy of Strong Mayor Plan

After many years of acquiescence in the reform movement, the
Democratic Party emerged to advocate a strong mayor. In 1957 the
Democrats proposed an amendment providing for a directly elected
mayor with veto power and the authority to appoint a chief administrative officer. Ironically, Democratic indecision and disorganization weakened this effort and strengthened the forces of reform.
Democratic leaders, aware of considerable reform sentiment in the
party, hesitated for months before calling a referendum. With little
money, few spokesmen, and a moribund organization, the Democrats conducted an ineffectual campaign. Although *The Blade* and
organized labor were sympathetic to the strong mayor plan, the
Democratic Party foundered on its own internal divisions and
disorganization.

In contrast, the Democratic charter amendment stimulated a
well-organized and highly successful campaign by the City Manager
League, a reform organization of business and professional people
which had revived a year earlier to promote the appointment of a
professional city manager. The City Manager League endorsed and
campaigned for five Republicans and four Democrats pledged to the
continuation of the council-manager plan. The four Democrats endorsed by the City Manager League were also endorsed by the
Democratic Party, accentuating the party schism on reform.
Thus four City Manager League Democrats, including three popular incumbents, openly opposed the party's charter amendment. On
the other side, the City Manager League had a unified slate of
candidates and a well-financed campaign to support them. The
Democratic Party, as an editorial in *The Blade* commented, had
"no spokesman really determined to carry the ball. They [the party
leaders] made little effort to unite the various factions of a divided
party and to get them to support what was supposed to be a party
program."[12]

---

[12] *The Blade*, November 7, 1957, p. 24.

Eight of the nine City Manager League candidates were elected. Only one anti-city manager candidate, a Democrat, survived the election. A promising young anti-city manager Democrat was narrowly defeated. The three remaining Democrats who supported the party's charter amendment came in 13th, 15th, and 16th in the balloting. The City Manager League was equally well rewarded in the voting results on the strong mayor amendment. The Democratic proposal was defeated by a vote of 57,592 to 24,783. Only 29.9 per cent of the voters favored the strong mayor plan. The survival of the council-manager form of government was temporarily assured and an active reform organization had again entered electoral politics.

The campaign of 1959. In 1959 Democratic leaders renewed their efforts to introduce the strong mayor plan. They found the situation greatly complicated by the presence of four City Manager League Democrats on city council. One of these councilmen, a fervent advocate of municipal reform, had been elected mayor.[13] The mayor and the party leadership were openly hostile. Democratic leaders believed that the mayor was filling city positions with Republicans and reformers. ''I have always thought,'' Mayor Yager said, ''that the party has felt that perhaps it could never fully trust me. I guess they think I am not a good Democrat, and I guess I am not, if you mean a professional Democrat.''[14]

By the spring of 1959, Democratic leaders had concluded that a successful campaign for the strong mayor amendment would require the expulsion of city manager Democrats from the party. The four reform councilmen, including the mayor, were asked to resign from the party's executive committee and denied party endorsement for the fall election. The mayor protested, claiming that he would be a good Democrat if he were to run for higher office. In city politics, he argued, there is no necessity for being a good Democrat.[15]

Mayor Yager responded to Democratic attacks by urging the City Manager League to function as a political party dedicated to the

---

[13] This was John W. Yager, elected president of the Greater Toledo Municipal League in 1964. Mayor Yager's father, Joseph Yager, had been active in the reform movement of earlier years.

[14] *The Blade*, April 12, 1959, Section 2, p. 3.

[15] *The Blade*, April 24, 1959, p. 1.

continuation of good government. After one political address, the mayor introduced the city manager, who expressed his opposition to a city government of partisanship and party responsibility. "Why this constant pressure by political leaders to control city hall?" asked the manager. The city manager then criticized the Democratic leadership for insisting on party responsibility among city councilmen and charged that "there are ulterior forces at work seeking to plant the seeds of graft and corruption."[16]

During the summer, advocates of the council-manager plan and the strong mayor proposal organized campaign committees cutting across party lines. A prominent county Republican and a Republican councilman (and former mayor) with 22 years on city council and a 1957 endorsement from the City Manager League supported the Citizens' Committee for Strong Mayor Government. A new Republican councilman elected with City Manager League support in 1957 also renounced the manager form of government. A former Republican councilman told a Democratic strong mayor committee: "City manager government has proved that it cannot cope with the problems of a city of this size. City manager government provides only a diffusion of leadership."[17]

On the other side, reform Democrats as well as Republicans continued to support the City Manager League. Mayor Yager and his three exiled colleagues appealed to Democrats to put their belief in good government ahead of partisanship. The president of the City Manager League, a former Republican councilman and mayor, urged voters to defeat "a proposal which should really be called the weak mayor, strong boss system."[18]

The Yager proposal. As strong mayor advocates were circulating petitions for their amendment, Mayor Yager introduced a rival proposal in city council.[19] The Yager proposal provided for the direct election of a mayor who would preside over city council and vote only in the case of a tie; the mayor would possess veto power over all legislation except that pertaining to the budget, but his veto

---

[16] *Ibid.*

[17] *The Blade*, August 12, 1959, p. 4.

[18] *The Blade*, August 13, 1959, p. 1.

[19] Charter amendments can be placed on the ballot by petition and by city council. The 1957 charter amendment was placed on the ballot by council. Petitions have often been used as a campaign tactic, as in the introduction of the council-manager plan.

could be overridden by a two-thirds vote of the council.[20] The votes of four City Manager League Democrats and two City Manager League Republicans placed the mayor's proposal on the ballot. Thus the voters would consider two alternative amendments, a condition usually sufficient to defeat proposals for charter revisions.

Proponents of the strong major plan immediately noted the danger of the Yager proposal. *The Blade*, originally a supporter of the council-manager plan but now an advocate of the strong mayor system, accused Mayor Yager of political tricks in introducing an amendment designed to "confuse the voters." Mayor Yager retorted that *The Blade* was attempting to act as a "fourth political party" in addition to being "the principal supporter and promoter of the so-called strong mayor plan."[21]

During the fall campaign, *The Blade* continued to praise the strong mayor plan and to chastise its opponents. The United Labor Committee (AFL-CIO) and the Teamsters also endorsed the strong mayor proposal. Although organized labor had never been sympathetic to the council-manager plan, the campaign of 1959 represented its greatest commitment to changing the system. In 1957 the United Labor Committee had endorsed two candidates committed to council-manager government and supported by the City Manager League. In 1959 all seven candidates endorsed by the United Labor Committee favored the strong mayor form of government. Union members were exhorted to register and vote and a former city manager was quoted in the *Toledo Union Journal* as saying that "the people behind the City Manager League are the same people who attempted to put through the right to work law."[22]

As the campaign progressed, heated statements were exchanged between leaders of the Citizens' Committee for Strong Mayor Government and the City Manager League. The chairman of the strong mayor committee charged that the Yager proposal "is an attempt to foist on the people a subterfuge in the form of a watered down strong mayor proposal."[23] The executive secretary of the City Manager League defended the council-manager plan, contending that a

[20] The Democratic strong mayor proposal was essentially the same as the 1957 charter amendment. The 1959 charter amendment provided for a mayor with power to appoint a chief administrator; and with veto power over all ordinances, with the provision that a vote of seven out of nine councilmen could override the mayor's veto.

[21] *The Blade*, August 23, 1959, p. 4, and August 25, 1959, p. 4.

[22] *Toledo Union Journal*, October 23, 1959, p. 1.

[23] *The Blade*, August 13, 1959, p. 1.

return to any version of "the executive mayor type of government" would amount to a vote for "crime, corruption, and misrule."[24] He cautioned Toledo voters against the danger of giving the mayor "virtually unlimited powers." Others in the City Manager League, including Mayor Yager, made a few gestures in behalf of the direct election of the mayor.

Neither the Yager proposal nor the strong mayor proposal passed. The strong mayor amendment was defeated by a vote of 49,626 to 41,289. The improved campaign effort, as well as the support of *The Blade* and organized labor, were evident in the increased percentage of support for the strong mayor plan. In 1957, 29.9 per cent of those voting had favored the Democratic proposal; two years later this percentage increased to 45.4.[25] The percentage favoring the strong mayor amendment increased in every ward.

The Yager amendment was defeated 54,895 to 24,496, drawing only 32.4 per cent of the vote. This percentage probably included voters who would have supported the strong mayor proposal if a choice between two amendments had not been offered. It is possible that the Yager amendment deflected support necessary to pass the strong mayor amendment.[26]

While defeating the strong mayor amendment, the voters elected five councilmen pledged to that form of government. Only four candidates, two Republicans and two Democrats, of the nine endorsed by the City Manager League were elected. A fifth candidate, a reform Democrat, was narrowly defeated. The remaining City Manager League candidates placed 18th, 19th, 21st and 22nd. In the new council, City Manager League councilmen were in a minority rather than an eight-to-one majority. This minority decreased to three when one City Manager League Democrat returned to the party. Thus the reform group included only John Yager and two Republicans.[27]

[24] *The Blade,* September 29, 1959, p. 14.

[25] Yet the sentiment for change had not grown since a charter issue in 1946, when 46 per cent of the voters favored a ward-based council with an elective executive.

[26] This assumes that a voter would not have supported both the strong mayor amendment and the Yager proposal. The issues and alignments of 1959 suggest that an affirmative vote on both proposals would have been unlikely. If both amendments had received a majority, the one receiving the highest number of votes would have prevailed. The presence of two issues and the course of the campaign posed a choice which may have detracted from support for the strong mayor amendment.

[27] Yager was third in the balloting; he was second in the 1957 election.

Pressure for Direct Election of the Mayor

Discussion of charter revision did not end with the divisive campaigns of 1957 and 1959. The political bargain by which the new mayor and vice-mayor were elected in 1959 attracted adverse comment. (The vice-mayor got his job in exchange for supporting the mayor for the job.) Even some of the orthodox in the City Manager League and the Municipal League began to question the indirect election of the mayor. Also, the ineptitude of the 1959–1961 city council and the uncertainty with which its successor elected a near-mayor and a mayor in 1961 again aroused discussion of charter revision.[28]

In early 1963, Republican leaders began to advocate a charter amendment providing for the direct election of the mayor. In contrast to the bitter controversies aroused by earlier proposals, the 1963 charter amendment attracted support from all community organizations. By 1963 contending groups had concluded, for differing reasons, that the direct election of the mayor would be a desirable step.

Leaders in the City Manager League, the Municipal League, and the League of Women Voters abandoned their earlier reservations about enhancing the mayor's prestige and power by direct election. An analysis made by the Municipal League emphasized the dissimilarity of the strong mayor form and the directly elected mayor. The direct election of the mayor was described as a suitable alternative to the selection of the mayor by council and "one which does not involve the abandonment of the council-manager form of government under which Toledo has operated since 1935." The League of Women Voters, a traditional advocate of the council-manager form of government, endorsed the charter proposal. A leader in the City Manager League declared that the direct election of the mayor is "a good move . . . which does not in any way detract from the form of government we now have."[29] The Chamber of Commerce, long sympathetic to the council-manager plan, also endorsed the charter amendment.

[28] For evidence of the uncertainty in the 1961 mayoralty choice, see *The Blade*, November 15, 1961, p. 1. The Republican choices for mayor and vice-mayor described in this article were later changed.

[29] *The Blade*, September 21, 1963, p. 3, and October 6, 1963, p. 21.

Reform leaders had concluded that the direct election of the mayor would correct admitted faults in the existing arrangement while staving off pressure for the strong mayor plan. If the amendment passed, the voters would no longer be affronted by a mayor chosen in backroom bargains. A mayor with the psychological and political advantages of direct election could provide the measure of leadership necessary to deflate demands for the strong mayor plan. Although leaders in the City Manager League and the Municipal League recognized that this course "could provide an opening wedge for doing away with the council-manager form of government," they gambled on it.[30]

The Republican Party had also considered the situation carefully. Party leaders decided that taking the initiative with direct election would be preferable to resisting repeated Democratic efforts to introduce the strong mayor plan. A directly elected mayor could provide a focus to city government without jeopardizing a system in which Republicans can win elections. Republican leaders hoped that the 1963 charter amendment would eliminate the most obvious defects and abuses of the council-manager plan, thus postponing and possibly preventing a public demand for more radical change. The Republican party chairman asserted that the direct election of the mayor is fully consistent with the Republican commitment to the city manager system. The change, he argued, will preserve the form of government while "paving the way for more vigorous, aggressive community leadership."[31] Other party leaders were skeptical about this strategy. One officeholder and member of the Executive Committee commented: "I wasn't convinced, but everyone jumped through the hoop, including such pure people as the Municipal League, the City Manager League, and the Republican Party. It makes you puke to think of it."

The reasoning of Democratic leaders justified the apprehension felt by some Republicans. After two unsuccessful efforts to introduce the strong mayor plan, Democratic leaders decided on the strategy of change by degrees. In this context, the direct election of the mayor could be considered a significant step toward a strong executive rather than a concession to reform, as Democrats had previously viewed it in 1959. Instead of entering another difficult charter campaign for the strong mayor plan, the Democratic Party

[30] *The Blade*, September 21, 1963, p. 3.
[31] *The Blade*, October 9, 1963, p. 7.

would cooperate in the less demanding task of passing a direct election amendment. The next step would be to elect a Democratic mayor with a Democratic majority on city council. The mayor with the support of party colleagues could then appoint a city manager of his own choosing. With the prestige of direct election and the backing of a Democratic majority, the mayor could gradually move Toledo toward the strong mayor system. The informal powers which would accrue to the mayor would make it less difficult to add formal powers such as the veto at a later time.

Organized labor also subscribed to this interpretation. The *Toledo Union Journal* (AFL-CIO) and the *Team and Wheel* (Teamsters) endorsed the amendment. "The direct election of the mayor," said one union leader, "marks the beginning of the end for the days when the mayor's job was to pass out glass keys and talk to little old ladies."[32] *The Blade* also concluded that gradual change would be preferable to divisive charter conflicts. Editorials in *The Blade* reflected the hope that the direct election of the mayor could lead to other improvements in city government.[33]

The 1963 Charter Amendment and Its Aftermath

On election day the charter amendment was approved by 24,406 voters and opposed by only 11,110 in a low turn-out.[34] Seventy-six per cent of those voting favored the change to direct election in one of the largest margins ever recorded for a charter amendment in Toledo. The unanimity of group support and general dissatisfaction with processes used in choosing recent mayors influenced the outcome. The voters had been assured that they could improve city leadership without departing from reform institutions.

Since the passage of the 1963 amendment, the organizations dedicated to these institutions have been quiescent. Leaders in the Toledo Municipal League and the City Manager League assert that

---

[32] Toledo, as a glass center, distributes glass keys to visiting dignitaries.

[33] See *The Blade*, September 30, 1963, p. 12.

[34] Only 45,516 voted on the 1963 charter amendment; 82,090 voted on the 1957 strong mayor proposal; 90,866 voted on the 1959 strong mayor proposal, and 81,281 voted on the Yager proposal.

their organizations are still alert to threats to the council-manager plan. But the City Manager League has been inactive in council elections since 1959. The 1965 mayoralty election, in which Toledo first tested a significant retraction from the 1935 charter provisions, produced no organized activity by the City Manager League or other advocates of municipal reform. The Democratic candidate's outspoken belief in a strong mayor and his campaign promise to fire the city manager aroused no public comment from the organizations and leaders active in earlier controversies.[35] The Republican candidate's charge that his Democratic opponent would, if elected, destroy nonpartisanship and the council-manager form of government was also received silently. The Republican candidate was elected without the open and active support of the City Manager League.[36]

The Republican Party has long advocated and benefited from the council-manager plan. When the reform movement was ascendent, the Republican Party accommodated itself to the tenets and organizations of reform. During those years, the Democratic Party suffered from the conflict of party and reform Democrats. The Democratic Party has now banished reformers, and the Republican Party may eventually carry the greater internal conflict.

The Democratic Party, weak and divided in 1957 and 1959, was equally unsuccessful in 1965. The party strategy for the 1965 election emphasized the need to avoid a divisive and possibly futile effort at charter revision. When a Democratic councilman revived the strong mayor issue in the winter of 1965, party leaders persuaded him to withdraw his proposal.[37] But Skeldon handled his campaign in such a way as to provoke the conflicts which the party sought to avoid. The promise to fire the city manager unnecessarily awakened reform opposition. In challenging the form of government, the Democrats have failed, regardless of party strategy.

[35] For the remarks in which Skeldon promised to fire the city manager, see *The Blade*, September 9, 1965, p. 1.

[36] For Potter's warning about the threat to nonpartisanship and council-manager government, see *The Blade*, September 22, 1965, p. 3. Although Potter did not have the organized support of the City Manager League, Skeldon's remarks probably intensified and enlarged Potter sentiment among groups sympathetic to reform. Thus Skeldon raised an issue which was not to his advantage.

[37] Councilman Neumann (D.) proposed that a strong mayor amendment be submitted to the voters in May 1966. His proposal is described in *The Blade*, January 4, 1966, p. 11.

Although organized labor supported the strong mayor amendments, it did not conduct a strenuous campaign for their passage. One union official explained labor's role this way:

> Labor has favored the strong mayor, but it hasn't been vehement about it. . . . Perhaps there is an underlying fear that a strong mayor of the opposite side could hurt labor. The City Manager League has capitalized on this.

Most Negro leaders were either sympathetic to the council-manager plan or indifferent to the form of government; few considered the charter issue significant for Negroes or for the community.

These conditions have contributed to the durability of reform institutions in Toledo. The City Manager League exploited the disorganization and disinterest of other groups in winning votes of confidence for the council-manager plan. In achieving the victories of 1957 and 1959, the City Manager League relied on the sympathy of many business and professional leaders and the active support of some. Reform leaders broadened this base of support by invoking good government sentiment, caution about change, and fear of corruption under the strong mayor plan. Some of these themes reappeared in the 1965 mayoralty campaign. But the reform organizations themselves have greatly deteriorated. In 1966 neither the City Manager League nor the Municipal League had the interest or the strength to confront issues not posed in a charter amendment.

Political developments arising from the direct election of the mayor and increased party activity have not revived reform organization. Many business leaders are less interested in either "good" government or community participation than they were in past decades. Business and political leaders once active in the reform movement express a sense of powerlessness in facing the local power of labor, Democratic strength, party voting in city elections, and the influence of minority and ethnic groups. Long-range efforts to compete with these influences are considered futile. A charter amendment on the form of government, in contrast to general political activity, presents a specific, immediate issue on which reformers feel the greatest commitment and confidence.[38]

The decision to elect the mayor directly may prove to be a signifi-

[38] Don K. Price noted reformers' preoccupation with charter questions and their neglect of other facets of city politics in "The Promotion of the City Manager Plan," *Public Opinion Quarterly*, V (Winter 1941), 563–578.

cant event in altering the circumstances of reform influence. The involvement of the political parties and organized labor in the 1965 and (quite possibly) future mayoralty elections will make Toledo politics less susceptible to the sporadic activities characteristic of the City Manager League in the past. A future revival of reform organizations would not find the inert political situation which greatly increased the impact of brief periods of reform activity during the 1930s and '50s.

Furthermore, the direct election of the mayor can help to bring about the governmental changes which reform organizations hoped to forestall when they endorsed the 1963 amendment. Any mayor elected by the voters will hold a more potent office than his predecessors chosen by city council. The elected mayor will have the prestige and position to provide increased cohesion and direction in city government. Mayor Potter has taken steps in this direction by placing the mayor first in council roll calls and instituting weekly meetings for the city manager, department heads, and himself.[39]

Reform sentiment, without the organized support of the City Manager League or the stimulus of an immediate charter proposal, will probably permit the gradual development of a strong executive. Under these circumstances, the city manager will defer to the mayor and become increasingly identified with him. The resulting political patterns will be far removed from the division of legislative and administrative authority and the equality of officeholders prescribed in the council-manager plan.

Thus the direct election of the mayor is the first step in the acquisition of executive powers and the possible abandonment of the council-manager plan. The influence of the reform tradition on voting, recruitment and election practices, and the local political ethos will not give way in the near future. Nor will the mayor have the formal powers, such as the veto, desirable for decisive leadership. But the direct election provides an opening for change.

[39] *The Blade,* December 29, 1965, p. 16.

8 THE CIVIC AND POLITICAL ROLE OF BUSINESS LEADERS

The diffuseness of Toledo's political structure is equalled by the fragmentation and impassiveness of its business leadership. Major business interests are loosely organized and only slightly interested in city affairs. Leaders in large industrial, financial, and retail institutions do not seek to control city government, either directly or indirectly. Most executives in major firms enter the public arena only to perform unassailable good deeds in civic drives; occasional defensive actions in politics are delegated to subordinates.

The Toledo Business Community

The business community of Toledo is not dominated by any one firm or group of firms. The city's large private employers include national corporations, local firms, retail companies, utilities, and financial institutions. For many of the major companies, Toledo is more than a plant location. Excluding governmental agencies, such as the Toledo Public Schools and national and state utilities (that is, Ohio Bell and the New York Central System), eight of the eleven largest employers in the city have Toledo headquarters.

111

Seven of the eight locally based industrial and business firms were founded and developed in Toledo. Among the firms historically associated with the city are the glass companies, (Libbey-Owens-Ford, Owens-Illinois, and Owens-Corning Fiberglas), the Toledo Scale Corporation, Champion Spark Plug, the DeVilbiss Company, and Toledo Edison.[1] All of these firms are now publicly owned and listed on the New York Stock Exchange. In some cases, such as Libbey-Owens-Ford Glass Company and the Toledo Scale Corporation, a large percentage of the company stock is locally owned. In a few, notably Champion and DeVilbiss, descendants of company founders occupy the executive offices. The three largest absentee corporations are Chevrolet Division of General Motors, Doehler-Jarvis Division of National Lead, and Kaiser Jeep Corporation, a subsidiary of Kaiser Industries, Inc.

Table 8.1 presents 1965 employment figures for the eleven largest industrial and business employers in the city.

TABLE 8.1

The Major Employers in Toledo, 1965

Company	Employment (August 1965)
Kaiser Jeep Corporation	6,924
Libbey-Owens-Ford Glass Co.*	6,350
Owens-Illinois, Inc.*	4,719
Chevrolet	3,361
Dana Corporation*	3,293
Doehler-Jarvis	1,957
Champion Spark Plug*	1,781
Toledo Edison*	1,550
Gladieux Corporation*	1,524
Toledo Scale Division, Toledo Scale Corp.*	1,320
DeVilbiss Company*	1,070

* The asterisk indicates that the firm is based in Toledo. (Source: *The Blade*, August 16, 1965, Section 2, p. 3.)

Some prominent firms in the industrial, retail, and financial fields do not appear among the city's largest employers. Owens-Corning

[1] Of these companies, only Owens-Corning Fiberglas is not among the top employers.

Fiberglas Corporation has its headquarters in Toledo and its many plants elsewhere. Consequently, its employment is well under a thousand. Large downtown retail stores with close to a thousand employees are LaSalle and Koch Company, a division of Macy's, and two local firms, Tiedtke's and Lamson Brothers Company. The Toledo Trust Company, Ohio Citizens Bank and Trust, and the National Bank of Toledo are the major financial institutions in the city.[2]

Attitudes of Toledo Businessmen

Toward civic affairs. Local firms are often thought to be more active in city affairs than absentee corporations.[3] Presumably, retail and financial institutions have a greater interest in the local community than industrial corporations with national markets.[4] These generalizations do not hold for Toledo. Although many firms have Toledo headquarters, their interest in the city has declined as their operations have increased. Toledo plants and headquarters are balanced by a multitude of plants and office buildings in other locations. Retail firms and banks are following their clients to the suburbs rather than participating in city programs to improve their original downtown sites. None of the large industrial, retail, or financial institutions displays a marked interest or involvement in the city. Twenty interviews with high executives in major firms revealed that the apathy of Toledo business leaders transcends the conventional distinctions about ownership, headquarters, product, and service.

Business leaders would deny this indictment. Only two of twenty executives described the leaders of major business interests as less than actively involved in community affairs. Most business leaders

2 A fourth bank, the Progress National Bank, was founded in 1965. Toledo banks have total assets of $75,868,499. In October 1965, bank deposits were as follows: Toledo Trust, $317.4 million; Ohio Citizens Trust, $315 million; First National Bank of Toledo, $144.1 million; and Progress National Bank, $3,376,610. These figures are from *The Blade*, October 11, 1965, Section 2, p. 3.

3 See, for example, Robert Schulze, ''The Bifurcation of Power in a Satellite City,'' in Morris Janowitz, ed., *Community Political Systems* (New York: The Free Press, 1961), pp. 19–81.

4 Edward C. Banfield and James Q. Wilson, *City Politics* (Cambridge, Mass.: Harvard University Press and M.I.T. Press, 1963), p. 263.

are convinced that they carry a heavy burden of community responsibilities in addition to demanding company obligations. One corporation executive and financier commented:

> Business leaders are terrifically active in this community. It's astounding—the spirit of the top business leaders. Participation is on the increase. There are some 30 or 40 people active in business leadership now—compared with the few aggressive, dominant ones in the years before 1945.

A bank president described business participation this way: "I'm afraid business leaders are very much involved in the community. In fact, too much so. With few exceptions, we carry the brunt in city activities."

Leaders in major firms cite many activities to their credit. Charitable organizations and fund drives are the most popular area of business participation. For many business leaders, the United Appeal, the Red Cross, and the hospital commissions were important examples of civic contribution. An Owens-Corning Fiberglas executive reviewed his civic activities and those of other business leaders:

> I've been very much involved, and I think many business leaders have—in the United Appeal, which is really operated by business. The hospital field is another area where I've been active and where business has had a large part. For example, Toledo business got through a law for the county to set up a hospital commission and issue tax exempt bonds.

Others referred to their work for Goodwill Industries, the YMCA, the Boy Scouts, the Boys' Clubs of Toledo and the Toledo Newsboys' Association.[5]

In some cases, cultural and educational institutions received the greatest emphasis:

> I've been especially interested in the Symphony Orchestra and the Opera. For many years I have served on the board of trustees of the University of Toledo and the Toledo Museum of Art. My

---

[5] The emphasis of Toledo business leaders on charitable and civic activities is in accord with findings of other studies. See Peter H. Rossi's observations on the community activities of the American Telephone and Telegraph Company, reported in National Opinion Research Center, Report No. 64, *Industry and Community*, October 1957.

firm and many others have long been involved in cultural activities
such as these and in the major charities.

A smaller number of executives stressed their interest and participation in public authorities and commissions, such as the Labor-
Management-Citizens Commission, the Toledo Metropolitan Housing Authority, the Toledo Area Development Corporation, and the
Toledo-Lucas County Port Authority.

Toledo business leaders, with few exceptions, confine their community activities to safe organizations and causes. Helping the
handicapped, the diseased, and the unfortunate through reputable
private organizations is considered an appropriate form of business
participation in the community. The cultural and educational institutions of the city, like the established charities, carry little risk of
public opposition or dissension. Few business leaders extend their
activity into organizations and areas where the way is not sure.
Those who supported private charities were generally unconcerned
or unsympathetic with the local war on poverty. Participation in
boys' organizations does not mean support of the agencies serving
the Negro youth of the central city. An avowed interest in the city
has not produced a business organization to advance urban redevelopment.

In rare cases local business leaders have made a contribution to
the community beyond the realm of charity. The interest of a few
prominent businessmen in the Labor-Management-Citizens Commission, a local mediation agency, during the late 1940s and '50s is an
example. More recently, some business leaders, with a boost from
The Blade, have contributed to the development of the Toledo-Lucas
County Port Authority. Such efforts would probably be more frequent under the stimulus of real political leadership, which has
been missing in Toledo for a long time.

As of 1966, the leaders of major firms appear to be less involved
in the community than ever before. Many local companies have
expanded to world-wide dimensions or merged with national corporations.[6] One official voiced the opinion of many:

> If you look at the big corporations here, the big glass firms and
> automotive parts companies, what happens in Toledo isn't of

---

[6] Textileather merged with General Tire and Rubber in 1954; Kaiser Jeep
Corporation bought Willys Motors in 1953.

major concern. These broad-based businesses do not depend on Toledo.

The individuals most active in business leadership during the past three decades have recently retired or serve only in advisory positions. The business leaders most interested in Toledo are older men, no longer active in their companies.

The new men in executive positions have a narrower concern for the community and a restricted conception of business participation. An executive at Libbey-Owens-Ford Glass Company described the increasingly circumscribed role of business in the community:

> In most companies involvement has become less of a personal thing and is done more on an organizational basis. It has become a management-directed public relations gesture—on the part of many. The great individual contributions are gone. John Biggers [former president of L-O-F] was extremely active. When Biggers was president, L-O-F was very active. Biggers' successor had a bit of *noblesse oblige*. The present president has very little contact with anything but the nuts and bolts of L-O-F.

The president of Owens-Illinois was described by a company official as "a man who believes that a businessman should be concerned with his job, family, and church." In other companies, the top leaders tend to be oriented to national and state affairs, as in the case of Owens-Corning Fiberglas, or concerned with company expansion rather than community participation: "Dana Corporation was in bad shape 14 years ago. Our tendency has been to emphasize that the business of the company is business." An executive in another large company commented:

> Our attitude on community affairs has been only fair at Toledo Scale. We've been very busy with company growth. But we're represented in various activities.

Absentee management (Kaiser Jeep Corp.), living in Ann Arbor, Michigan, or more distant points, has naturally had little time or concern for Toledo. Even the hereditary executives of the smaller home-based firms, both industrial and financial, seem to be drained of community spirit.

Most businessmen feel cautious about all major local issues. Leaders in a number of companies expressed reservations about present and future urban renewal projects as inappropriate areas for business involvement. Others were skeptical about the expressway program. Traffic congestion, slums, and blight are recognized as problems, but the remedies appear to be unsettling, slow, and riddled with politics. Urban renewal and expressway construction involve the dislocation and conflict feared by business. Change through industrial development may present similar problems. Although officials in banking and utility companies were interested in industrial development, leaders in several major industrial companies were more cautious, hoping that Toledo "would not grow too fast," "change too much," or "become an unpleasant place to live." Most business leaders are not interested in change and the possible disadvantages it might bring.

Business leaders admit that they avoid organizations and programs which might arouse public disputes: "I do not personally participate actively in controversial issues. What we want is good will. Controversies do not produce good will." All companies want their community activities to result in "good will" and "good public relations."[7] The president of a large corporation said:

> We believe firms should be involved. Yet I admit that it's public relations to a great degree for us and for most companies. I wouldn't be honest if I didn't say so. It's public relations and perhaps a desire on the part of the leadership to do their job properly and in total.

By participating in the United Appeal and the Red Cross a company leader can show that his firm is a "good corporate citizen." Involvement in such areas as urban renewal, civil rights, and party politics would reduce the acceptability of this image and the good will benefits expected from civic activity.[8]

Toward politics. Politics is considered particularly unsuited to company purposes. In contrast to charitable and civic activities, politics is likely to be divisive; and instead of being an ennobling

[7] Corporation executives' fear of controversy and concern with public relations are discussed in various studies. See Norton E. Long, "The Corporation, Its Satellites, and the Local Community," in Edward S. Mason, ed., *The Corporation in Modern Society* (Cambridge, Mass.: Harvard University Press, 1959), pp. 202–217.

[8] For another illustration of this pattern see Long, "The Corporation, Its Satellites, and the Local Community." Long writes that the corporation executive finds himself involved in "ritualistic do-goodism in community affairs."

concern, in the manner of the Crippled Children's Society or the Crusade of Mercy, it appears sordid. Business leaders fear that party politics "alienates people instead of building friendships." As a result, business activity in politics is discreet. Those interested in politics direct their attention to the finance committee of the local Republican Party or, in rare cases, to the national affairs of the Republican Party. Overt activity in campaigns and elections is rare. Of the 20 business leaders interviewed, only three mentioned party activity beyond membership on the Republican finance committee; of these only two had been openly involved in Republican campaigns in Toledo, one as a senatorial candidate and one as chairman of the Citizens' Committee for Goldwater-Miller. Participation in the Democratic Party is beyond the pale. One executive reminisced about his experiences in publicly supporting the Johnson-Humphrey ticket: "The campaign was very emotional. I caused a lot of comment. It's quite unpopular to associate with the Democratic Party if you're a business leader."

Most business leaders view politics with disinterest and distaste. In addition to being incompatible with public relations, politics is an unappealing realm abounding in Democrats, union officials, and assorted double-dealers. One Owens-Illinois executive commented:

> I'm interested in politics as a personal matter. . . . I believe more businessmen should be interested in politics. They have a stake in it, but they don't recognize it. In general, businessmen are short-sighted about social revolutions. They let them sneak up and bite them before they know what's happening.

A bank president explained some of the reasons why politics is unappealing to him: "In politics there's always a drive toward patronage, special favors, the pressuring of officials, corruption."

Toward the political parties. In spite of their distaste for politics, many business leaders have pronounced opinions on political parties. In contrast to leaders in other groups, business executives are likely to emphasize the differences between the local Democratic and Republican parties. Leaders in major firms consider the local Democratic Party, like the national party, closely linked to organized labor, if not identical with it. In the opinion of one glass company vice-president: "The Democratic Party in Toledo has pretty much abdicated to COPE.'"[9] More than one executive believed the local Democratic Party to be a weak organization dominated by radical labor unions.

Most business leaders express only disdain for the Democratic alliance of labor, ethnic groups, and Negroes. The Democratic coalition is described as an immutable and controlling force extending from the local community to the federal government. Business leaders find the local and national policies of the Democratic Party as repugnant as the groups supporting them. According to the president of one firm: "All Democratic programs, locally and nationally, boil down to this: are you willing to pay for things which people should and are, for the most part, able to provide for themselves."

The local Republican Party is a more congenial organization for business leaders, although it does not generate enthusiasm or political activity from most of them. They regard the Republican Party, locally as well as nationally, as sounder, more sympathetic to business thinking, and more responsible in fiscal matters. Furthermore, John Andrews, the local Republican leader, is a man who might have had a successful business career if he had not chosen otherwise. Those business leaders most enthusiastic about the local Republican organization and most active in party affairs are at Andrews' former company, Owens-Corning Fiberglas Corporation.

Apathy and discontent are common among officials from firms other than Owens-Corning Fiberglas. A majority of business leaders vote Republican, but are indifferent to the local party, its officials, candidates, and electoral activity. The local Republican Party, although vastly preferable to the Democratic Party, is considered irrelevant to matters of consequence. A Republican defeat in city elections will not jeopardize crucial company interests. Nor will it affect personal interests, for, as many business leaders pointed out, "I live in Ottawa Hills rather than Toledo."[10]

Those mild, reassuring, and nonessential Republican qualities which appeal to apathetic businessmen are objectionable to the few who are interested in politics. This minority finds its party deficient in organization and appeal. According to one executive:

[9] The political arm of AFL-CIO unions in Toledo is called the United Labor Committee, not COPE (Committee on Political Education).

[10] Robert A. Dahl reports similar reactions of apathy and detachment in his discussion of the public role of economic notables in New Haven. *Who Governs?* (New Haven, Conn.: Yale University Press, 1961), pp. 69–79.

The Democratic Party in Toledo just seems to be smarter and to
have better politicians. The Republican organization here seems to
attract a bunch of fat heads. John [Andrews] is a businessman.
He's no organization politician. He doesn't know how to carry a
precinct. He's never gotten his hands dirty at the precinct level.

Other critics argued that the Republican emphasis on respectability, efficiency, and wholesomeness has fostered business indifference.
In the opinion of one corporation president: "What Toledo needs is
good partisan politics and politicians, not politicians who pretend to
be businesslike. Most Republicans and businessmen resist this
idea." One business critic urged a more energetic Republican
effort to win the political support of organized labor and minority
groups. But this suggestion is far removed from the thinking of
most business leaders.

Toward labor. Although they appreciate the assistance of union
officials and organizations in philanthropic drives, business leaders
consider the political influence of labor excessive. In city politics,
unlike civic affairs, labor is not an adjunct to business leadership.
The political detachment of business leaders increases their ignorance and suspicion of the relatively minor efforts of other groups.

Business leaders have only sketchy and, in many instances,
inaccurate information about the labor unions of Toledo. The relation of local unions to international unions is a source of confusion.
Prominent businessmen often contrast the UAW with the CIO and
describe the local AFL-CIO council as one union among others. All
Toledo unions are believed to be under the domination of a tyran-
nical local leader and an omnipotent national headquarters. Business leaders recognize the economic power of labor organizations
and officials and fear their political power in areas which have not
seemed to warrant business attention.

Most business leaders exaggerate labor's political activity and
suspect its motives and goals. Organized labor is seen as seeking
or actually exercising control of the city for "its own selfish interests." One corporation president believed that the local political
situation "couldn't possibly be dominated by unions more than it
is now." A senior vice-president in another company argued:

> Organized labor has prevented Toledo from growing as it
> should. The basic trouble here is that the fellows in the Auto
> Workers are always vying for control of the city. They don't
> think in terms of the good of the community as a whole.

Local unions, generally enumerated as the Teamsters, the UAW, and the CIO, are seen as united for local political action in spite of personal differences between leaders in the three unions. Although the UAW appears stronger than other unions, several prominent businessmen think that "its loyalties run to Detroit." According to the president of one firm: "CIO headquarters in Detroit rather than the good of the community determine the political moves of Toledo unions."

While leaders in the major firms do not believe that labor is working for specific policies that would be injurious to business interests, the pervasive influence of labor is regarded as damaging in less obvious ways. The "business climate" suffers. Seeing "city officials, Republicans as well as Democrats, swayed by union influence" is distasteful. A Republican mayor offended several prominent businessmen by reappointing a convicted UAW official to the Port Authority. The union leaders who command the political respect of both parties are unaesthetic and uncongenial to most business executives:

> X————— [a leader in the UAW] is impossible to deal with. He's low, crude, coarse, vulgar—with a criminal record. He never wears a coat and tie, speaks crudely. He's a low-type man who has hurt Toledo.

Labor influence has not resulted in civic policies hostile to major business interests, but it has meant a psychological reduction of the prestige and power of business leaders—especially since business leaders have shown no inclination to combat labor's influence by increasing business activity in politics. Thus when business leaders enter the political sphere, their power is shared rather than total; a Republican mayor supported by business interests is still responsive to the United Auto Workers. Even in civic affairs, labor leaders must be considered and included. One bank official commented:

> If organized labor is opposed to any civic project, it probably can't be passed. The UAW is helping us on this year's drive for hospitals. Without their support you can't do very much. In Toledo labor leaders are not just left out of the Community Chest, hospital commissions, or the Red Cross. Labor leaders are taken in, invited to be part of civic projects in this community.

Yet labor participation in drives and organizations which are "really operated by business" is more comfortable than political action by union officials or the United Labor Committee. Business leaders hope that labor's local interests will turn from politics to civic affairs as it grows more "mature" and "responsible." In this view, union members and union leaders are becoming more community-oriented than they were in the past. A company president said:

> Richard Gosser [UAW] became an outstanding example of the labor statesman. In earlier years he was hungry. He wanted and got his men in city and county government. Around '52, he started taking a lead in encouraging and assisting in community projects. Larry Steinberg [the leader of the Teamsters] is also, by and large, a broad-minded person with the interest of the community at heart.

Another businessman spoke of the new era in which "Gosser and Steinberg are trying to outdo each other as civic leaders, working together and competing at the same time." In the new period of "labor statesmanship," business spokesmen hope that unions will forsake electoral politics and overt political influence for the community-wide charitable and civic goals of business.

Thus many business leaders would like (if it were possible) to recast labor participation along lines similar but subordinate to their own. Although they do not fear adverse effects from city issues and elections, business executives are apprehensive about the role of organized labor in city politics.

Toward civil rights. The detachment of business leaders has a severe effect on their understanding of local civil rights problems. Top executives are almost completely divorced from the leaders, organizations, and problems in race relations.[11] The group which Negro leaders look upon as the "power structure" is, for the most part, unsympathetic to their cause and unwilling to support or join local efforts in civil rights. Most leading businessmen have little acquaintance with Negro leaders and slight respect for local civil rights organizations. Economic conditions do not require contact with the representatives of Negro organizations, as several company officials pointed out:

---

[11] For other accounts of the alienation of business leaders from community groups, see Schulze, "The Bifurcation of Power in a Satellite City," and Long, "The Corporation, Its Satellites, and the Local Community."

> We meet only with the UAW. We deal with Negroes only through the UAW. We have no direct acquaintance with Negro organizations, the NAACP or anything else. Outside of Harold Moss [a Negro in the UAW leadership] I wouldn't know who the Negro leaders here are supposed to be.

In some firms, such as banks, the union contact is also lacking:

> Not having a union in the bank, we stay out of this civil rights thing. I don't know what the major [civil rights] organizations in town are.

Whatever actions are taken are more likely to result from federal and (to a lesser degree) state coercion than the community responsibility of business leaders. Thus the large firms with government contracts, such as Dana Corporation, appear more responsive to local civil rights problems than historic Toledo companies (for example, Champion, DeVilbiss) with an alleged tie to the community.

Some business leaders expressed an understanding of the barriers which Negroes have encountered in housing and employment, but most did not. The president of one firm commented: "The main trouble with colored employees here and elsewhere is that they all want to start as vice-president without learning how. They don't want to work their way up." In housing, the difficulty was described this way: "There's a lot of colored housing in Toledo. We had it early here. But, damn it, they don't keep up their places. They're not ready for home ownership."

Most leaders in major firms do not believe that Toledo has or needs strong civil rights organizations. Negro leaders recognized by business are "decent," "responsible," "not the type that says he favors nonviolence and then leads the masses into a situation where violence is bound to occur." In the judgment of business leaders, the local situation does not justify militant organizations or leadership. Although a few prominent businessmen thought that more and faster progress is needed in race relations, most were reasonably satisfied with existing conditions. In the opinion of a senior vice-president in one company: "We've never had much segregation in Toledo." A high official in another firm believed that "Toledo is pretty well integrated in every respect." According to one businessman:

> The situation here in race relations is generally good. In housing, a Negro can go into any part of the city and buy a house that he can afford. This is my belief.

Employment problems are "not the manufacturer's fault, but the result of educational drawbacks among Negroes." The absence of qualified Negroes rather than discriminatory employment accounts for Negro difficulties in the job market.

Businessmen generally believe that city government and other local agencies have been extremely responsive, if not too responsive, to the grievances of Negroes. In city council "Negroes have always been represented, long before national publicity was given to these problems." "We've had a colored on municipal court and school board as well as city council," one businessman commented. In addition, both parties have sought Negro support and "both Republican and Democratic councils have worked very hard to please Negro voters."

Although the impact of local civil rights actions on major firms is negligible in comparison with state and federal legislation, it is a source of irritation for some business leaders. Several company officials expressed annoyance at a local equal employment pledge signed in 1963, asserting that it had not and would not alter employment practices and represented only "a public relations gesture which we were forced into." Federal investigation of employment is accepted as inevitable, but inquiries by local leaders are considered "police state tactics." The passage of a city fair housing ordinance in 1961, although approved by some business leaders, was frequently described as "an effort to legislate morality." Few businessmen thought that it was appropriate for city government to play a significant part in civil rights questions:

> City government in Toledo has been pretty sensitive to Negroes. I'm not sure that they [city council] have shown leadership, however. I'm not sure that city government should be showing leadership in something like civil rights. I don't think so.

Interestingly, a white minister and a white businessman involved in local voluntary and governmental civil rights agencies were described as Negro leaders by several businessmen!

Toward the city government. Toledo executives want a city government which is sympathetic to business interests. They ask nothing specific of this government; nor do they wish to contribute anything to it. Broad municipal programs are not expected or supported. Business leaders have not attempted to promote or encourage government action by an organization similar to Civic Progress in St. Louis or the Allegheny Conference in Pittsburgh.[12] They ask only that the city government refrain from damaging increases in water and sewer rates, increased taxes on pipelines, and other measures annoying or injurious to business.

The "climate" of local government is more important to business leaders than its policies. A good climate depends on "understanding" councilmen. Periods of city government are distinguished by the presence or absence of understanding councilmen rather than by party majorities or policies enacted. Although many business leaders did not know the names of more than a few councilmen or the party division (6R—3D) of city council, they were unanimous in finding the 1965 council "very cooperative." A previous council in which a UAW administrator served as mayor and a Negro as vice-mayor was considered "unsympathetic." Yet a number of executives found that they had relatively little contact with city council, sympathetic or not.

While business leaders are aloof from the major problems of the city and confine their activities to the charitable field, their ideology holds otherwise. Most prominent businessmen endorse the ideals of the reform movement, especially the movement that sought to open local politics to the respected business and professional leaders of the community. Toledo business leaders recognize a disparity between reform ideals and actual practice in their city. For a majority, however, the presence of reform institutions is reassuring enough to justify continued support or to cause them to have serious reservations about possible charter revision.

Although they do not fulfill their part in the reform scheme, many businessmen believe that nonpartisanship and the city manager plan have nevertheless produced a more businesslike, competent, and efficient city government. Because of the nonpartisan ballot, "we've had better city councils than we would have had otherwise." People have been willing "to vote for the qualified individual rather than the party." Furthermore, the city manager form of government has provided "a very competent and successful approach in city government." A company president argued:

---

[12] For a discussion of these and similar organizations and the businessman as a "civic statesman," see Banfield and Wilson, *City Politics*, pp. 267–270.

> The city manager form is associated with a good local govern-
> ment climate from the business standpoint. The city manager
> form gets government farther removed from politics. It makes it
> more like a business operation.

Because of the city manager system, "Toledo is run as efficiently as
you can run a political body."

In contrast, the strong mayor form of government is seen as "too
political, with too much patronage." Such a system could lead to
"preponderant control by the UAW and the Democratic Party" or
"a return to the corruption of the twenties." One company president said:

> I am opposed to the strong mayor form of government. I see a
> certain similarity between this [strong mayor] and a strong
> federal government or even dictatorship. You could perhaps get
> decisions faster. City management may muddle through more, but
> we aren't looking for great orators or demagogues, but for good
> management.

A small minority of executives is inclined to question business
arguments for the city manager plan. A few favor the strong mayor
form, although not without reservations. Those who see value in a
strong political executive are usually careful to emphasize that they
have mixed feelings on the subject or do not consider the question
crucial. Thus the president of one company said:

> I'm for the strong mayor rather than the city manager system
> . . . because government is political. But I have no deep convic-
> tions about it. I've been here fifteen years. I'm sort of an outsider,
> really.

Others insisted that they could support the strong mayor plan only
if they were assured that the possible candidates would be sympathetic to business interests.

On this issue, as well as others, business leaders fear that change
could be unfavorable. Businessmen sympathetic to the strong mayor
plan are unwilling or reluctant to support a change which would
arouse controversy and could, if approved, disrupt conditions now
considered to be satisfactory. On the other side, those business
leaders who defend the council-manager plan and nonpartisanship
offer no evidence about their actual operation in Toledo. It is the
ideology rather than the performance of local reform institutions

that they find appealing. The form of government is supported not as an opportunity for business participation, but as a system not threatening to business interests.

It is doubtful that business leaders would participate in a holding action to save reform institutions. Council-manager government, like the Republican Party, is preferable, but does not justify a significant effort by executives in large companies. Very few of the top business leaders have been involved in the charter issues of recent years. Nor are they concerned about the impact of a directly elected mayor on the reform institutions. A change, if supported and adopted by the community, would be acceptable, for, as one executive predicted, "We'd find that the form of government is not that important to the big companies." According to a leader in another company: "Either type of government can be operated successfully and to the satisfaction of business."

Summary

In Toledo there is a dearth of business leadership rather than a community power elite of top executives. Business leaders do not initiate or control local policies;[13] nor do they usually find them of interest. In discussing the top business leaders, one local executive had this comment:

> They really don't know what is going on. Their prestige is out of proportion to their knowledge or ability to use their power. Business leaders are sitting in Toledo with power, not knowing how to use power or what to do with it, and damn busy.

Leaders in organized labor, the political parties, the mass media, and other groups, with the notable exception of Negro organizations, believe that Toledo has suffered from a shortage of business leadership in the community. This was not the expectation of reform doctrine or a hypothesis of this research which predicted that

[13] The peripheral role of Toledo executives is far removed from Floyd Hunter's account of a cohesive, controlling elite of business leaders in Atlanta: *Community Power Structure* (Chapel Hill: University of North Carolina Press, 1953). Nor do Toledo business leaders have the significant, although not controlling, role described in Kent Jennings' reinterpretation of Atlanta: *Community Influentials: The Elites of Atlanta* (New York: The Free Press, 1964).

reform institutions would enhance the influence of business leaders.[14]

Actually the effect has been quite the contrary. The council-manager plan has probably inhibited rather than encouraged business responsibility in the community. Business leaders were lulled by a form of government which did not demand their active participation. With the council-manager system, it seemed safe for business to have a respectable rather than a responsible role. The theory that business leadership would come forward once parties were weakened proved false. One executive commented:

> Industrialists, business executives as a profession are not any different from other groups. There's no *noblesse oblige* in this country—among businessmen or others. Business leaders feel no obligation for public participation.

In the opinion of a consultant to the major firms:

> Businessmen do not flex their muscles just to flex them. If a business leader can hire someone, he won't do anything. Businessmen have looked on the city manager as their hired hand. Business did everything calculated to shove responsibility onto someone else. They were always interested in getting someone else to take responsibility and the city manager plan facilitated this.

Thus the doctrine and institutions of reform have contributed to business indifference. Business leaders would perhaps do more in the community if the political system compelled their attention. A strong political leader, in contrast to a ceremonial mayor and a city manager, could command their respect. An active mayor with political support and prestige could break the impassiveness of business leaders. Similarly, a city government which departed from the largely caretaker role of recent decades would alter one of the conditions which has affected business withdrawal. Change and the fear which it arouses in business circles could at least initiate an advance from the present apathy. In the judgment of one businessman: "Business leaders need to be startled, not soothed. They would do more if they were afraid."

---

[14] The assumption that reform institutions will enlarge the role of business leaders is common. See, for example, Banfield and Wilson, *City Politics*, p. 275.

9 THE FAILURE OF COMMUNITY LEADERSHIP: URBAN RENEWAL IN TOLEDO

Toledo's urban renewal program reveals the consequences of an amorphous political system and apathetic private leadership. Federal urban renewal legislation requires a sustained response from the local community which is difficult to maintain without local leadership and interest. Although the 1949, 1954, and 1965 housing laws offer the prospect of substantial federal aid, the planning, initiation, and execution of urban renewal are the responsibility of individual cities.[1] To qualify for federal aid, each community must receive and retain Housing and Home Finance Agency approval of a "workable program" for urban renewal.[2] In executing an urban renewal project, the city

---

[1] For a discussion of the 1949 and 1954 acts and changing federal concepts of urban renewal, see Coleman Woodbury, "Human Relations and Urban Renewal," in Oliver P. Williams and Charles Press, eds., *Democracy in Urban America* (Chicago: Rand McNally & Co., 1961), pp. 489–502.

[2] The "workable program" is to consist of codes and ordinances for building and housing standards; a comprehensive community plan; neighborhood analyses of blight; administrative organizations capable of enforcing codes and executing renewal; financing; relocation plans; citizen participation.

must prepare initial plans and surveys, win the approval of the Urban Renewal Administration for loans with which to produce additional surveys and plans, provide the local share (one third) of the project cost, satisfy Urban Renewal Administration requirements on land acquisition, clearance, relocation, and land disposition, achieve the cooperation of the Public Housing Administration and/or attract private developers, and assist mortgage arrangements for redevelopers.

Urban renewal is a complex effort at planned change. The local community must establish its own, often controversial, renewal goals. Questions such as industrial or residential redevelopment, public housing or middle- and upper-income private housing are politically potent. Urban renewal, whatever its objective, is disruptive and damaging to some interests. Community leaders must assess these effects and the possible responses of groups within the city; they must attract the necessary group support to aid in the execution of urban renewal and contribute to redevelopment. In addition, urban renewal requires a measure of continuity and professional competence in city leadership. Local officials must fend for themselves in a diffuse, intricate administrative environment including several federal agencies and many technical restrictions and choices.

Successful Urban Renewal Programs

Studies indicate that successful urban renewal is associated with leadership capable of negotiating support and facilitating coordinated action.[3] Extensive urban renewal programs are most often found in cities with stable, centralized political systems. Robert A. Dahl has emphasized the importance of Mayor Richard Lee's leadership in New Haven's remarkable urban renewal program.[4] In his first term in office Lee made urban redevelopment the central policy of his administration. The mayor's dominant role in this field served to increase his political influence in other areas, such as

---

[3] The use of the word successful in discussing urban renewal refers to the *extent* of renewal programs rather than their social or aesthetic effects.

[4] See Robert A. Dahl, *Who Governs?* (New Haven, Conn.: Yale University Press, 1961), pp. 115–141.

public education and party affairs. Decision-making by diverse and uncoordinated organizations (or "rival sovereignties," to use Dahl's term) gave way to a durable executive-centered coalition. From 1953 on, Mayor Lee and his urban redevelopment program held the paramount position in local politics. Dahl has described Lee's performance: "He took on more and more of the task of negotiating with the 'Feds'; he knew how to cut through the interminable delays characteristic of bureaucratic agencies, and he exploited statutes and rules to gain concessions for New Haven that cut down the actual contribution the city was required to make. . . . The city was able to move far partly because its agents moved fast."[5] Under the continuing impetus of Lee's leadership, New Haven developed one of the largest urban renewal programs in the country.

Edward C. Banfield has discussed the way in which the Cook County Democratic Party overcame the fragmentation of governmental institutions in Chicago.[6] There, the rival sovereignties were subdued by the "structure of control" achieved by Mayor Daley and his party organization. Formal decentralization in urban renewal and other fields is counteracted by informal centralization. Mayor Daley, like Mayor Lee, committed his administration to urban renewal.[7] Instead of fostering dispersed authority, as his predecessor had done, Mayor Daley used his political and organizational resources to achieve increased coordination in urban renewal. In Chicago, as in New Haven, urban renewal is attached to the fortunes of an adroit politician who has dominated the local scene for approximately a decade (Lee was first elected in 1953, Daley in 1956).

Other examples also confirm the importance of executive power and continuity of leadership. In St. Louis, Mayor Raymond R. Tucker presided over a 12-year period in which massive slum clearance, urban renewal, and other innovations were undertaken. Although he did not have the party organization of either Daley or Lee, Mayor Tucker used the powers of his office (strong mayor) and a reform alliance of business leaders, upper- and middle-income

---

[5] Dahl, p. 130.

[6] Edward C. Banfield, *Political Influence* (New York: The Free Press, 1961). See also Martin Meyerson and Edward C. Banfield, *Politics, Planning, and the Public Interest* (New York: The Free Press, 1955).

[7] Peter H. Rossi and Robert A. Dentler, *The Politics of Urban Renewal* (New York: The Free Press, 1961), p. 250.

residents, the press, and (some) Negro and union leaders to dominate the policy process.[8] Pittsburgh's renowned urban renewal program benefited from the continuity and cohesion supplied by David
Lawrence's Democratic organization.[9] In Newark the development
of a successful program was dependent on the support of a mayor
occupying a newly strengthened office.[10]

In all of these cases, the political system is centralized. Power is
concentrated, either formally, as in Newark, or informally, as in
Chicago. In power and prestige the political executives of New
Haven, Chicago, Newark, Pittsburgh, and St. Louis stand above
other elective officials. The political leaders of these cities are committed to urban renewal and are able to act on that commitment.
They have assumed initiative and responsibility in guiding community decisions.

The presence of a stable, clear locus of political power has often
enhanced the contribution of professional urban renewal administrators. With the assurance of political direction and support,
urban renewal professionals can develop the skills and procedures
to fulfill the highly technical requirements of the program. Thus
Mayor Lee of New Haven provided the political conditions for an
effective Development Administrator. Dahl writes:

> No one but the mayor could have given redevelopment the
> priority it received. In another administration, the Development
> Administrator could have been frustrated and helpless. In Lee's,
> the Development Administrator's furious drive and energy found
> infinite outlets in redevelopment.[11]

Similarly, the administrative staff of the Newark Housing Authority has been a major source of policy and initiative in Newark's
urban renewal program. But in Harold Kaplan's judgment, the
system rests to a large extent on the mayor's ability to obtain city

[8] On the St. Louis political scene, see Robert H. Salisbury, "St. Louis
Politics: Relationships Among Interests, Parties, and Governmental Structure," *Western Political Quarterly*, XIII (June 1960), 498–507, and Ernest
Calloway, "A Reform Period Closes," *Focus Midwest*, III, Nos. 10 and 11
(1965), 14–15.

[9] Edward C. Banfield and James Q. Wilson, *City Politics* (Cambridge,
Mass.: Harvard University and M.I.T. Press, 1963), p. 274.

[10] See Harold Kaplan, *Urban Renewal Politics* (New York: Columbia University Press, 1963). Newark adopted a strong mayor charter in 1954.

[11] Dahl, *Who Governs?*, p. 127.

hall approval of NHA's plans and his willingness to give NHA a free hand in policy formation. Kaplan writes: "The strong mayor charter adopted in 1954 helped stabilize the renewal system by concentrating power at City Hall . . . and relieved NHA of the necessity of dealing directly with the Council."[12]

In addition to its administrative benefits, centralized political leadership of urban renewal has interested and involved community groups in the program. In cities with successful urban renewal programs, mayors have induced the leaders of diverse community organizations to give their endorsement and assistance. Through persuasion, publicity, advisory committees, and political bargaining, Mayors Lee and Daley built community support for renewal. In some cities, business leaders have made significant contributions. For example, powerful leaders in Pittsburgh politics and business have cooperated in a vast urban renewal program, and the business leaders of Newark and St. Louis have been drawn into urban renewal by skilled political leadership.

Urban renewal is, in sum, a political problem. The task of establishing objectives and consolidating support for a difficult community program is essentially political. In cities where leadership is ineffectual, either because of the inadequate formal powers of the mayor or his indifference, urban renewal is unlikely to flourish. In contrast, a strong political leader with an active commitment to urban renewal can supply a crucial stimulus to the program. He can encourage both administrative competence and group support.

The Renewal Program in Toledo

In Toledo, all of the conditions related to successful programs—political leadership, clarity and continuity of direction, administrative competence, and group support—have been lacking. The Toledo urban renewal program has been small and halting. By

[12] Kaplan, *Urban Renewal Politics*, p. 181. In other cities, stability has been obtained under the council-manager plan. Managers and urban renewal administrators with long tenure and established authority have contributed to the success of urban renewal in Hartford, Connecticut, and Kansas City, Missouri. For a discussion of urban renewal in Hartford, see Carleton F. Sharpe, "Teamwork in Urban Renewal," *Public Management*, XLIV (September 1962), 198–202.

June 1965, approximately $16 million in federal funds had been allotted to urban renewal in Toledo, including projects in the planning stages, underway, and completed.[13] Table 9.1 indicates the

TABLE 9.1

The Twenty Leading Urban Renewal Cities and Toledo, 1965

(1) City	(2) Total Federal Funds Disbursed (in millions of dollars)	(3) Total Federal Funds Reserved (in millions of dollars)	(4) Funds Disbursed Per Capita* (in dollars and cents)
1. New York	122.3	281.1	15.72
2. Chicago	79.8	149.3	22.47
3. Philadelphia	53.2	198.5	26.55
4. Baltimore	37.9	70.8	40.36
5. Boston	37.0	149.5	53.11
6. New Haven	36.5	77.4	239.89
7. Pittsburgh	32.3	99.3	53.49
8. Washington	27.6	82.7	36.12
9. Detroit	26.5	88.5	15.87
10. St. Louis	22.9	57.0	30.58
11. Norfolk	21.7	38.7	71.32
12. Newark	20.0	97.0	49.27
13. Cincinnati	19.5	73.6	38.89
14. Minneapolis	16.0	35.3	33.04
15. Providence	15.2	46.7	73.29
16. Cleveland	15.0	58.9	16.65
17. San Francisco	12.4	93.7	16.80
18. Atlanta	11.7	41.0	24.01
19. Dayton	9.1	25.8	34.58
20. Columbus	8.8	20.7	18.58
21. TOLEDO	4.0	15.9	12.66

* This is computed by dividing column 2 by the city's 1960 population.

Source: U.S. Housing and Home Finance Agency, Urban Renewal Administration, *Urban Renewal Project Directory* (Washington, D.C.: March 31, 1965).

[13] Urban Renewal Administration financial estimates and evaluations of progress in Toledo are presented in *The Blade*, July 3, 1965, Section 2, p. 9.

meager extent of the Toledo program in comparison with the programs in 20 leading urban renewal cities.[14]

In the years since the passage of the 1949 Housing Act, Toledo has undertaken six urban renewal projects of which one has been completed.[15] The completed project, Gunckel, involved a relatively small clearance area (38 acres) with redevelopment by the Toledo Metropolitan Housing Authority and the expansion of a grade school playground. Other projects now in progress include: Ironville, a 67-acre port-oriented industrial redevelopment project started in 1960; Vistula Meadows, an extensive (99 acres) downtown renewal project started in 1959; Riverview, a small (13 acres) downtown renewal project initiated in 1963; and Roosevelt, a conservation project designated and surveyed in 1962. The oldest project and the one which best reveals Toledo's difficulties in urban renewal is Chase Park, a 127-acre residential redevelopment project three and one-half miles north of the downtown business district.

The Chase Park project. Chase Park was conceived in 1951, when the area was designated a study project of substandard housing. At that time Toledo renewal hopes were focused on plans for a large industrial redevelopment area, the Canton project. In August 1955, an official in the Chicago office of the Urban Renewal Administration advised the director of the Toledo Housing Improvement and Urban Renewal Commission that the Chase Park area would also be an appropriate site for urban renewal. City officials then turned their attention to the Chase Park project, which they visualized as an effort to rehabilitate deteriorating property adjacent to a rat-infested dump. Plans were submitted to federal Housing and Home Finance Agency officials, who questioned the emphasis on rehabilitation instead of clearance and redevelopment.[16] Nevertheless, after a year's delay the Chase Park project received federal

---

[14] The cities in Table 9.1 are ranked according to total disbursements of federal funds. Because of this, some cities with smaller totals, but large per capita expenditures do not appear in the table. In Hartford, Connecticut, for example, federal funds disbursed for urban renewal amount to $46.27 per capita. The totals for federal funds reserved indicate the future dimensions of urban renewal programs.

[15] This total does not include two abortive efforts; the Canton Project was dropped in favor of the Chase Park effort, discussed below; the Spring conservation project was dropped for lack of federal approval. The Gunckel project was completed on July 31, 1964.

[16] *The Blade,* December 30, 1956, Section 5, p. 1.

approval, a capital grant for two thirds of the cost, and an advance planning loan from the Urban Renewal Administration.[17]

At the local level, controversies were stirring. After an uncertain period in which it had three directors in one year, the Housing Improvement and Urban Renewal Commission began to reconsider the Chase Park project. Proponents of clearance and redevelopment were now in a majority on the commission and on city council. In December 1957, the director of the Housing Improvement and Urban Renewal Commission concluded that it would be necessary to revise the Chase Park plan to meet both the longstanding HHFA preference for redevelopment and the changed appraisal of HIURC members and city councilmen.[18] Instead of being a rehabilitation project with spot clearance, Chase Park was to be a clearance project with spot rehabilitation. In March 1958, the amended application was approved by the HHFA.

In 1958 the city also altered its administrative arrangements. The Housing Improvement and Urban Renewal Commission was replaced by the Urban Renewal Agency, a city department. The role of the former HIUR commissioners was to be fulfilled by a newly established Urban Renewal Advisory Commission, appointed by the mayor with the approval of the city council.

Meanwhile, the Chase Park project was being challenged on new grounds. In the fall of 1958, some councilmen and renewal officials began to consider the industrial potential of the Chase Park area. The chairman of the City Plan Commission and a Democratic city councilman emerged as the leading advocates for a change of plans.[19] They emphasized the proximity of Chase Park to the Maumee River and port development as well as existing industry on the periphery of the project. Those favoring residential redevelopment pointed to nearby parks and residential areas and the greater resale value of residential property. After several months of discussion, city council voted eight to one to approve the Chase Park plans as predominantly residential.[20]

Yet the issue was not settled. While the proponents of industrial redevelopment continued to object to residential plans, citizens living in the vicinity of Chase Park mobilized to resist any change

[17] *The Blade*, June 6, 1957, p. 20.
[18] *The Blade*, December 29, 1957, p. 36.
[19] *The Blade*, March 29, 1959, Section 1, p. 2.
[20] This vote took place in December 1958.

in renewal objectives. In September 1959, two Democratic council-men staged a desperate effort for industrial development by moving to table the residential project. Their seven colleagues on city council remained unconvinced by arguments that Chase Park is "the most logical place for port-oriented industry," as they voted to proceed with residential redevelopment.[21]

Despite continuing dissension over renewal objectives, Toledo was ready to move into the implementation stage of the Chase Park project in 1960.[22] A fragile Democratic majority had replaced the 8–1 City Manager League council of the previous two years; the Democratic mayor, elected with the support of a maverick Republican and a City Manager League Democrat, had an active interest in urban renewal. During 1960 the city began acquiring property, although it encountered resistance and a law suit from one of the largest property owners in the area.[23] Aside from this difficulty, the project seemed to be advancing at last and the Toledo urban renewal director had reason to believe that "things are going better than we ever dreamed possible."[24] By 1961 a large part of the property had been acquired and the relocation of more than 300 families was proceeding smoothly.

Demolition commenced in 1961, a decade after the project had first been discussed. But it soon became evident that hopes for the rapid conclusion of the Chase Park project were premature. In April 1961, after several months of work, demolition was halted by a report that the contractor was selling salvaged siding, windows, and shrubs without authorization. After a conference between the urban renewal director and the contractor, demolition activities resumed.[25] Within weeks, however, new allegations were made. Two city officials, the municipal demolition supervisor and the administrative assistant to the city manager, were found to have been making a little money on the side. The Toledo demolition supervisor had accepted a kick-back of $100.00 in the illicit sale of a garage. In addition, the administrative assistant to the city manager and the demolition supervisor had formed a partnership to buy Chase Park

[21] *The Blade*, September 9, 1959, p. 1.

[22] For a discussion of continuing dissension over redevelopment objectives see *The Blade*, December 31, 1961, p. 22.

[23] For a review of these difficulties, see *The Blade*, September 12, 1962, p. 3.

[24] *The Blade*, February 3, 1961, p. 17.

[25] *The Blade*, April 20, 1961, p. 25.

homes and move them elsewhere for sale. Upon disclosure of these activities, the demolition supervisor quickly resigned and the city manager, after some hesitation, called for the resignation of his administrative assistant.[26]

Additional questions led to a second suspension of the contract with Surety Salvage and Lumber Company. The urban renewal director was disturbed by the moving and sale of garages and houses by the demolition contractor; the dismantling of property by unauthorized persons and the sale of salvageable materials on the site also seemed questionable under the contract. But in spite of these and other problems, such as the demolition of 27 houses which the city intended to exempt and resell, Toledo legal and renewal officials recognized that a "loosely drawn" and "ambiguous" contract was at least partly responsible.[27] Thus the city and the contractor again negotiated their differences and demolition resumed.

The city manager attempted to reassure critics by "placing the Chase Park renewal, especially demolition, under the direct supervision of his administration."[28] A registered engineer was to supervise demolition activities and report directly to the city manager. *The Blade* was unimpressed with these moves:

> From the outset, the city ordinance on urban renewal vested in the manager top responsibility for administering the program. And if a registered engineer is required—as Mr. Alspach [the city manager] now finds—why is this necessity discovered so late in the program? . . .
>
> Although the city administration . . . failed to exercise effective supervision and delayed remedies, this is no occasion for Council to indulge in sanctimonious pronouncements.
>
> Some councilmen have personally intervened in the selection of urban renewal employees and Council as a whole has seemed more concerned with its own system of overseeing urban renewal projects than with demanding top quality professionals to do the job.[29]

The Blade's suspicion that "all was not going well with the project" soon received additional confirmation. In the fall of 1961, demolition activities were suspended as city officials investigated numerous contract violations disclosed by *Blade* reporters. An ini-

---

[26] *The Blade*, June 24, 1961, p. 13, and June 26, 1961, p. 1.

[27] *The Blade*, December 31, 1961, p. 22.

[28] *The Blade*, July 3, 1961, p. 1.

[29] *The Blade*, July 5, 1961, p. 20.

tial survey of the clearance area revealed 78 instances in which the contractor had failed to remove the foundations of razed buildings to the 36-inch required depth and to comply with specifications for filling excavations and grading surfaces. After inspecting the complete foundations of several supposedly demolished buildings, the city manager commented: "We're in the position of having the wool pulled over our eyes."[30]

Nevertheless, a majority of administrative and elective officials did not think that the project would benefit from a change of contractors. Surety Salvage and Lumber was directed to correct contract violations in 154 of 158 demolished structures at its own expense and to resume demolition under the scrutiny of city supervisors. The city law director assured critics that demolition in Chase Park was actually ahead of schedule; the vice-mayor emphasized city council's responsibility in urban renewal and its determination to correct past mistakes.

A maverick Republican councilman led the opposition to these explanations, contending that Chase Park had long been afflicted with "buck passing, excuses, unnecessary delays, and a high degree of incompetence." Democratic and Republican councilmen supporting the administration countered that the opposition was merely trying to make the city manager, the law director, and the urban renewal director "scapegoats" instead of concentrating on the task of reassuring the public.[31]

As the turmoil over demolition appeared to subside, another issue revived. Although the city had endorsed residential redevelopment in Chase Park three years earlier, in December 1961 the law department recommended that the City Plan Commission approve a major change in previous plans. On the eve of a condemnation suit, the city succumbed to the pleas of the Ayling-Reichert factory and recommended that small industry be allowed to remain in the project area. A *Blade* editorial criticized the sudden shift in which the city asked that a 40-year old factory be permitted to remain in the center of an area designated for private residential redevelopment.[32]

Others insisted that the factory would preserve jobs and promote industrial development. *The Blade* recalled that it had questioned

---

[30] *The Blade*, October 3, 1961, p. 1.

[31] *The Blade*, November 11, 1961, p. 1.

[32] *The Blade*, December 17, 1961, Section 2, p. 4.

the original decision to designate the area for residential rather than industrial development. Yet, it concluded, "once the project is undertaken it makes no sense to permit a factory to remain where it has been a nonconforming use since the beginning of zoning."[33] The City Plan Commission refused to accept the recommendation, and *The Blade* offered a critical appraisal of urban renewal in Toledo:

> Toledo has been playing at urban renewal like a dilettante for nearly twelve years. From one administration to another, the city has changed plans and programs so often that it has lost a whole decade of progress during which other communities forged ahead with Federal assistance.[34]

The aura of scandal and incompetence during the Democratic administration of 1960–1961 had contributed to the election of eight Republicans to the city council which assumed office in January 1962. All incumbent Democrats, including the mayor, had been defeated in an election which only one Democrat survived. The new Republican administration listed urban renewal as its top priority. Days after assuming office it was faced with a new problem in demolition operations.[35] A new Republican councilman, Andy Douglas, charged Surety with again violating the contract and defrauding its employees by substandard wages. The councilman cited intimidation and wage cuts suffered by demolition employees. These infractions, added to previous difficulties, led to a cancellation of the $70,000 contract with only half of the job complete. Councilman Douglas, chairman of city council's urban renewal committee, was unsuccessful, however, in his effort to initiate an investigation of urban renewal operations.

The Republican administration hoped to hasten Chase Park progress by the appointment of a new city manager and a revised and improved demolition contract. During the winter months, city officials worked on the task of rewriting the demolition contract, submitting it for federal approval, and seeking bids for a new contractor. Surety Salvage and Lumber Company responded to its dismissal with a law suit asking the Common Pleas Court to pro-

[33] *Ibid.*

[34] *Ibid.* (Reprinted with permission of Toledo Blade Company. © Toledo Blade Co.)

[35] *The Blade*, January 2, 1962, p. 11.

hibit Toledo from hiring another demolition contractor.[36] In March a Common Pleas judge rejected Surety's contention that Toledo had illegally breached the contract.[37] Bids for the demolition of the remaining 161 buildings indicated that the change in contractors would cost the city an additional $23,000. But the revised contract itself was said to be a great improvement, since renewal officials understood it to prohibit the moving and sale of houses and garages.[38]

During the spring of 1962, demolition remained at a standstill and old controversies continued. In April 1962, city council's urban renewal committee revived a recommendation to include public housing for senior citizens in the Chase Park renewal area. Officials for the real estate and building industries (and others) protested the damaging effect of public housing on the prospects for private redevelopment.[39] City council ignored these arguments and approved the recommendation of its urban renewal committee, although it had defeated a similar proposal the previous year. At the end of April, city council's urban renewal committee revived another old issue by recommending that the Ayling-Reichert factory be allowed to remain in the Chase Park area under certain conditions. City council rejected this recommendation in a vote calling for the removal of the factory.[40]

In May, after more than four months of delay, demolition resumed with a new contractor, the Cleveland Wrecking Company. Only weeks later a proposal to purchase and ship houses to Michigan for sale to an unnamed buyer brought the work to a standstill again. The city and the contractor were at odds on the terms of the demolition contract, but the question was resolved by the disappearance of the buyer.[41] After this episode *The Blade* commented:

> The Chase Park project may look simple on paper, but it's hard to recall a single undertaking by the city in recent years that got bogged down in such a mass of confusions, frustrations, blunders, and boo-boos as has struck activities in Chase Park.

[36] *The Blade*, January 19, 1962, p. 8.
[37] *The Blade*, March 20, 1962, p. 17.
[38] *The Blade*, March 28, 1962, p. 37.
[39] *The Blade*, April 10, 1962, p. 37.
[40] *The Blade*, April 30, 1962, p. 13, and May 2, 1962, p. 37.
[41] *The Blade*, June 25, 1962, p. 13.

> . . . If the administration and city council have any thoughts
> of taking the voters to the top of the mountain and holding up
> Chase Park as an example of what urban renewal can mean, they
> had best forget them for the present.[42]

The resignation of the urban renewal director in June left the
Republican administration with a critical vacancy. In August 1962,
the appointment of Thurmond Hawkins was announced. Although
Mr. Hawkins had had no previous experience in urban renewal or
city planning, he was said to have been selected for his other
professional qualifications. The city manager noted the new director's administrative experience in business and the army. After
ending a five-year army career as a major and public relations field
representative in Paris, Mr. Hawkins had served in executive and
sales capacities in the real estate and insurance business. Moreover,
he was secretary of the Republican Central Committee, seventh
ward chairman, and a precinct committeeman.[43] *The Blade* casti-
gated the appointment of a real estate and home salesman with no
experience in government and administration who "concedes that
his background in selling, public relations, and office management
encompasses no comparable experience in handling the major contracts or large projects involved in urban renewal."[44]

Demolition, rehabilitation, and relocation continued during 1963.
Six of the eight Republican incumbents survived the fall election in
which they defended the urban renewal progress achieved by a
"competent" and "responsible" administration. Applications for
federal approval, loans, and grants on new projects moved more
quickly than events in Chase Park, however. After the completion
of clearance and site improvements, Chase Park land was opened
for bids in the summer of 1964, with disappointing results. There
were only three initial bids on one section of land and no bids at all
on about half the acreage advertised for disposition.[45]

In July 1964, federal authorities approved the sale of land to two
local redevelopers, Clifford C. Loss, Inc., and Scholz-Chase, Inc. The
Loss Company purchased 19 lots on which it began to construct
$13,000–$14,000 ranch homes, two of which were opened for display

---

[42] *The Blade*, June 27, 1962, p. 20.

[43] For an account of Hawkins' political positions and activity, see *The Blade*, May 24, 1964, Section C, p. 1.

[44] *The Blade*, July 10, 1964, p. 14.

[45] *Ibid.*

in September 1964. Scholz-Chase purchased 14 acres on which to build a 240-unit apartment complex. Construction, first scheduled to begin in September 1964, had not yet started in September 1966.[46] Other redevelopment in the Chase Park area is by public agencies. The Toledo Metropolitan Housing Authority has constructed a 50-unit housing project for elderly persons, and the Toledo public school system has completed a new elementary school. The final record will indicate that the Chase Park project was at least 15 or 16 years in the making.

Other renewal projects in Toledo. Progress on Toledo's other urban renewal projects has been hindered by many of the problems seen in Chase Park: disagreement over objectives; uncertainty in policy and administrative decisions; resistance from property owners; questions and objections from federal officials; demolition difficulties; and an undercurrent of political acrimony. In addition, a 1914 charter provision (Section 79), which prohibited city expenditures of more than $500,000 on public improvement without voter approval, impeded local financing of urban renewal projects.[47] From 1960 to 1964 the major effort on Ironville (industrial redevelopment) and Vistula Meadows (downtown renewal) was devoted to circumventing Section 79 by subdividing and rearranging the projects.[48] The city was freed from the tortuous process of evading the $500,000 spending limit when the voters repealed Section 79 in May 1964.

In 1966 several large projects entered or approached the execution stage. In Ironville, started in 1960, structures were razed, and the area was finally advertised for redevelopers in 1967. Buildings were also demolished in a one-block area of Vistula Meadows, which will be the site of an experimental public housing project for the aged and handicapped. The city is awaiting federal permission to proceed with land acquisition, relocation, and clearance in the large area remaining. Federal officials expect that Vistula Meadows, in the planning stages since 1959, will be completed in 1972.[49] In October 1965, a demolition contract was signed for Riverview, a

---

[46] For a comment on repeated delays in starting construction, see *The Blade*, September 14, 1966, p. 14. Donald J. Scholz offers his explanation in *The Blade*, September 21, 1966, p. 16.

[47] *The Blade*, June 9, 1963, Section 2, p. 1.

[48] *The Blade*, August 9, 1963, p. 3.

[49] *The Blade*, September 28, 1965, p. 1.

three-block downtown renewal project conceived in 1963. Property
in the Riverview area was offered and sold to prospective developers
in 1966.[50]

The Appeal of Renewal Projects in Toledo

To the politicians. Toledo's urban renewal program has touched
the imagination of only one group, the politicians. Yet most politicians have been more intrigued with its possibilities for discrediting
the opposition than with its potential for advancing their own
ambitions. No Toledo politician has had the power to direct urban
renewal in the manner of Mayor Lee of New Haven or Mayor Daley
of Chicago. Only two mayors, Michael Damas (D., 1960–1961) and
John Potter (R., 1962–1967) have attempted to identify themselves
with urban renewal. Mayor Damas, who served during the inglo-
rious demolition activities in Chase Park, did so with disastrous
results. His association with the inept administration of urban
renewal contributed to the abrupt end of his political career in the
only primary defeat ever suffered by a mayor.[51]

John Potter also attached his political fortunes to urban renewal,
but with more favorable results. In 1963 Mayor Potter unveiled the
Riverview project as his personal contribution to urban renewal in
Toledo. In introducing the project, which he described as being
inspired by a depressing midnight walk through downtown Toledo,
the mayor gave assurances that he had a commitment from a rede-
veloper who was willing to spend millions to rebuild and revive the
area. Later he announced a gift from the Charities Foundation for
the purchase of an old post office in the Riverview area. After the
1963 municipal election, Mayor Potter succeeded in removing the
dissident Councilman Douglas from the chairmanship of the urban
renewal committee and assuming that position himself. The mayor
conferred with urban renewal officials in Chicago and Washington,
addressed business and citizens' groups, and cajoled local adminis-

[50] *The Blade*, January 25, 1966, Section 2, p. 1. John Galbreath and
Company of Columbus immediately announced its interest in redeveloping the
entire area.

[51] Mayor Damas's distinction was noted in *The Blade*, October 24, 1965, p. 1.

trators in an effort to facilitate urban renewal. He managed to raise the program from the nadir of ineptitude. Yet he had limited success in accelerating the major projects or interesting community organizations in urban renewal.

The extreme decentralization of the political system, rather than the errors of incumbent mayors, is in large part responsible for the shortcomings of urban renewal in Toledo. The mayor, even when he has had a strong commitment to urban renewal, has not had the authority to dominate the crucial decisions. Power has been dispersed among nine councilmen and several administrators. The division of authority between city council and the city manager and between the city manager and the urban renewal director have been unclear. The resulting confusion has engendered a politics of petty reprisal and quarrelsomeness rather than permitting the emergence of a political leader who could confidently stake his career on a record of achievement in urban renewal. Instead of being a field for political achievement, as in New Haven, urban renewal has been an ideal target for attack during the past fifteen years.

To business. The peculiar futility and political backbiting characteristic of urban renewal in Toledo have appealed to few community organizations. The tortuous, uncertain process of making decisions in the absence of executive direction and administrative competence has not created the kind of business support for urban renewal seen in many communities. In New Haven (and other cities with successful programs), political and administrative officials have worked together in a cohesive, centralized effort to achieve coordinated decisions and group support. Thus Mayor Lee employed the Citizens Action Commission with its membership of leading bankers, industrialists, and businessmen to assure acceptability for urban redevelopment.[52] The Newark Economic Development Committee and the Newark Commission on Neighborhood Conservation and Rehabilitation were used to build business support in that city.[53]

In Toledo the Urban Renewal Advisory Commission and the councils for the individual projects have been ineffectual. The potential effect of these groups is negated by the absence of strong political leadership to utilize them. Although many business leaders

---

[52] Dahl, *Who Governs?*, p. 133.
[53] Kaplan, *Urban Renewal Politics*, pp. 70–75.

belong to councils or committees, most of them frankly admit their disinterest in urban renewal. Thus a vice-president in one company said:

> The business leaders, the top people, haven't been very interested in urban renewal. Business people could have done more, much more. The whole program has been entirely too slow. Toledo needs a strong individual to start ramming it through. We need more aggressiveness and a top level executive for the urban renewal agency.

Many executives believe that "more action and less talk" would be the best method to attract the interest of business leaders who have become "bored by years of planning without results." Others argue that business leaders would give more support if "their opinions and assistance had been solicited more frequently and in a more concrete manner."

But the withdrawal of business leaders is also a matter of their own choice. Urban renewal, as one corporation president expressed it, "is an area, which, while it may be desirable, is not a matter of any great concern to business leaders." No specific project or plan has held their interest; no leader has successfully challenged their detachment. The difficulties of the urban renewal program have confirmed their justification for "not touching it" instead of suggesting the need for increased private interest as well as improved public leadership.

The absence of business support has contributed to Toledo's unimpressive showing in urban renewal. The director of urban development in Pittsburgh has cited the money, time, talent, and interest which business and industry have given to the city's renewal program. No such contribution has taken place in Toledo. A *Blade* editorial commented:

> Here in Toledo urban renewal is plodding along. One reason is that the program simply has not had the active participation and vigorous leadership of the uppermost echelons of our industrial and business community. It has had their vocal support, to be sure; but when it came down to the nuts and bolts of putting a program in shape, of encouraging the city to bring in an experienced professional director, of moving toward substantial investments of private funds in redevelopment projects, of contributing materially in other ways, Toledo's over-all effort suffers immeasurably in comparison to that of Pittsburgh.[54]

[54] *The Blade,* October 20, 1964, p. 16.

To labor. Organized labor's interest in urban renewal has been equally dispirited. In New Haven redevelopment attracted what one labor leader described as universal support from union members and officials.[55] In Toledo labor leaders express differing degrees of dissatisfaction. An official in the Teamsters described Toledo's renewal program:

> It's a business-oriented operation, with little attention to the human aspects. The objective is to clear the property and then turn it over to the real estate speculators. Labor isn't consulted much. They haven't really tried to bring organized labor into the program.

A leader in the Electrical Workers asked: "What urban renewal program? Our system of city government isn't organized for getting things like that done." In the opinion of a UAW official: "John Potter has tried to make urban renewal move and to bring labor in, but he's been sabotaged by Thurmond Hawkins [the urban renewal director]." Officials in the Building Trades Council have found dramatic benefits from redevelopment slow in coming.

Leaders in the various unions are mildly interested in urban renewal and mildly concerned about its slow progress. But few of them think that urban renewal warrants significant attention and support from organized labor.

To Negroes. Because of the slow pace and limited scope of the program in Toledo, it has not displaced significant numbers of Negro residents, as it has in some cities. Thus, urban renewal has not been of particular concern to Negro leaders and organizations. Most prominent Negro leaders in civil rights organizations, religious associations, social agencies, and public positions regard the urban renewal program with satisfaction or indifference: They either praise the program in general terms or confess that they have not followed it closely. Few are interested in the impact of urban renewal on local civil rights problems. Several of the younger leaders, however, are critical and concerned:

> The urban renewal program here is not completely satisfactory from the Negro's standpoint or from anyone else's. Mr. Hawkins does not recognize the Negro as a person. He has not recognized Negro leadership. Even in urban conservation programs in largely

55 Dahl, *Who Governs?*, p. 136.

Negro areas, there is no consultation. Relocation has not dispersed
people enough. Deterioration is increasing rapidly. Housing is a
major problem and urban renewal has done nothing to alleviate it.
In general, the whole urban renewal program is moving too
slowly.

To voters. The voters have had few occasions to record their
judgment of urban renewal. Until 1965 Toledo voters did not have
the opportunity to express a verdict on a variety of programs
through mayoralty elections. But they have defeated councilmen
unpleasantly identified with urban renewal. From the response of a
wide variety of community organizations, including labor unions,
Negro organizations, the Chamber of Commerce, fraternal associations, and nationality clubs, there is reason to believe that popular
demand for urban renewal is relatively small. In 1962 only 47.5 per
cent of those voting, instead of the required 55 per cent, approved a
payroll income tax increase to finance the local cost of slum clearance and urban renewal.

Summary

In Toledo the various mayors and renewal administrators have
not had the political strength and skill to attract the support of the
organized interests and the electorate. Between the passage of the
1949 Housing Act and 1965, city council has selected six mayors, of
whom only two served consecutive terms. Toledo mayors have been
ephemeral and powerless in comparison with the executives of cities
whose renewal programs have been successful: Mayor Lee of New
Haven (1953–   ); Mayor Daley of Chicago (1956–   ); Mayor Car-
lin of Newark (1953–1962); and Mayor Tucker of St. Louis
(1953–1965).

The mayors of New Haven, Chicago, and St. Louis succeeded in
integrating fragmented decision-making processes in urban renewal
and in other fields because they started with considerably more
authority than their counterparts in Toledo. They were elective
executives and possessed formal powers lacking in Toledo. Chicago
has been described as a city with "extreme decentralization of
authority";[56] yet the mayor of Chicago, in contrast to the mayor of

[56] Banfield and Wilson, *City Politics*, p. 104.

Toledo, has several essential formal powers, including a veto, which can be overriden only by a two-thirds vote of the aldermen, and an item veto over appropriation acts.[57] In transforming the political system of New Haven from a pattern of "rival sovereignties" to an "executive-centered coalition," Mayor Lee also was aided by formal powers—as well as by his political skill, which Dahl so admires. Dahl mentions "the patronage and wide assortment of other favors and punishments available to the chief executive of the city" and "the resources at the Mayor's disposal [which] are much too great for any dissident faction in his party to overcome."[58] Such could never be said of the mayor of Toledo.

Furthermore, the mayors of Chicago and New Haven could rely on strong party organizations in creating an informal centralization of power. The atrophied party system of Toledo did not provide this alternative. Nor could the mayor of Toledo draw on an active good government alliance, as Mayor Tucker did for many years. Business and labor organizations, active participants in some cities, have provided an uncertain source of community support in Toledo.

On the administrative side, Toledo's urban renewal program has suffered from incompetence and instability. Between the passage of the 1949 Housing Act and 1965, Toledo had five city managers and five urban renewal directors. The managers, lacking decisive directives from the mayor and council, have been unwilling or unable to provide effective supervision of urban renewal. City council and the city manager have deferred to each other for both policy and administrative decisions, with unsatisfactory results. Urban renewal directors, like city managers, have been selected for their political rather than their professional qualifications. In the mid-1960s, a former Republican councilman as manager and a Republican ward chairman and ex-real estate man as urban renewal director reveal the discrepancy between reform ideals and actual practice. These officials have displayed neither the competence nor the "furious drive and energy" of, for example, New Haven administrators.

By his own account, Thurmond Hawkins, the Toledo renewal director, "started from scratch on urban renewal in 1962."[59] Be-

---

[57] Meyerson and Banfield, *Politics, Planning, and the Public Interest*, p. 66.

[58] Dahl, *Who Governs?*, p. 111.

[59] Hawkins resigned in May 1966, to become urban renewal director in Rochester, Minnesota. He was replaced by Walter Edelson, a young city planner.

cause of the inexperience of its director and staff, the urban renewal agency relied heavily on a New Jersey consulting firm, Candeub and Fleissig, in the preparation of renewal plans and applications. Candeub and Fleissig, hired for their professional skills, submitted report after report to the Urban Renewal Administration only to have them returned for revision.[60]

Toledo's political system is poorly suited to the demands of the urban renewal program, as the 15-year history of the Chase Park project suggests. Reform institutions, which were intended to assure an effective municipal response to city problems, have yielded the opposite in urban renewal.[61] The council-manager form of government, with its division of authority between a city council of equals and an administrator, has produced a governmental system which is political, without having a focus of power. Contrary to reform expectations, the absence of a preeminent political leader has not facilitated the appointment of a professional administrator; nor has it assured the autonomy and authority of the city manager. Municipal reformers attempted to remove politics from city government and destroyed political leadership instead. The result was most unfortunate for urban renewal.

[60] *The Blade*, May 24, 1964, Section C, p. 1.

[61] None of the council-manager cities over 250,000 in population is among the top ten urban renewal cities. The council-manager cities in this population category include four cities of over 500,000: Dallas, Cincinnati, San Antonio, and San Diego. Cities in the 250,000 to 500,000 category include Kansas City, Phoenix, Oakland, Fort Worth, Long Beach, Oklahoma City, Rochester, Norfolk, Miami, Dayton, Wichita, and Toledo. Of the council-manager cities, Norfolk has the most impressive record in urban renewal (See Table 9.1, p. 134).

10 THE LOCAL INTERESTS OF ORGANIZED LABOR

Business leaders and politicians alike describe organized labor as a dominant, if not controlling, influence in Toledo; but, actually, labor's sporadic and often half-hearted activities in local politics are in sharp contrast to its image as a power which determines election results and dictates policies. The local labor unions have economic power, numerical and financial strength, and notable political influence in state and national elections.[1] Yet organized labor has made no major effort to extend its power to city politics. Contrary to its reputation, labor is relatively uninterested in local politics and policies, which rarely impinge on the crucial economic and social issues that interest labor as a group. Furthermore, organized labor in Toledo does not have the unity, organization, and party alliances to exercise consistent or decisive local influence; and the political institutions and ethos of reform are highly resistant to the fluctuating efforts of organized labor. At-large, nonpartisan elections and an abiding tradition of independent voting accentuate labor's lack of political influence and interest.

[1] Toledo, as a highly unionized city, presents a sharp contrast to many other cities, particularly in the South. For a comparison, see Kenneth E. Gray and David Greenstone's discussion of Houston: "Organized Labor in City Politics," in Edward Banfield, ed., *Urban Government* (New York: The Free Press, 1961), pp. 377–379.

Organized Labor in Toledo

The disunity characteristic of the political and business spheres in Toledo is also true of organized labor—power is dispersed and incompletely mobilized. Toledo's economy is sufficiently diversified to provide a base for a number of unions. Thus the approximately 70,000 union members in the greater Toledo area in 1965 were divided among the United Auto Workers (23,000); the Teamsters (14,000); the Building Trades (6,500); the Maritime Trades (5,000); the United (flat) Glass Workers (5,000); the Electrical Workers (2,500); the Flint (bottle) Glass Workers (2,000); and other smaller unions.[2]

The UAW, with eight locals and the vast majority of its 23,000 members living within the city limits, is the dominant union on the local scene. Although it has not achieved the controlling position of its Detroit counterpart, the UAW has long been conspicuous within labor and in the community. The bitter strikes at Toledo parts plants in 1934 and at the Chevrolet plant in 1935 were crucial to the formation of the UAW.[3] Out of the turmoil of these early struggles emerged the man who is still dominant, Richard T. Gosser. As president of Local 12 (1937–1942), regional director (1942–1947), and an international vice-president (1947–1964), Gosser led the UAW in Toledo to power and respectability.[4] After three decades of controversy and achievement, he was convicted of conspiring to obtain confidential information from the Internal Revenue Service.[5] Despite his failing health, he began a 3-year prison term in November 1965. However, with the assistance of friends and associates who date from the early days of the union, Gosser is still the major source of leadership in the UAW.

The Teamsters, the second largest union in Toledo, are led by

[2] The membership figures are from officials in the unions cited; figures on union membership within city limits were not available.

[3] For a discussion of the early Toledo strikes, see Sidney Fine, *The Origins of the United Automobile Workers* (Ann Arbor: The Institute of Labor and Industrial Relations, University of Michigan and Wayne State University, 1960), p. 279.

[4] Gosser's role in the international is discussed by Jack Stieber, *Governing the UAW* (New York: John Wiley, 1962), pp. 13, 62, 98, 103, and 141.

[5] For a discussion of Gosser's career and the conspiracy charges, see *The Blade*, January 27, 1963, Section B, p. 1.

Lawrence Steinberg. Steinberg was formerly a director of the old CIO Retail, Wholesale, and Department Store Workers Union. When that union was expelled from the CIO on charges of communism, Steinberg led Toledo members into the Teamsters, where he consolidated his power in Local 20. In 1953 he wrested the presidency of Joint Council 44 from Harry W. Card, a longtime Teamster leader. In addition to directing extensive organizing activity in the Toledo area and elsewhere, Steinberg has served as a personal representative and trouble-shooter for Teamster general president, James Hoffa.[6]

Other local unions have neither the powerful leadership nor the membership of the UAW and the Teamsters. The Building Trades Council is a loose confederation of 24 craft and construction unions. The Port Council of maritime trade unions is a similar federated arrangement, which is further weakened by the long or permanent absences of sea-going members. Many United Glass Workers employed at the Libbey-Owens-Ford plants in East Toledo and Rossford live outside the city limits. Furthermore, a provision requiring the annual election of union officials has helped keep the leadership of the United Glass Workers in perpetual flux. The Electrical Workers, although they have continuity of leadership, are small in number, as are the Flint Glass Workers. Yet in sum these smaller unions represent over 30,000 workers in greater Toledo.

The many and diverse unions of Toledo are not drawn together effectively. The Toledo Area AFL-CIO Council was established in 1958, three years after the national merger, on orders from George Meany.[7] Although the UAW is the controlling force in the Council, it has not achieved the dominance of the UAW in the Wayne County (Detroit) AFL-CIO Council.[8] The move of craft unions into the Council, motivated by AFL-CIO assistance during a strike, has not altered their strong sense of autonomy or the suspicion with

---

[6] Sam Romer, *The International Brotherhood of Teamsters* (New York: John Wiley, 1962), p. 67. For a fascinating study, see Ralph and Estelle James, *Hoffa and the Teamsters* (Princeton, N.J.: D. Van Nostrand Co., 1965).

[7] For a review of the local merger and the growth of the Toledo Area AFL-CIO Council, see *The Blade*, May 3, 1964, p. 3. At the end of 1965, membership in the AFL-CIO Council ranged between 60,000 and 65,000; this membership figure is for the greater Toledo area rather than the city alone. *The Blade*, January 2, 1966, Section H, p. 37.

[8] For a discussion of the Wayne County AFL-CIO Council, see Gray and Greenstone, ''Organized Labor in City Politics,'' pp. 369–370.

which they regard the UAW.[9] The AFL-CIO Council reflects rather than resolves the jurisdictional and personal antagonisms between Toledo unions and their officials.

The Political Goals of Toledo Unions

In the absence of a predominant union or labor organization, the various Toledo unions pursue their own political objectives. Studies of other cities have produced certain generalizations about the involvement of labor unions in the community.[10] Craft unions are said to have a greater stake in the local community than industrial unions.[11] For industrial unions, the local community is of marginal importance. Economic conditions, for labor as well as for management, depend on national rather than local developments. Local contracts and employment are affected by national markets and industry-wide practices. Craft unions, operating in competitive local markets, are more affected by the local bureaucracy, police, and wages and hours. Yet industrial unions, rather than craft unions, are more likely to have an ideology favoring aggressive political action at all levels of government.[12] In Toledo these distinctions are muted by a pervasive disinterest in the local community.

No union is committed to aggressive political action and community responsibility. Objectives are limited and closely related to union needs—sympathetic city officials, policemen, and judges. In describing the local interests of labor, union leaders emphasize the importance of a friendly Safety Director to supervise the Police Department, especially in the event of a strike. Recent and ancient misdeeds by policemen in interfering with picket lines are recited to explain labor's anxiety about this aspect of local government. Simi-

[9] Suspicions arise partly from a longstanding dispute between the building trades and the UAW about maintenance work in industrial plants.

[10] A review of these generalizations is presented by Edward C. Banfield and James Q. Wilson, *City Politics* (Cambridge, Mass.: Harvard University Press and M.I.T. Press, 1963), pp. 278–279.

[11] The varying roles of different kinds of unions are discussed by Richard Baisden, "Labor Unions in Los Angeles Politics," unpublished Ph.D. dissertation, Department of Political Science, University of Chicago, 1958.

[12] See, for example, the discussion of United Steelworkers and UAW locals in the Chicago area by Joel Seidman, *et al.*, *The Worker Views His Union* (Chicago: University of Chicago Press, 1958), pp. 227–236.

larly, all unions want municipal and common pleas judges who will not issue antistrike injunctions without hearings and due consideration for the rights and interests of labor. The fear of hostile city actions in obstructing a strike is the most universal and powerful local concern of labor.

The Teamsters and the building trade unions have an immediate interest in other local considerations. The Building Trades are interested in the provisions of building, plumbing, and housing codes and in the appointment of sympathetic inspectors. One official in a craft union expressed satisfaction that ''our political efforts paid off when the Republicans appointed two of our fellows building inspectors even though they're Democrats.'' Furthermore, the city is a key source of large construction contracts. The Building Trades have a decided interest in local capital improvements programs and in maintaining cordial relations with the city manager, mayor, and councilmen. The Teamsters have a specific stake in local government through their 300 members employed in the refuse, water, and street departments and the Toledo Zoo. Notices on city bulletin boards asserting that the Teamsters have ''always done a job for all city employees, speaking with a powerful voice'' suggest that the Teamsters are interested in expanding their membership among city employees.[13] The Teamsters and the Building Trades are clearly much closer to the local arena than the UAW or the glass workers' unions.

Yet no union, either craft or industrial, has any specific policies to advance at the local level. The concern with such questions as the Safety Director, building inspectors, construction contracts, and refuse collectors has not generated an interest in the functions and programs of city government. City officials and union leaders agree that the only council action of particular interest to labor in recent years was the passage in 1964 of an ordinance prohibiting the use of professional strike-breakers in labor-management disputes. Controversies concerning pay increases for city employees attract some attention, but little notice is given to the vast majority of issues which do not directly affect labor. City councilmen have concluded with surprise that ''labor actually is not interested in proposing or

[13] *The Blade*, October 28, 1965, p. 23. About 800 city employees belong to Local 7, Public Employees Union. On the conflict of the Teamsters and Local 7, see *The Blade*, November 12, 1965, p. 16; and *Toledo Union Journal*, November 12, 1965, p. 1.

supporting municipal policies.'' One councilman observed: ''It's not what I expected, but none of the unions has much to say about what we are doing.''

To union leaders, city government activities are not especially important. As one official in the UAW noted:

> City government just isn't as crucial to labor as state and national politics. Labor-management questions and welfare policies are handled in national and state government. We depend on the county more than the city, because of the county's welfare and relief activities. The functions of the city are much more restrictive.

A leader in an old AFL union echoed this judgment:

> City government is not as important for us. We've got to think about state and national issues. The state in many ways is the most important, I think, since it handles workmen's compensation, unemployment, and such things.

Issues such as right-to-work, minimum wage legislation, unemployment compensation provisions, improved social security coverage and benefits, and medicare fall to the national and state governments. Local controversies over whether to build a municipal or a county incinerator seem irrelevant to the social and economic programs with which labor seeks to complement and protect its collective bargaining achievements. With the exception of matters of direct concern to labor (e.g., the Safety Director, an ordinance against strike-breaking), union leaders see no immediate justification for labor to devote its resources to city government.

Nevertheless, in some cities labor unions have developed an ideology which includes or even emphasizes city politics. The UAW in Detroit is concerned with political action and public policy at all levels of government. The leaders of the St. Louis Teamsters Local 688, like UAW officials in Detroit, regard the union as a social and political force in the community as well as in state and national politics.[14] The ideology of these unions recognizes that programs achieved at the national and state levels often require local action, if they are to be effective. In addition, the local community offers

---

[14] For a discussion of the Teamsters in St. Louis, see Gray and Greenstone, ''Organized Labor in City Politics,'' pp. 373–377.

many areas in which unions can take the initiative in behalf of their membership and the city as a whole. In recent years, Teamsters Local 688 has demanded and obtained enforcement of the St. Louis rat control ordinance; called for a graduated city income tax; recommended a metropolitan government plan; protested cut-backs in garbage collection; threatened legal action if the city did not enforce its air pollution ordinance; and constructed a massive senior citizens housing project.[15]

There is little evidence of a comparable ideology or performance among Toledo unions. The UAW is a bread-and-butter union in Toledo. It lacks the militancy of the international and the many locals which were organized and led by radicals with a commitment to broad political goals. Toledo UAW officials never displayed an affinity for the ideological and policy concerns which shaped the character of the union in Detroit, Lansing, Windsor, Chicago, and elsewhere.[16] The leaders who arose from the Toledo plants during the difficult days of the 1930s were and continued to be interested in building a union with increasing benefits and facilities for its membership.[17] After years of growth and consolidation, some outstanding facilities, such as the diagnostic clinic and retirees' center, were made available to the entire community.[18] Yet neither ideology nor self-interest provided an impetus for a broad role in the community. The UAW's political activity at the local level is defined by union issues, narrowly construed, while its other undertakings, such as the Children's Summer Camp, are noncontroversial in nature.

The Teamsters have a more explicit ideological commitment to political action than the UAW. Lawrence Steinberg, like Teamster Executive Vice-President Harold Gibbons of St. Louis, believes that the union should assert itself politically and civically as well as at the bargaining table. One official commented:

[15] *Ibid.*

[16] For a discussion of the UAW in other cities, see William H. Form, "Organized Labor's Place in the Community Power Structure," *Industrial and Labor Relations Review*, XII (July 1959), 526–539; C. M. M. Hart, "Industrial Relations Research and Social Theory," *Canadian Journal of Economics and Political Science*, XV (February 1949), 53–73; and Seidman, *et al.*, *The Worker Views His Union.*

[17] The history of the UAW in Toledo and the development of various union activities are reviewed by Bernard Stern in two articles on UAW Local 12, *Toledo Union Journal*, June 7, 1956, and June 14, 1956.

[18] For a discussion of the Toledo Health and Retiree Center, see *The Blade*, April 25, 1965, Section B, p. 1.

> The union movement in Toledo has lacked the political con-
> sciousness which is essential for its survival. We [the Teamsters]
> have learned that we must attend to both the bargaining table and
> legislative activity, and this includes city government. We want
> the rank and file to see the connection between bread and butter
> and political action.

It is easier, however, to demonstrate this connection in opposing
the Landrum-Griffin bill, urging the election of Lyndon Johnson,
and advocating repeal of Section 14(b) of the Taft-Hartley Act
than in considering the issues of city politics. In recent years, the
Toledo Teamsters supported the city ordinance prohibiting the
importation of strike-breakers; they opposed the 1964 amendment
to repeal Section 79 of the Charter, the $500,000 spending limit, as
a "downtown conspiracy" which will "prepare the way for an
increase in the fraudulent [nongraduated] payroll income tax."[19]
But they have shown little interest or involvement in the broad
range of municipal questions which have concerned their fellow
Teamsters in St. Louis.

In Toledo the local orientation of the Teamsters and the UAW is
not too dissimilar from the restrictive political view of the Building
Trades. Toledo unions rarely attempt to advance or alter local
programs on urban renewal, recreation, race relations, water pollution, or code enforcement. Labor, like business, is unwilling to take
the initiative in urging or opposing actions by the city government.
A good local government atmosphere is considered more important
than what the government does. Organized labor, believed by some
executives to be "taking over the community for its own selfish
interests," is in fact seeking the same innocuous objectives as business.

The union leader, like his counterpart in management, wants a
local "climate" which will not deter economic developments which
he considers advantageous. The expansion of Toledo Edison and
Libbey-Owens-Ford and the location of a large new Chrysler plant
five miles from Toledo are seen as benefits of a favorable climate.
Some union leaders believe that an overt flexing of labor's muscles
in city politics would hinder goals best advanced through the Toledo Area Development Corporation and good labor-management
relations. The concept of a good local climate common to both labor

---

[19] For the Teamster position on Section 79, see the *Team and Wheel*, May 31,
1964.

and industry emphasizes an avoidance of disruptive issues and politics as such; it suggests no specific commitments or responsibilities by any party.

Labor and management also share a preference for "understanding" or "sympathetic" city councilmen rather than particular policies. Although union leaders rarely ask anything of city council, they want to feel that they could, if a question should arise. Union leaders want city councilmen sympathetic to the interests of labor and willing to consult them on occasion. One official in the UAW described recent city government this way:

> We've had good relations with the mayor and most of the councilmen. We've conferred with them every now and then. We haven't asked them for anything special and they haven't done anything against labor.

A city councilman commented: "Labor's role in the city is odder than people recognize. Labor really wants consultation and recognition more than anything else."

Labor wants an understanding city council rather than a council for which it must take responsibility. All union leaders explain that they "do not support a labor city government but a government that is good for labor and the general public." A voice in city council is preferable to control:

> With city council we fight a little shy of it. We would rather have influence on council than have our own city council. That way we don't have to suffer the blame for mistakes. We've gotten as much or more consideration from Republican councils as we have from Democratic or labor-oriented councils, such as the Damas [a UAW administrator who served as mayor] council, and haven't had to suffer for their mistakes.

Labor Activity in Local Elections

To assure a considerate city council, regardless of party, the major unions engage in electoral activity. The AFL-CIO Council, the Teamsters, and the Building Trades Council have special procedures or organizations for evaluating candidates and issues in local elections. Other unions, such as the United Glass Workers and the

Electrical Workers, endorse local candidates on a less consistent basis.

The United Labor Committee. The United Labor Committee is the political arm of the AFL-CIO Council. Individual AFL-CIO locals or units of amalgamated locals affiliate, by choice, with the United Labor Committee, in which they are represented according to their numbers; central bodies, such as the Building Trades Council, receive one delegate. The UAW dominates the United Labor Committee numerically and by tradition. The ULC was conceived in 1940 by Richard T. Gosser as a means of achieving labor unity in politics without aggravating jurisdictional or union controversies. The ULC, Gosser hoped, would provide a new, voluntary organization in which different unions could cooperate for political action. After the war, the United Labor Committee, a miscellaneous force of AFL and CIO unions led by the UAW, entered the political arena.[20] Efforts first concentrated on presidential and congressional elections were extended to include local elections in 1949. When the AFL-CIO Council was established in 1958, the United Labor Committee became its political adjunct.

The United Labor Committee follows certain established procedures in endorsing local candidates. Before 1965 primary endorsements were avoided. One ULC official explained:

> Endorsements for primary elections are very difficult for us. Many new candidates come forward and it's hard to determine who to support without stepping on toes all around and causing divisions before the election. We could end up putting our weight behind people who wouldn't make it through the primary.

Thus, prior to 1965, when the mayoralty election attracted increased attention from labor, the ULC steering committee on endorsements made no recommendations until mid-October. Recommendations are ostensibly made on the basis of assessments which consider each candidate's relations with labor, his past performance on council, if an incumbent, and his activities, achievements, and concerns. The steering committee's recommendations are formally presented to the membership of the United Labor Commit-

<hr>

[20] The origins and early campaigns of the United Labor Committee are described by Stern, *Toledo Union Journal*, June 7, 1956, and June 14, 1956. For an account of early postwar activities, see *The Blade*, October 8, 1950, p. 3.

tee and then referred to the AFL-CIO Council for approval.[21]

After making its endorsements, the ULC prints circulars and handbills bearing its slate and distributes these to the various plants which have political committees to inform the workers. Weekly issues of the *Toledo Union Journal* carry campaign articles, copies of the ULC slate, and appeals for a heavy turn-out on election day. Door-to-door campaigning is conducted in areas of labor strength, although not on the scale of ULC efforts in national and state elections.

The Political Information League of the Teamsters. Organized political activity by the Teamsters is a more recent development. The Political Information League of the Teamsters (PILOT) was established only in 1960. Before 1961, the Teamsters made no formal endorsements in local elections, although they ''occasionally supported certain candidates by word of mouth.'' A Teamster official described PILOT activities in local elections this way:

> We do not work on a blank check with either party. PILOT is primarily interested in the individual candidate. After we've endorsed men who will serve the best interest of labor and the community, we provide financial, moral, physical assistance for these candidates. The stewards put up signs and distribute literature. We arrange meetings at the hall. The *Team and Wheel* carries editorials.

The Building Trades Council. Although most building trade unions are now affiliated with the AFL-CIO Council, the Building Trades Council continues to make its own endorsements and to carry on its own campaign effort. Building Trades officials, like those of the Teamsters, explain that their support is granted on the basis of individual qualifications rather than party affiliation. ''We follow the Gompers philosophy of rewarding our friends and punishing our enemies,'' said one official in the Building Trades Council. In the past, building trade unions also relied on a political alliance with the Teamsters. The Mutual Assistance Committee of the Teamsters and the Building Trades Council had about 35 affiliated locals at its peak in 1961–1962.[22] As the building trade unions

---

21 The AFL-CIO Council has never rejected ULC recommendations on endorsements.

22 *The Blade*, May 3, 1964, p. 3.

affiliated with the AFL-CIO Council and as the Teamsters developed a permanent political organization of their own, the formal aspects of the alliance disintegrated. Yet informal ties and cooperation continue.[23]

The goals and procedures of the three major unions in endorsing and supporting local candidates are basically the same: All groups want a responsive city council. But there are some differences on the means to achieve this. The United Labor Committee has cast its lot almost entirely with the Democratic Party. Although the Teamsters and the Building Trades also have leaned to the Democratic side, they have produced more balanced tickets than the ULC. The Teamsters, unlike the United Labor Committee, have urged the election of a labor representative, specifically a Teamster, to city council. Thus in 1961 the only PILOT endorsement went to the Teamsters' business agent, who also serves as the Director of PILOT. After the failure of the 1961 effort, the Teamsters launched a massive campaign which achieved the election of their business agent in 1963. Since 1953, the ULC has endorsed six candidates from organized labor, of whom only one was elected.

The divergence of labor endorsements in city elections indicates more than differences of approach. Few candidates receive all three labor endorsements, although there is often considerable overlap between the Teamsters and the Building Trades. The separate slates reflect antagonisms between unions rather than conflicting visions of city government or differences in the candidates endorsed by each organization. City politics is a harmless field for rivalry between the UAW and the Teamsters, two powerful unions contending for dominance in organized labor. Organizing conflicts between the Teamsters and AFL-CIO unions such as the Brewery Workers, Painters and Decorators, Public Employees, and Glass Bottle Blowers are unhealed by any overriding political issue. The relatively inconsequential questions and innocuous candidates of city politics provide a luxurious opportunity for the animosities which labor cannot afford in campaigning against right-to-work or Barry Goldwater.

The local endorsements of the United Labor Committee and the Teamsters are influenced by the suspicion with which they view

---

[23] In 1965, for example, the Teamsters and the Building Trades Council endorsed five of the same candidates for city council.

each other. The Teamsters, as outcasts from the AFL-CIO, distrust the United Labor Committee and suspect that it will not work for their candidates, even when it endorses them. They claim that in 1961 the ULC reluctantly endorsed Teamster business agent Frank Rossler only to exclude him from later campaign efforts, thereby costing Rossler the election. United Labor Committee officials contend that the Teamsters reneged on *their* 1961 promise to support ULC candidates in return for AFL-CIO support of Rossler. In this atmosphere of mutual distrust the ULC and the Teamsters generally reserve their endorsements for candidates not closely identified with the other side. Labor's nebulous goals and the similarity of local candidates facilitate this kind of political maneuvering.

The Success of Labor's Political Activity

Organized labor has not achieved remarkable success in electing its candidates to city council. Of the 20 candidates endorsed by the Teamsters since 1961, ten have been elected. Forty-three ULC endorsements since 1953 have produced only 23 victories. Neither the Teamsters nor the United Labor Committee has a political organization even vaguely comparable to the extensive, elaborate precinct structure of the UAW in Detroit. Such organizations as Toledo unions do have are rarely fully mobilized for a city election.[24] One official at the UAW observed:

> Having campaign workers in the wards and neighborhoods is very costly. We seldom go to the expense of doing this on any large scale in city elections. Political action in city politics is chiefly to keep in shape for the next year. Our main effort is every four years, on special issues such as right-to-work and reapportionment, congressional and state elections. Activity in city elections is to keep things going.

[24] In addition to the ULC organization, forces led by the UAW can work through ward and precinct chapters of Sixty Now, an organization founded by Richard Gosser to advocate an amendment to Social Security provisions which would permit retirement and adequate pensions at age 60. Yet these organizations are skeletal in comparison with those of the UAW in Detroit and the Teamsters in St. Louis. See Gray and Greenstone, ''Organized Labor in City Politics.''

Even in 1965, when all labor organizations were especially interested in Toledo's first mayoralty election in three decades, prominent union leaders were preoccupied with other matters. Richard Gosser was faced with the prospect of a three-year prison sentence when the United States Supreme Court declined to review his case.[25] UAW attention focused on a request for reconsideration and a stay of the sentence, which the Supreme Court granted in mid-October.[26] During the summer and fall of 1965, Lawrence Steinberg of the Teamsters was directing raiding and organizing activities at the Johns-Mansville plants in Defiance and Waterville, Ohio.[27] The chairman of the United Labor Committee was preoccupied with building united AFL-CIO resistance to the Teamsters' organizing efforts and achieving local AFL-CIO affiliation for unions threatened by the Teamsters.[28] The UAW voiced its support of AFL-CIO unions in a contest in which some labor leaders saw the Teamsters threatening a longstanding no-raid agreement in Toledo as well as UAW predominance in Northwestern Ohio. To many labor officials, the struggle between the unions seemed more significant and more interesting than the municipal election.

Thus, even when labor makes an unprecedented effort in a municipal election, with primary endorsements and campaign activities in the plants and neighborhoods, other questions are likely to take priority. The electoral returns in areas that United Labor Committee officials consider union strongholds—the 4th, 5th, 8th, 14th, and 20th wards—do not reflect high or consistent support of ULC slates. The absence of a clear connection between endorsements and an issue or principle important to labor perhaps accounts for the tendency of union members to vote their own choices. Endorsements made by the leadership on the basis of union antagonisms or personal friendships do not carry any compelling justification to the rank and file. In 1965, for example, it seems likely that many members of the UAW and other AFL-CIO unions disregarded the ULC endorsement of Ned Skeldon (D.) to support John W. Potter,

[25] *The Blade,* October 11, 1965, p. 1.

[26] See the *Toledo Union Journal,* October 15, 1965, p. 1. On November 15, 1965, the Supreme Court denied Gosser's petition for a rehearing. *The Blade,* November 15, 1965, p. 1.

[27] *The Blade,* October 28, 1965, p. 23. The Teamsters were challenging the Glass Bottle Blowers Association in both cases.

[28] *Toledo Union Journal,* October 15, 1965, p. 1. The Teamster viewpoint in these contests is presented in the *Team and Wheel,* October 30, 1965.

the Republican candidate, endorsed by the Teamsters.[29] The slight impact of ULC slates on the outcome of city elections from 1953 through 1965 is summarized in Table 10.1.

TABLE 10.1

United Labor Committee Endorsements, 1953–1965*

	Number	Victories	Percentage of Victories
ULC endorsement for incumbents			
Democrats	12	8	66
Republicans	5	4	80
Total	17	12	71
ULC endorsement for non-incumbents			
Democrats	22	11	50
Republicans	4	0	0
Total	26	11	42
Total ULC endorsements			
Democrats	34	19	56
Republicans	9	4	44
Total	43	23	53
No ULC endorsement			
Democrats	20	6	30
Republicans	43	24	56
Total	63	30	47

* No endorsements were made in the 1963 municipal election. UAW grievances over the Gosser case and labor participation in the Democratic Party led to ULC inactivity.

Source: Interviews with UAW leaders.

An additional explanation of labor's poor showing in city elections lies in the absence of a strong alliance between labor organizations and the political parties. The influence of the UAW in Detroit is the product of its political militancy, size, ward organization, and

[29] Skeldon's percentage of the vote in areas of presumed labor strength was as follows: 4th ward, 65 per cent; 5th ward, 47; 8th ward, 61; 14th ward, 48; 20th ward, 58.

powerful position in the Democratic Party.[30] The UAW in Toledo, in addition to lacking both militancy and organization, suffers from an estranged relationship with the Democratic Party. UAW officials have long resented the suspicious treatment they have received from the party which their union has supported for over 20 years. Democratic party chairman John Patrick Kelly, anxious to protect the party from UAW captivity, has successfully excluded most union officials from executive, ward, and precinct positions, while relying on their assistance at election time.[31] With a solid entourage of incumbent ward chairmen and precinct committeemen, the party chairman has easily disposed of occasional UAW slates in precinct races.[32] The UAW, normally preoccupied with union matters, has not launched a full-scale effort to gain a greater role in the Democratic Party. One UAW official commented:

> Kelly's ward and precinct organization is very run down. We have a better organization in the ULC and the ward and precinct chapters of Sixty Now. We don't want to get into that business or we could take them [the Democratic Party] over in a week. We would like to have something to say about different issues and decisions, but we don't want to take over any party.

The inability of the UAW to achieve its limited objectives in the party organization has left an atmosphere of resentment and frustration. As one official at the UAW observed: "We're sick of putting up the money, working the registration drives, campaigning for Democratic candidates, and then being shut out of party councils."

UAW disenchantment with the Democratic Party increased when Richard Gosser was prosecuted by the Kennedy administration. UAW leaders believe that the officials and elected representatives of the local Democratic Party could have mobilized their political forces to dissuade the Attorney General or the President, if they

[30] J. David Greenstone, "Party Pressure on Organized Labor in Three Cities," in M. Kent Jennings and Harmon Zeigler, eds., *The Electoral Process* (Englewood Cliffs, N.J.: Prentice-Hall, 1966), pp. 55–81.

[31] The Toledo situation is in sharp contrast to that in Detroit, where 17 per cent of the Democratic precinct leaders are labor union officers and 56 per cent are union members. Samuel J. Eldersveld, *Political Parties* (Chicago: Rand McNally & Co., 1964), p. 504.

[32] The UAW failure in 1962 is reviewed in *The Blade*, June 3, 1963, p. 3.

had exerted themselves. But on this matter of grave importance to labor, party leaders responded with indifference, perhaps feeling that "it would be easier to have Gosser out of the way."

To many in the UAW, Ned Skeldon seemed to offer the possibility of deliverance from the paranoiac and hostile Kelly leadership. In 1964 there was considerable optimism that Skeldon could circumvent Kelly to build a stronger alliance between the Democratic Party and labor. Yet even this is now in doubt. Skeldon's decisive defeat in the 1965 mayoralty election did not enhance his position for extending his control of the party. The repudiation of Skeldon and five members of his slate for the council left Kelly's influence intact and unthreatened. Furthermore, there are those in the UAW who are not eager for Skeldon to dominate the Democratic Party. In the lower echelons of the UAW, Skeldon's "disinterest in union problems and meetings," his practice of "cozying up to the top leadership, while ignoring others," and his willingness to depart from UAW and Democratic positions on such questions as reapportionment are seen as evidence of an intent to exploit labor for his own ends.

Dissatisfaction with the Democratic Party has produced UAW support for a few Republican candidates in the city and county, but no direct contact with the Republican Party organization. Although UAW leaders consider the Republicans to be the party of business, finance, and antilabor sentiment, they recognize that ambitious Republicans must take at least a moderately liberal stance for success in Toledo. The able, tested Republican incumbent may compare favorably with some of the candidates of a Democratic organization noted for its suspicion of labor. In the opinion of one UAW leader: "At the local level the Republican Party has come up with some damn good men, competent, liberal, friendly to labor."

Nevertheless, the UAW's commitment to the Democratic Party as the "friend of labor" in national and state politics militates against close or frequent association with Republican candidates at the local level. The local political inclination of all AFL-CIO unions, including the building trades, is, in large part, a product of the national and state alliance of organized labor and the Democratic Party. The stakes of this alliance are such that the United Labor Committee and its member unions are rarely willing to experiment in city politics, despite their grievances with the local Democratic organization.

The Teamsters have been more uncertain in their political alignment. As a decentralized AFL union, the Teamsters have lacked the
political direction and unity achieved by the UAW and other CIO
unions which have greater power concentrated in their international organizations.[33] The highly autonomous locals of the Teamsters have pursued diverse and sometimes conflicting political objectives. In Toledo Teamster leaders have been casting about for a
party alliance. In the early 1960s Steinberg hoped to establish a tie
with the Democratic Party. Teamster business agent Frank Rossler,
the instrument of Steinberg's political aspirations, ran for city
council in 1961 and 1963 as a Democrat.

The Teamsters were not received with enthusiasm in the Democratic Party. Older party leaders referred to Rossler as ''a promising young Teamster'' rather than a promising young Democrat.
Prominent Democrats did not conceal their distaste at having
Teamsters in their midst. A Democratic elected official commented:
''Everyone avoids the Teamsters like the plague. Their organization
is only out for itself. We don't want to mix with that.'' Another
prominent Democrat, in discussing labor's role in politics, remarked: ''Hell, who needs the Teamsters? We've got the UAW.''
The Teamsters suffered their last rebuff when Skeldon and Ashley
prevented Steinberg from being a delegate to the Democratic national convention in August 1964.[34]

After the 1964 election, the Teamsters began to shift their direction. In April 1965 Steinberg announced that the Teamsters favored the passage of four state issues supported by Governor
James Rhodes (R.), including a Republican reapportionment plan
strongly opposed by the state and local AFL-CIO organizations.[35]
At the same time Steinberg indicated that he would support the
election of Mayor John W. Potter (R.), ''one of the best friends of
labor in Toledo.'' The future of Democratic councilman Rossler was
caught between Steinberg's desire for continued representation on
city council and his support for Potter. The Teamsters' distaste for

---

[33] The structure of the Teamsters is discussed by Romer, *International
Brotherhood of Teamsters*. For an analysis of the centralizing influence of
James Hoffa, see James and James, *Hoffa and the Teamsters*.

[34] The Teamster reaction is recorded in the *Team and Wheel*, February 29,
1964, p. 1. Skeldon and Ashley later explained that their action was based on
Steinberg's erratic and last minute record of supporting Democrats. *The
Blade*, October 30, 1965, p. 3.

[35] *The Blade*, April 22, 1965, p. 3.

Skeldon, which he reciprocated, put Rossler in a delicate position with the party, although he still intended to seek reelection as late as March 1965. The conflict was resolved, under Steinberg's guidance, when Rossler dropped out of the race and instead organized rallies of Democrats for Potter.[36]

It is unlikely that the Teamsters have found a permanent ally in the Republican Party. Many national issues, such as the repeal of Section 14(b) of the Taft-Hartley Act, draw the Teamsters to the Democratic Party. Furthermore, the local Republican organization has not welcomed the Teamsters with unbounded hospitality. One Republican councilman commented: "Steinberg's been calling on John Andrews [state and local Republican leader] lately, but I doubt that he'll get very far with that angle." Several Republicans questioned the ties which a few of their colleagues have established with the Teamsters. Many Republicans would like to benefit from Teamster campaign assistance without being closely identified with what they consider a rough, violent organization under power-hungry leadership.

In Toledo the political weakness of the parties and of organized labor has contributed to their estrangement. The leaders of a decadent party system have felt free to rebuff or insult labor supporters. Union officials have made no major effort to transform the party organizations which repelled their overtures. Personal animosities and organizational jealousies, rather than ideological differences, have stood in the way of strong political alliances. In discussing the relationship of organized labor and the Democratic Party in Detroit, Chicago, and Los Angeles, David Greenstone observed:

> Both organizations [Committee on Political Education (COPE) and the Democratic Party] controlled resources more lasting than personal popularity or a particular politician's possession of a public office. Because each organization had funds, campaign workers, and the loyalty of many voters, neither one could afford to ignore the other.[37]

The absence of these conditions in Toledo accounts for a strained relationship between the Democratic Party and organized labor—a strain that is particularly evident in city politics.

---

[36] *The Blade*, October 28, 1965, p. 3.
[37] Greenstone, "Party Pressure on Organized Labor," p. 75.

Labor's Civic Participation

In other cities, organized labor has attempted to extend both its political influence and its civic activities. McKee and Form have described labor efforts to achieve greater representation on community boards and charitable agencies in Lorain, Ohio, and Lansing, Michigan.[38] Organized labor in Toledo has not displayed a comparable concern with civic participation, although the top officials have been active in certain areas. Steinberg and Gosser both contributed to the establishment and development of the Labor-Management-Citizens Commission, a local mediation agency. Gosser held executive positions in the Toledo Area Development Corporation and the Port Authority. The president and the executive secretary of the AFL-CIO Council and the president of the Hod Carriers' Union serve on the Board of Community Relations.[39]

But as of 1966, labor was unrepresented on the Toledo-Lucas County Plan Commission, the Toledo Metropolitan Housing Authority, the Urban Renewal Advisory Commission, the University of Toledo Board of Trustees, and many other municipal boards and commissions. Union officials serve on the boards of very few civic and charitable agencies; labor participation in this area is largely restricted to the Community Chest, the Red Cross, the Central Hospital Bureau, and Council of Social Agencies. Even in these agencies, labor has only nominal representation.[40]

Developments in late 1965 and early 1966 suggested a possible change in labor's civic participation. After studying the boards of more then 70 agencies and organizations, UAW leaders concluded that labor was grossly underrepresented. In addition to recommending increased labor participation and responsibility, the UAW statement proposed that the AFL-CIO Council provide advice and endorsements for labor representatives appointed to public, civic,

[38] James B. McKee, "Status and Power in the Industrial Community: A Comment on Drucker's Thesis," *American Journal of Sociology*, LVIII (January 1953), 363–370; and Form, "Organized Labor's Place in the Community Power Structure."

[39] Labor representation on the Board of Community Relations is required by city ordinance (1951).

[40] These judgments are based on an examination of the boards of 45 civic and charitable organizations.

and charitable organizations.[41] Despite this statement, Toledo labor leaders have generally been more concerned with union matters or with projects developed by labor, such as the Health and Retiree Center, than with business-dominated charitable and civic organizations.

Although union leaders may enjoy the respect or even the friendship of some executives, business management is still regarded as the adversary; and the charitable and civic projects of business are consequently regarded by labor people with a certain amount of suspicion. They note that the business executive may lend his name to worthy projects, but he is, in the words of one union official, "more interested in cavorting on the national scene and getting his name in the *Wall Street Journal* than considering his employees or his city." Pleasant luncheon meetings to discuss the United Appeal do not obliterate the experiences of three decades in the labor movement. One UAW official, discussing his association with a prominent business executive in several community undertakings, remarked: "As I think of him now, my mind goes back to the pension fight of 1950 when he fought us for months on end with everything he had." In dress and speech, as well as outlook, leading union officials express their commitment to organized labor rather than the middle-class respectability expected by business and party leaders.[42]

Labor and Civil Rights

Although most union leaders, with the exception of those in the craft unions, are moderately committed to civil rights, they hope to advance this cause by the general goals of labor: more jobs, better working conditions, higher wages, younger retirement, earlier social security, improved low-cost medical care and educational opportunities. Union leaders have rarely taken the initiative in urging local civil rights measures, such as the fair housing ordinance of 1961 or

[41] The UAW study of labor's civic participation and the new rules set forth for community service are described in detail in the *Toledo Union Journal*, January 28, 1966. See also *The Blade*, December 1, 1965, p. 16, and January 16, 1966, p. 20.

[42] The outspoken personalities of several union leaders and their failure to wear ties caused widespread comment from party leaders and business executives.

the equal employment pledge of 1963. Nor have they been prominent in civil rights organizations or in social, governmental, or religious agencies concerned with race relations. Demonstrations are discouraged as injurious to the good atmosphere which Toledo has achieved in race as well as labor-management relations.

Thus, civil rights problems, like other local problems, are appraised from the perspective of the union. Labor leaders emphasize the contributions of the unions in advancing equal employment, but they also emphasize that their role in solving Negro problems is necessarily limited:

> We've come a long way. I remember when the first Negro went to work at the Spicer plant in 1933 or so—they burned him in effigy. The UAW's been for equality since the beginning, but it's management that does the hiring.

Labor and Reform Institutions

Because union leaders devote relatively little of their time and resources to the local community, they dislike the reform institutions which seem to hinder labor's half-hearted ventures in city politics. At-large elections, nonpartisanship, and the council-manager plan make it more difficult for labor to accomplish its ends with a limited effort. The leaders of some unions would prefer a return to wards:

> The at-large election makes it more difficult for us. It weakens low-income group representation—there's no doubt about that. With wards and a Tammany Hall system of responsibility we could have greater representation for all groups, not just those in the 12th and 16th [prosperous, Republican] wards.

Wards, many union leaders noted, would eliminate the handicap of nonvoting in the lower-income areas of the city. In a ward system, labor could achieve victories in union and lower-income districts without the costs of its present city-wide effort.

The nonpartisan ballot is also believed to obstruct labor's political activities. Labor organizations must impress a particular slate on their members without the assistance of identifying labels on the ballot. Several union officials contend that nonpartisanship and the

reform tradition have left workers and other voters with an incorri-
gible habit of disregarding party and union slates:

> I don't know whether our ULC slate has an effect or not. I'm
> beginning to wonder. Certain names and personalities like Andy
> Douglas [R.] and Bob Savage [D.] take hold and draw well from
> both parties and all parts of town. John Potter's another example.

The council-manager plan also complicates labor's task at the
local level. Power is diffused, so union leaders must maintain contact with several different officials. The direct election of the mayor
is seen as a step which will simplify labor's access to city government without resolving the problem completely. Labor will not be
able to ignore the powers still held by other councilmen and the city
manager. The city manager, an appointed official with considerable
authority, is an annoyance to labor and a possible threat. There is a
danger that the post will be filled with an allegedly professional
manager hostile to organized labor. Although the most recent
manager, Frank Backstrom (1962–1967), was considered reasonably agreeable, one of his predecessors during the late 1950s is
invariably cited as the prime example of labor's fears. This manager, in the opinion of the leadership in every union, was "very
antilabor," an "errand boy for big business" who would never
listen to labor.[43]

The council-manager plan is distasteful to labor in theory as well
as practice. The reform ideal of a professional city manager safely
insulated from direct political influence does not strike a responsive
chord with labor leaders. Rhetoric about city decisions made on the
basis of technical rather than political considerations has slight
appeal to those who see it as a facade for business interests rather
than an explanation of how government actually operates. The
reform objective of emulating business in government is understood
as a tactic to exclude labor and lower-income groups from political
decisions. A political ideal which proposes that administrative decisions be made by professionals and public officials elected for individual qualifications rather than association with "special inter-

---

[43] Labor suspicion of city managers and the council-manager plan is com-
mon. See Oliver P. Williams and Charles R. Adrian, *Four Cities* (Philadelphia:
University of Pennsylvania Press, 1963), p. 146; and John Bartlow Martin,
"The Town That Tried 'Good Government,' " in Edward C. Banfield, ed.,
Urban Government (New York: The Free Press, 1961), pp. 276–284.

ests'' leaves little room for organized labor. The general emphasis of
the reform ethos on the good of the city as a whole provides, as one
union official noted, an effective method for depreciating the role of
organized labor.

Despite their disgruntlement with reform ideas and institutions,
union leaders are not dissatisfied with their role in city government.
Many are reluctant to say that reform institutions have restricted
labor's influence in the city, although they have implied it in other
statements:

> I don't think the city manager thing is good for labor, but on
> the other hand, I can't see that it has had a restrictive effect on
> labor. The weight of labor has been felt in this community. It will
> be felt under any form of government.

Union leaders are generally content that labor has achieved the
local policies and consideration which it desires. Relations with city
council over the past 15 years have been friendly and cooperative;
few, if any, actions distinctly unfavorable to labor have been taken.
Reform institutions, although distasteful, have presented no problem warranting serious concern.

Because of its general satisfaction, organized labor has been less
than adamant in its interest in the strong mayor plan. It would be
more convenient for labor to have the ear of a strong mayor than to
work through a weak mayor, several councilmen, and the city manager. Yet labor would have no new policies or interests to advocate
under such a system. A strong executive system in an openly
partisan city government would appear more congenial to labor, but
it might also be more threatening. The 1965 election results indicate
that a concerted effort on one office does not increase labor's effectiveness in local elections, as some union leaders had hoped. The
failure of labor's political activities could be more costly under the
strong mayor plan. The specter of a strong mayor unfriendly to
labor has checked enthusiasm for charter revision. Union leaders,
with their relatively small stake in city politics, are cautious about
introducing new uncertainties into a basically satisfactory situation, in which union leaders are free to concentrate on contracts,
union expansion, union programs and facilities, conflicts within and
between unions, reapportionment, medicare, 14(b), and other state
and national issues.

Summary

At the local level, labor wants a government that refrains from certain offenses, such as interfering with picket lines, rather than a government that enacts certain programs. City government under reform institutions has fulfilled this goal and offered no justification for broader expectations. Reform institutions have in fact accentuated labor's negative orientation to city politics. Recent city councils have done little to attract either the wrath or the interest of labor. The city's halting progress on important local programs, such as urban renewal, has not produced a view of local action that would cause either labor or business to revise its low estimate of city government.

Toledo unions, lacking militant ideological motives for participating in city politics, have received no alternative incentive from a caretaker city government. City politicians with limited power and personal organizations have not drawn labor into a governing coalition. Nor has a strong party alliance interested labor unions in a political arena removed from their immediate bread and butter concerns.[44]

Furthermore, the ethos and institutions of reform have blunted the activities that labor has undertaken in city politics.[45] The long-standing tradition of maverick politicians and independent voting can withstand even strong labor efforts, such as the United Labor Committee campaign for Skeldon. The reform tradition brands labor as "a special interest group," seeking its own ends instead of the good of the community. In a political system characterized by individual efforts rather than strong political organizations, labor's intentions and activities are suspect. Self-styled politicians and atrophied political parties tend to be cautious about a close association with labor, which could jeopardize the image of independence valued in Toledo. Candidates and parties want the assistance of

---

[44] Compare Toledo and Chicago. See Banfield and Wilson, *City Politics*, p. 289.

[45] This has also been the case in Detroit, where the UAW has been far less successful in city politics than it has in county, state, and national politics. For an account of the UAW's difficulties in nonpartisan local elections in Detroit, see Banfield and Wilson, *City Politics*, pp. 287, 288.

labor but fear the effects of an overdose. Party leaders are anxious to preserve their organizations for themselves, even at the cost of the electoral success that could be possible through a closer alliance with labor. Candidates hope to receive a labor endorsement while avoiding a damaging identification with a "special interest," "lower class" group—an identification that could hurt their showing in the prosperous, high turn-out wards which are important to success in at-large elections.

Organized labor in Toledo is not the integral part of the local political system that it is in some cities. The narrow political orientation of Toledo unions and the local political tradition have combined to give organized labor a less significant community role than its members and resources warrant.

11 THE CIVIC AND POLITICAL ROLE OF NEGRO LEADERS

Through the years, the reform movement has expressed the political values and aspirations of the middle class. The reform ethos, founded on Yankee-Protestant political traditions, emphasized civic responsibility and abstract standards in political life.[1] The decades since these ideals were first propounded have seen the growth of large, lower-income populations in many American cities. Foremost among these groups contributing to the changing character of urban politics are Negroes. In major American cities, Negroes comprise an increasing percentage of the total population. Between 1950 and 1960, the 12 largest cities in the United States showed a net loss of more than two million whites and a net gain of nearly two million Negroes.[2]

Toledo's Negro Population

Although Toledo has a relatively small Negro population in comparison with many Northern cities, it has grown

[1] Richard Hofstadter, *The Age of Reform* (New York: Vintage Books, 1960), p. 9.
[2] Edward C. Banfield and James Q. Wilson, *City Politics* (Cambridge, Mass.: Harvard University Press and M.I.T. Press, 1963), p. 293.

rapidly in the last 20 years. In the decade between 1940 and 1950, there was a 60 per cent increase in the Negro population, followed by an additional 61 per cent increase in the years 1950 to 1960.[3] At the time of the 1960 Census, 40,013 Negroes constituted 13 per cent of Toledo's total population. Table 11.1 indicates the size of Toledo's Negro population in comparison with that of other cities.

TABLE 11.1

Negroes as a Percentage of City Populations, 1960*

City	Negroes as a Percentage of Population	City	Negroes as a Percentage of Population
Memphis	37.1	Youngstown	19.0
Baltimore	35.7	Columbus	17.0
Newark	34.1	New York	14.0
Detroit	28.9	Akron	13.5
Cleveland	28.6	Los Angeles	13.5
St. Louis	28.6	TOLEDO	13.0
Philadelphia	26.4	Boston	9.1
Norfolk	25.8	Milwaukee	8.4
Chicago	22.9	Rochester	7.4
Dayton	22.5	Louisville	7.3
Cincinnati	21.6	Denver	6.1
Indianapolis	20.6	Hartford	5.7

* Source: Computed from figures of the U.S. Bureau of the Census, *U.S. Censuses of Population and Housing*, 1960.

The rapid growth of the Negro population in the last 20 years has resulted in a concentration of approximately 80 per cent of the Negroes in a small, compact section of the core city, outlined in Figure 11.1. The number of Negroes in this area increased from 11,908 in 1940 to 32,754 in 1960, while the white population decreased from 30,603 to 8,589.[4] Negro residential districts in the outlying areas are few. By political boundaries, the 6th ward, with

[3] These figures from *U.S. Censuses of Population and Housing*, 1940, 1950, and 1960.

[4] Toledo Council of Social Agencies, *Report of Urban Planning Committee: Older City Area* (Toledo: mimeographed, 1963), p. 11.

FIGURE 11.1

Census Tract Areas in which 80 Per Cent of Toledo Negroes Live*

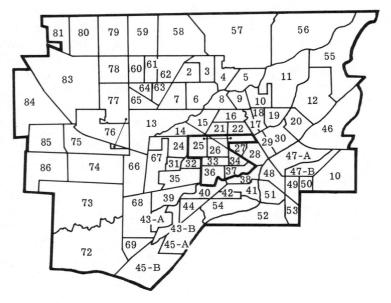

* Data from U.S. Census reports, 1960.

a population that is 63 per cent Negro, and the 8th ward, with a
population that is 86 per cent Negro, are the centers of Toledo's
ghetto.[5]

Negroes are distinguished from the rest of the population economically as well as geographically. In the 6th and 8th wards 76 per
cent of the families have an annual income of $5,000 and less; in the
20 predominantly white wards, the percentage at this level falls
between 10 and 51. Unemployment and Aid to Dependent Children
rates in Negro areas are vastly higher than those elsewhere in the
city and county.[6] Racial differences in education are also evident,

[5] The 6th ward is not primarily a residential area. Population is concentrated
in the 8th ward.

[6] The 1960 unemployment rate in the area where 80 per cent of Toledo
Negroes live was 14.6 per cent, as compared to Lucas County's rate of 6.5 per
cent. The dependency rate in 1960 was 209 children per 1,000 children; the
county average for 1960 was 40 children per 1,000 children. *Report of Urban
Planning Committee*, pp. 14–17.

although less striking than income differences, as Table 11.2 reveals.

The Negro population of Toledo, although economically depressed, is of sufficient size and density to have produced several sources of leadership. A variety of different organizations and their leaders contribute to the civic and political role of Negroes. Negroes in the political parties, organized labor, the church, the press, social agencies, professional positions, and civil rights organizations offer competing claims to speak for their community. In Toledo and elsewhere, the Negro role is shaped by the character of the Negro population, its rate of growth, stability, educational and economic levels, and pattern of segregation. But to a large degree, the civic and political life of Negroes reflects that of the city as a whole.[7] The structure and style of Negro politics are determined by the nature of city politics. A Negro political machine, such as the Dawson organization in Chicago, is dependent upon the existence of a white machine. Negroes enter politics under rules and practices prescribed by the distinctive political system of the city where they live. Similarly, Negro civic activity is powerfully influenced by the character of white civic leadership, the presence or absence of allies in labor and business, and the accessibility and sympathy of city politicians.

The prevailing disorganization and inertia of Toledo politics, business, and labor are clearly mirrored in the civic and political leadership of Negroes. The predominance of oldtimers is as pro-

TABLE 11.2

The Distribution of Income and Education among
Whites and Nonwhites in Toledo, 1960*

| | Per Cent | |
	Whites	*Nonwhites*
Income of families		
$3,000 per year and under	13.4	34.8
$10,000 per year and more	17.7	3.4
Education of persons 25 and over		
Less than one year of high school	38.4	54.4
Four years of college or more	6.4	2.5

* Source: U.S. Bureau of the Census, *U.S. Censuses of Population and Housing, 1960*, Table P-4.

[7] This follows the argument of James Q. Wilson, *Negro Politics* (New York: The Free Press, 1960).

nounced in Negro organizations as it is in the political parties and labor unions. Negro leaders are less militant and more divided than their counterparts in organized labor. Their commitment to a nonpolitical and noncontroversial course of action equals that of business executives. The disinterest of Negro leaders in political organization and electoral activity accurately reflects the attitudes of party officials, as does their preference for preserving their own positions at the expense of the cause or organization they lead.

The Civil Rights Movement in Toledo

In some Northern cities, the civil rights movement has opened the way to a very different situation. In Philadelphia, New York, Chicago, and St. Louis, civil rights leaders are making their views known through civic and political organization and/or direct action. The source of Negro leadership in the North is often found in professional race relations organizations, such as the Congress of Racial Equality (CORE) and the National Association for the Advancement of Colored People (NAACP).[8]

The NAACP. In Toledo, professional civil rights organizations are weak or nonexistent. There is no Urban League, and in 1966 the local chapter of CORE was struggling into the third year of a precarious existence. The Toledo chapter of the NAACP, founded in 1915, is one of the oldest in the country, but certainly not one of the strongest.[9] Despite its longevity, the Toledo NAACP is a relatively small and inconspicuous organization. The chapter claims a membership of 3,000, drawn largely from the middle class rather than lower-income groups.[10] The active membership is far smaller, however. Only 450 members voted in a closely contested presidential election in December 1964. Chapter meetings, activities, and newsletters are infrequent.

NAACP leaders are, with few exceptions, well-established men in professional or comfortably middle-class positions. Several are at-

---

[8] See Wilson's discussion, *Negro Politics*, pp. 295–319.

[9] For an account of the 50-year history of the NAACP in Toledo, see *The Blade*, September 19, 1965, Section H, p. 1.

[10] Some whites, particularly politicians, belong to the NAACP, but white participation is insignificant.

torneys in successful firms or partnerships; one man is the minister of one of the most prosperous churches in the Negro community. The president who served from 1962 to 1966 was a deputy sheriff in Lucas County. The NAACP leadership differs from the majority of Negroes in its occupational security and status and in its party affiliation. Most of the top officials in the chapter are active Republicans in what they describe as the "Lincoln tradition." The chapter president (1962–1966) served under a Republican sheriff in Lucas County; three other local NAACP officials sought office as Republicans, while others have held or aspire to Republican appointments on the bench and in city and state government.[11]

Local NAACP officials are closely, although quietly, allied with leading Republicans. In other cities, by way of contrast, the NAACP and similar groups have often attempted to present facts and raise issues which would "put the heat on the politicians."[12] The NAACP in Chicago, for example, has excoriated Congressman Dawson for his alleged "softness" on race issues and his "subservience" to the Democratic National Committee.[13] In Toledo there is an identity of interests between Republican politicians and NAACP officials. Both have a common concern with the party and the jobs and political advancement it can bring. Race goals are softened by an interest in avoiding politically embarrassing issues and controversies.

The economic position and political involvement of local NAACP leaders contribute to what they call "behind the scenes" activity. NAACP officials, confident of their political ties and community respectability, are convinced that goals such as equal employment and fair housing can be achieved without destructive conflict. The white community, in their judgment, generally listens to and understands the problems of the Negro. Demonstrations may only irritate the officials with whom the NAACP needs an effective relationship. The president of the NAACP explained:

> It is our belief that if you demonstrate with as many as 10,000 marching, picketing persons, you demonstrate little more than that a problem exists, and more often create a feeling of hostility.[14]

[11] NAACP officials have run for state legislature (1964), city council (1965), and municipal judge (1965).

[12] Wilson, *Negro Politics*, pp. 111–117.

[13] Wilson, p. 115.

[14] *The Blade*, July 5, 1964, Section C, p. 3.

NAACP leaders believe that elected officials have shown themselves willing to confer and negotiate. They also consider the "power structure," consisting of high executives in the major companies, accessible. In the opinion of one NAACP official:

> We've had cooperative action in Toledo. We've had communication with the white leadership. We can disagree agreeably and negotiate again. We can develop knowledge of each other without harassment of particular individuals and companies. We know we can sit down with the presidents of major companies, and we've proven that we won't harass them. We believe in persuasion—causing a change of opinion for lasting results. There's no need for sensationalism when you are on your way.

The use of direct action, described by one NAACP leader as "the noisemaking and dancing in the street approach," is considered a last resort unjustified by the civil rights situation in Toledo.

The severity of such problems as housing, employment, and education is to a large extent counteracted by the "lines of communication" highly valued by NAACP leaders. One of these leaders, in summarizing his favorable appraisal of race relations in Toledo, referred to housing and employment as "our only problems." To middle-class Negro leaders, such as those in the NAACP, the possibility of communication is an achievement in itself which makes other problems appear less urgent. Many in the NAACP who recall the days of rigid segregation are unwilling to jeopardize the gains of recent years by militant actions with unpredictable consequences.

The few overt moves of the NAACP are cautious and restrained. Demonstrations indicate sympathy for Selma, Alabama, rather than dissatisfaction with local conditions. Boycotts, such as the NAACP selective buying campaign against Sealtest in 1961, are infrequent.[15] Political education drives are sporadic, often occurring only weeks before the registration deadline or election day.[16] NAACP-requested surveys, such as the 1964 study of the employment and promotion of Negroes in city government, are not followed by aggressive action or public discussion.

In the winter and spring of 1965, NAACP attention focused on

[15] For an account of the boycott of Sealtest, see the local Negro newspaper, *The Bronze Raven*, December 23, 1961, p. 1.

[16] *The Bronze Raven* has criticized the NAACP for its weak political efforts. For editorial comments on the NAACP, political organization, and the 1965 campaign, see *The Bronze Raven*, October 2, 1965; October 16, 1965; and October 30, 1965.

the problem of "motivating the Negro community in a cooperative effort as it relates to the moral obligation for respect and responsibility."[17] The president of the NAACP contended that "a tendency to give lighter sentences when a Negro murders a Negro than when a Negro murders a white man" had weakened the forces of law and order in Negro neighborhoods. Leaders in the NAACP called for equal prosecution and punishment for all crimes and a unified campaign by social agencies and civil rights organizations to combat crime and delinquency in the Negro community. In this case, as in its other actions, the NAACP has revealed a "sensible" and "responsible" orientation reassuring to white leaders in business, politics, and labor.

The Federated Council. Similar to the NAACP in leadership and outlook is the Federated Council, established in 1963 to achieve greater unity among various organizations and agencies in the civil rights field. The Council is a loose association of attorneys, officials in social agencies and public positions, NAACP leaders and a few ministers under the leadership of a prominent local psychologist and the executive director of the Frederick Douglass Community Association. The organization of the Council resulted from several convictions:

> We believed that there are problems in Toledo, but over the years we had built good relations here. We had a number of people widely accepted by the total community—people who might not want to go into the streets and sing hymns. We wanted to use these people to get at the whole racial situation. We felt that techniques used in Montgomery, Alabama, would not be appropriate to Toledo.

The professional men who took the initiative in establishing the Council saw the need for educated, articulate leaders to argue the Negro case. Like the NAACP leaders who have supported and assisted them, Council officials are committed to the process of discussion and negotiation, particularly with what they call the power structure, "the concentration of influence built around people who control money in the glass industries and financial institutions." In dealing with the power structure, Council officials think that the Negro community should be represented by its most effec-

---

[17] NAACP statement, February 1965, mimeographed.

tive spokesmen rather than those "who would be hampered by their lack of education—the way some of the ministers are."

Leaders in the Council believe that corporation executives are responsive to the skillful use of the conference method. To support their view, Council leaders point to their meetings with corporation officials during the winter of 1964, which resulted in an equal employment pledge signed by 41 companies.[18] As a result of a series of carefully planned discussions, corporation executives were "willing to commit themselves to equal opportunity at the local level, which did a lot to establish a healthy, productive atmosphere."

The Federated Council, like the NAACP, has tried its hand at conducting a voter registration drive without making an intensive or continuing effort in this area. The Council also shares the NAACP's strategy of combining negotiation with an up-by-the-bootstraps emphasis for the Negro community. Active support was given to the NAACP's effort against crime and to other steps considered necessary to "improve the Negro's image of himself and his community."

Council leaders, however, have failed to fulfill the purposes of their organization. After 1964, efforts at coordinating or initiating civil rights activity became much less frequent. The prolonged inactivity of the Council during most of 1965 and 1966 suggest that it is moribund, if not defunct.[19]

The Interdenominational Ministerial Alliance. The Interdenominational Ministerial Alliance, an association of some 40 Negro ministers established in the early 1940s, has become increasingly involved in civil rights in recent years. The ministers in the IMA, unlike the professional, middle-class leaders of the NAACP and the Federated Council, can reach a wide segment of the Negro community on a weekly basis.

With other groups emphasizing conferences and negotiation, the

---

[18] See *The Blade*, March 2, 1964, p. 12. Many large companies with government contracts (such as Kaiser Jeep Corporation) were already bound by federal regulations.

[19] The weakness of Toledo's Federated Council presents a marked contrast with the success of such councils in New Orleans and Durham. For a discussion of the Coordinating Council of Greater New Orleans, see Daniel C. Thompson, *The Negro Leadership Class* (Englewood Cliffs, N.J.: Prentice-Hall, 1963). Durham's influential council, including all major Negro organizations in the community, is discussed by M. Elaine Burgess, *Negro Leadership in a Southern City* (Chapel Hill: University of North Carolina Press, 1960).

IMA has sought to establish itself as the aggressive advocate of civil rights in Toledo. By the use of militant language and periodic threats of demonstrations, the ministers rebuke those in the NAACP and Federated Council who question their education and their ability to speak for the Negro. In its civil rights actions, the IMA is anxious to demonstrate the independence and achievements of the churches. Cooperative ventures, such as participation in the Federated Council, the Toledo Ministerial Association, the Council of Churches, and a Toledo University convocation on race relations are spurned. Negro ministers are suspicious of organizations and events which could displace them as the preeminent spokesmen for their community.

Leaders in the IMA cite several local incidents to illustrate their indispensable role in civil rights. They contend that a threatened IMA demonstration over discriminatory practices by Windsor House, a luxury apartment building, produced an equal accommodations pledge by the owners of the city's four largest apartment complexes. Ministers argue that quiet suggestions by officials in the NAACP and Federated Council were given force by the possibility that the IMA might invoke a demonstration. Similarly, a local radio station, WSPD, was warned of "possible reprisals" by the IMA if it persisted in the use of "racial tags" in crime reporting; the station agreed to revise its policy shortly after the IMA called a mass protest meeting.

But the militant tone which the IMA assumes on occasion is intended primarily for its critics and potential rivals in the Negro community. By calling mass protest meetings and threatening demonstrations or upheavals (which have yet to take place), Negro ministers assert that they are "the leaders of the people." In practice, the ministers are fearful of demonstrations, which "could get out of hand," and are dedicated to what they call "the Toledo way" in race relations. This means discussions and negotiation through the Board of Community Relations, on which prominent Negro ministers have been active.[20] Several Negro ministers believe that the Board of Community Relations has contributed significantly to "the unusually good atmosphere which Toledo has achieved in race relations." Negro ministers, like officials in the NAACP and the Federated Council, consider the lines of communi-

---

[20] The Board of Community Relations, the municipal race relations agency, was established in 1951; the IMA and other organizations are represented on the Board.

cation between white and Negro leaders to be cause for an optimistic appraisal of race relations in Toledo. Many Negro ministers also share the Republican loyalties of the lay leaders whom they distrust.

The slight differences of style between the IMA and other organizations indicate the relative insecurity which Negro ministers feel about their position as negotiators rather than a dissatisfaction with the method and its results. Indeed, the limited education and isolation of some ministers (in comparison with attorneys and other professional men) may lead them to place an even higher value on their few contacts with whites and on the significance of presenting "the Negro view" to them. Thus one minister commented:

> A white leader in this community invited me to his home after a meeting. We had coffee and talked. He introduced me to his wife and children. I could tell that he and his family accepted me as a person. This, to me, indicates what we can do in Toledo. I have confidence in the civil rights progress we can make with this kind of situation.

CORE. A small group of the young and discontented are organized in the local chapter of CORE, which has 50 to 75 members.[21] A few of the members have been active in the civil rights movement in the South, where they have spent time in Albany (Georgia) or Birmingham (Alabama) jails; others are students, both Negro and white, at the University of Toledo or young working people eager to accelerate civil rights progress in Toledo. The first Toledo CORE chapter, established in 1961, lost its charter from the national organization as a result of the divisive, controversial conduct of its leaders. It was reestablished in 1963 but has lacked continuity of leadership. It has also encountered hostility and suspicion from other Negro leaders. Leaders in the NAACP and the Federated Council have distrusted CORE's inclination for direct action and disliked its implication that they were insufficiently militant. Negro ministers and others have called attention to the youth of CORE leaders, "supported by white students, not by Negroes." Leaders in the IMA have made it clear that they will not sanction direct action, actual or threatened, if it is not under church control.[22]

---

[21] Membership estimates are from a local CORE official.

[22] CORE's interest in direct action is a matter of inclination rather than practice in Toledo. A CORE leader was instrumental in organizing a sympathy march for Selma, Alabama, but this is the extent of its direct action.

CORE leaders have grasped for local issues to bolster their position and enlarge their following. They have attempted, with little success, to focus attention on civil rights questions in urban renewal and the school system. NAACP leaders are disparaged as "Uncle Toms seeking personal gratification"; ministers are criticized for their support of elected officials and local agencies willing to give them "only token integration." Local CORE leaders, in accordance with the policy of the national organization, have attempted to develop plans for political action; yet this hope and others are unfulfilled. CORE has not yet developed an organization capable of commanding widespread attention from Negroes, and many white leaders do not know of its existence.[23]

Interrelationships among civil rights groups. Leaders in the NAACP, Federated Council, IMA, and CORE are conscious of strains between their organizations. But underlying these differences are widely shared values and aspirations. Race consciousness, the inescapable impact of being a Negro, is a consistent theme.[24] One lawyer reiterated this conviction:

> I've led an integrated life, to quite a degree. Some people in my position have tried to disavow race, to disavow any connection with it. But I know this is impossible. It involves me. It will involve my children. Discrimination by its very nature does not recognize educational differences. It's a problem for all Negroes alike.

Negroes who achieve distinction are both admired and resented; their accomplishments are a source of pride and anxiety:

> Dr. X [a medical doctor] has had a remarkable career. You've got to admire him, what he's done. But sometimes I get the impression that he doesn't think he's a Negro any more. But he is. It's something that's always with you.

Other leaders explained that in addition to the inescapability of a black skin, there is "a colored way of thinking" which whites can neither know nor imagine.

---

[23] The departure of the CORE president in 1966 left the organization near collapse.

[24] This conclusion is in accord with the findings of Wilson, *Negro Politics*, pp. 169–214, and St. Clair Drake and Horace R. Cayton, *Black Metropolis* (New York: Harper & Row, 1945), pp. 718–728.

Negro leaders insist that their aspirations are simple. "What we want," one Negro minister explained "is just what any other American citizen wants—minus nothing, plus nothing."[25] Others called for the end of race prejudice and the brotherhood of all men. Several leaders recounted personal experiences of maltreatment and humiliation to explain their deep condemnation of discrimination. Yet the hope that color barriers will be destroyed does not imply that Negro leaders seek assimilation into white society or the end of a specifically Negro community and consciousness. Some leaders believe or hope that Negroes will choose to maintain segregated living patterns, if granted an option. Those in the churches and professions who have achieved positions of leadership have no desire to destroy the community which has given them a comfortable, satisfying life. The sense of race consciousness which influences their efforts to end discrimination often heightens their interest in the continuation of the Negro community. The Negro leader may have a greater economic and psychological attachment to the Negro community than others who live there.

Widespread agreement on general aspirations provides no assurance of unity on specific objectives and methods, however. Negro leaders, like union leaders, find it easier to deal with national and state issues than with local questions. The race position, as well as the labor position, is fairly well defined in national and state politics. Negro leaders can, with little difficulty or disagreement, oppose Barry Goldwater; urge the passage of the civil rights bill of 1964, the voting rights bill of 1965, and a state fair housing law; and express support for Southern demonstrations and boycotts led by Martin Luther King.

For most Negro leaders, civil rights at the local level means specific grievances to be corrected. Negro officials seek to eliminate certain offensive local practices in much the same way that business and labor leaders do. The larger urban context in which discrimination and poverty appear receives little attention. Very few of the leaders interviewed indicated a concern for advancing the cause of the Negro by community programs in urban renewal, recreation, public education, and housing. Negro leaders in Toledo are not strongly committed to either status goals, such as fair housing, or welfare goals, such as improved streets and schools in Negro areas. For the most part, their attention has been directed to token goals,

[25] *The Bronze Raven,* July 10, 1965, p. 1.

such as the equal employment pledge by major companies (many of which were already bound by the President's pledge for equal opportunity), the fair practices pledge signed by luxury apartments, and the satisfaction of consultation and recognition from white leaders. The question of a wider, continuing role by Negro leaders and organizations is unresolved.[26]

Views of Negro Critics

A few Negro critics in organized labor, the ministry, and the Negro press have questioned the impact of civil rights leadership without a strong civic or political organization behind it. Skeptics reject the common assumption that Toledo is, as one Negro leader described it, "a very homey place, where communication is rapid and there is no barrier between the Negro leader and the top white leadership." To a minority of Negro leaders, the "behind the scenes" approach has produced few striking advances and little follow-through on gains such as the equal employment pledge. Furthermore, it provides a veil of mystery for what the leaders are actually doing. An editorial in *The Bronze Raven,* referring to a discussion of *de facto* segregation, commented:

> J. Frank Troy, president of the Toledo NAACP, horned in about working quietly behind the scenes on the question. Mr. Troy is forever working quietly behind the scenes. Why is it that the business of the NAACP has to be carried on behind the scenes? If this is true, a lot of people are going to be asking for their membership refunds.[27]

Critics urge greater unity and militancy in the major civil rights organizations rather than a new effort through CORE. The IMA, they suggest, should confront the whole problem instead of determining its actions on the basis of occupational jealousy. According to one critic:

---

[26] The discussion and differences in Toledo are mild in comparison with some cities. See Jack L. Walker, "Protest and Negotiation: A Case Study of Negro Leadership in Atlanta, Georgia," *Midwest Journal of Political Science,* VII (May 1963), 99–124.

[27] *The Bronze Raven,* November 13, 1965, p. 2. *The Bronze Raven* has been a frequent critic of Troy. See the editorial comment on June 19, 1965, p. 2.

> The Ministerial Alliance has been governed more by personal ambition, underlying rivalries and fears than a belief that the Negro must move forward. The ministers want to be the spokesmen in civil rights, but the approach has been passive, personal.

Dissenters argue that the IMA, if it is to be effective, must overcome its isolation and work with other organizations, such as the Federated Council and the NAACP, which also need strengthening.

An NAACP under the leadership of a deputy sheriff appears particularly unsatisfactory. Partisan overtones and political conflicts have, in the judgment of critics—especially Democrats—seriously weakened the impact of the NAACP. In December 1964, Negro leaders in the UAW supported a progressive, well-educated young minister for the presidency of the NAACP. Although the candidate was defeated in a four-way contest, President Troy's victory margin represented less than 50 per cent of the votes cast. The conflict continued in September 1965, when a UAW official defeated one of Troy's deputies in a contest for representation on the state executive board of the NAACP.[28]

But even dissident Negro leaders favor a slight rather than a radical change of emphasis in local civil rights activity. They want more aggressive leadership, willing and ready to talk, but also able to hold out the possibility of demonstrations:

> The greatest tool of the NAACP or any civil rights organization is demonstrations—to show up the inequities heaped upon Negroes. Troy is politically hog-tied as a member of the sheriff's department. He can't advocate demonstrations without being damaged politically. I'm not advocating demonstrations, but generally progress can't be and isn't made until the possibility of demonstrations exists.

The critics' prescription calls for more vigorous civic and political organization with which to support efforts at negotiation. Dissenters in organized labor, the NAACP, and the churches believe that the established Negro leaders have failed to realize the significance of

---

[28] For a discussion of conflicts in the Ohio NAACP, see *The Blade*, September 18, 1965, p. 3, and September 19, 1965, p. 2. Local Negro leaders prominent in organized labor include a UAW international representative and the UAW chief steward at Kaiser Jeep. In 1966 the balance of power in the Toledo NAACP appeared to be shifting away from the Troy faction. Troy declined to seek another term, and Robert A. Culp, the minister defeated in 1964, was elected president.

mass support and political strength in achieving improvements in civil rights. The publisher of *The Bronze Raven* has repeatedly emphasized the need for political organization and activity.[29]

But most Negro leaders are more entranced with the gains possible through meeting with corporation executives than with the task of political organization. Furthermore, Negro leaders, like union and business leaders, consider most of the activities of city council inconsequential. Although they are pleased with the consultation and recognition received from a friendly mayor, such as John W. Potter, few Negro leaders see any compelling reason to work for the election of council candidates of their race or party. Most Negroes active in politics hold subordinate positions in political parties which have never won victories by the strength of their ward and precinct organization or their local campaign efforts. Political organization is weak in Negro areas, and party structures are even more tenuous in Negro wards than they are elsewhere.

Negroes in Politics

In Toledo, Negroes suffer the political disadvantages of weak party organizations and an at-large electoral system. James Wilson has observed that the entrance of Negroes into city politics is related to the density of the Negro area, the size of the basic political unit, and the character of the party system.[30] In Chicago a Negro was first elected to city council in 1915.[31] The concentration of Negroes in small wards with representation on the city council facilitated the early and continued election of Negroes in Chicago. Negro candidates have also been successful in the ward-based poli-

---

[29] *The Bronze Raven,* October 16, 1965, p. 2, and November 6, 1965, p. 2. Editorials in *The Bronze Raven* suggesting that the IMA and the NAACP lead a united community campaign for the election of two Negro candidates to city council in November 1965 went unheeded by most Negro leaders.

[30] See James Q. Wilson, *Negro Politics,* pp. 21–47. Wilson points out that the large districts and diverse minority groups of New York may have delayed the development of Negro political influence in that city. On the subject of governmental structure and Negro politics, also see Wilson, ''The Flamboyant Mr. Powell,'' *Commentary,* XLI (January 1966), 31–36.

[31] The development of Negro politics in Chicago is discussed by Harold Gosnell, *Negro Politics: The Rise of Negro Politics in Chicago* (Chicago: University of Chicago Press, 1935).

tics of St. Louis, Cleveland, and New York.[32] Furthermore, the party organizations in large cities such as Chicago, New York, and Cleveland have attempted to widen their support by "balanced tickets" and a careful distribution of "recognition" to minority groups.[33] In Los Angeles, however, there are neither small wards nor active city-wide party organizations. The dispersion of the Negro population, large, heterogeneous electoral districts, and nonpartisanship have impeded the development of Negro political influence. Negro candidates have also fared poorly in the nonpartisan, at-large politics of Detroit, where a Negro was not elected to Common Council until 1957. An at-large, nonpartisan electoral system has effectively excluded Negroes from the Boston Common Council.

Toledo has had one Negro councilman, James B. Simmons, Jr., an attorney first elected in 1945. Simmons' entry into politics was facilitated by the system of proportional representation initiated with the council-manager charter of 1935 and abandoned after the 1949 election. Cincinnati had the PR system from 1925 to 1957, and one or two Negroes served on ten of the 15 councils elected during the 32 years that PR was in effect.[34] Negro candidates in Cincinnati were elected to city council with as little as ten per cent of the vote. In 1945 Simmons and his supporters hoped to achieve a similar result in Toledo. With strong support from the Negro churches and voters, Simmons placed ninth in the balloting and was elected. Although his margin of victory increased in the 1947 and 1949 elections, Councilman Simmons was defeated in 1951, when PR was no longer in effect.

In 1953 Simmons returned to office with the support of groups which had earlier regarded him with caution. During the early and middle 1950s, he had the endorsement of *The Blade*, the United

[32] For a discussion of the early days of Negro politics in New York, see Gilbert Osofsky, *Harlem: The Making of a Ghetto* (New York: Harper & Row, 1966), pp. 159–179.

[33] Raymond E. Wolfinger presents an interpretation of this in "Some Consequences of Ethnic Politics," M. Kent Jennings and Harmon Zeigler, eds., *The Electoral Process* (Englewood Cliffs, N.J.: Prentice-Hall, 1966), pp. 42–55. Also of interest is the discussion by Nathan Glazer and Daniel P. Moynihan, *Beyond the Melting Pot* (Cambridge, Mass.: Harvard University Press and M.I.T. Press, 1963).

[34] Ralph A. Straetz, *PR Politics in Cincinnati* (New York: New York University Press, 1958), pp. 109–126. The possibility that a Negro could be elected mayor of Cincinnati was exploited in the campaign resulting in the repeal of PR. A Negro councilman, Ted Berry (R.), had run second in the previous election (1955) and had served as vice-mayor.

Labor Committee, the City Manager League, and the Democratic Party in addition to consistent support in the Negro wards. Simmons' political career became more complicated when he sided with the City Manager League against the Democratic Party in the bitter charter conflict of 1959. He rejoined party ranks by voting for a party (strong-mayor) Democrat to serve as mayor in the divided council of 1959–1961. This bargain made Simmons vice-mayor, but it cost him his good government support and twinge-of-conscience votes in white wards. Toledo voters and community leaders were willing to sanction Negro representation on city council, but a Negro vice-mayor and the thought of a Negro mayor were cause for alarm. The poor performance of the 1959–1961 council did little to overcome bad feeling caused by the methods and results of the 1959 election for mayor and vice-mayor. Simmons was easily defeated in 1961.[35]

Negro leaders both criticize and defend Councilman Simmons' political career. He is described as an excellent councilman and the leading Uncle Tom; but he is accused of "selling out" on the City Manager League and on the Negro community. One Negro leader commented: "Before Simmons got enmeshed in personal politics, he always had wide community support and endorsements from those who favor good government. He made a fatal mistake when he sold out to become vice-mayor." In another opinion: "After J. B. [Simmons] got elected, he forgot what he was there for. He sold out on us without a second thought."

Simmons, despite the charges against him, is credited with a contribution to the Negro community. His accomplishments and his sell-outs are rarely substantiated with specific examples. Simmons' career in itself was a source of satisfaction and apprehension. The pride in having a Negro on city council was counteracted by the fear that a Negro could not be in such a position without considering his own "personal gratification" (a phrase used frequently by Negro leaders) over the interests of the race. Among Negroes the race interests of men who have satisfied their personal aspirations are suspect. The fact that most Negro leaders in Toledo have satis-

[35] In the 1961 election, Simmons placed 17th out of 18 candidates. There is a widespread feeling among both white and Negro leaders that Simmons' term as vice-mayor and the possibility of a Negro mayor were unspoken factors in the passage of the 1963 charter amendment providing for a directly elected mayor.

fied their personal goals perhaps accounts for the frequency with which they charge each other with "selling out."[36]

Three Negro candidates have run for city council in the two elections since Simmons' defeat. Wyatt Johnston (D.) placed 14th out of 18 candidates in 1963. Clayton Umbles (D.) placed 11th and Eddie Cole (R.) 16th among 16 candidates in 1965. Johnston and Umbles, particularly, received the editorial support of *The Blade*. Umbles also had the United Labor Committee endorsement, while Cole and Johnston were supported by the Teamsters. The crucial votes in the Negro wards were lacking, however. Johnston drew a notably feeble response from Negro leaders and neither Cole nor Umbles had the benefit of a strenuous community effort in the 6th and 8th wards. Several leaders who praised both Umbles and Cole predicted their defeat long before the campaign started. The weakness of political organization and bloc voting for Negro candidates was evident in the election results. The 8th ward, with a percentage turn-out of 59.6, and the 6th ward, with a percentage turn-out of 51.3, ranked 20th and 22nd (out of 22 wards) in voting participation.[37] Umbles received 86.5 per cent of the total vote in the 8th ward, but Cole drew only 61.8 per cent. Cole's support was nearly equalled by the Democratic mayoralty candidate, Ned Skeldon, who received 60.8 per cent of the votes cast.[38]

The 1961 Fair Housing Controversy

Although most Negro leaders have not attached great importance to political organization and representation, they have occasionally wanted certain actions from city council. The 1961 controversy over

[36] For a discussion of this phenomenon, see Wilson, *Negro Politics*, p. 176.

[37] Turn-out in partisan elections is generally higher. In the 1964 presidential election, there was a turn-out of 74.8 per cent in the 6th ward and 85.7 per cent in the 8th ward.

[38] See William E. Wright, *Memphis Politics: A Study in Racial Bloc Voting* (New York: McGraw-Hill Co., 1962). The effectiveness of bloc voting in Durham, North Carolina, is discussed by Burgess, *Negro Leadership*, pp. 65–67. Also see William J. McKenna, "The Negro Vote in Philadelphia Elections," *Pennsylvania History*, XXXII (October 1965), 407–415; and John O'Shea, "Newark's Negroes Move toward Power," *Atlantic*, XXVI (November 1965), 90–98.

a fair housing ordinance illustrates the civic and political role of Negro leaders and their impact on council decisions. In April 1961, the Board of Community Relations voted to submit suggestions for a fair housing ordinance to city council.[39] Vice-Mayor Simmons responded by expressing his regret that these suggestions had been introduced in an election year, when embarrassing political implications could arise.[40] Fair housing, the vice-mayor predicted, would raise a difficult issue for councilmen seeking reelection.[41] Despite the reservations of some councilmen, a city council committee opened hearings on the BCR recommendations for legislation to prohibit discrimination in the sale, lease, transfer, or negotiation of real estate.[42] Negro spokesmen urged city council to consider the severe shortage in housing available to the rapidly increasing Negro population. The Teamsters, the AFL-CIO Council, and Catholic, Jewish, and Protestant organizations joined the NAACP and the IMA in testifying in behalf of the ordinance, while the Board of Realtors and the Toledo Association of Home Builders indicated their expected disapproval.

In July 1961, the city council committee voted two to one to recommend approval of an ordinance forbidding real estate operators from refusing to sell, lease, rent, list, advertise, or show property for discriminatory reasons; prohibiting financial institutions from discrimination in extending financial assistance for the purchase, construction, or maintenance of real property; and forbidding discriminatory advertising by all persons, real estate operators, and financial institutions.[43] The recommendations of the Board of Community Relations, NAACP, and IMA were disregarded in provisions establishing a maximum penalty of $100, with 30-day imprisonment for failure to pay the fine.

The mildness of the penalty did not allay the objections of opponents in city council and in the community. The first reading of the ordinance in city council provoked a three and one-half hour debate in which five councilmen were at one point opposed to the legislation. Only after exemptions were granted for homeowners selling their own property, for property owners renting less than

[39] *The Blade*, April 26, 1961, p. 29.
[40] *The Blade*, May 10, 1961, p. 35.
[41] *The Blade*, May 15, 1961, p. 13.
[42] *The Blade*, July 27, 1961, p. 25.
[43] *Ibid.*

five family units, and for advertising by private persons did a majority of councilmen approve the ordinance.

In the weeks following the first reading of the ordinance, the opposition reiterated its objections. Several councilmen contended that the ordinance was "a deprivation of the seller's right of private contract" and "a subterfuge destroying the property owner's basic freedom to sell property to the person of his choice."[44] Others predicted that such an ordinance would inflame rather than alleviate racial tension. Realtors and home builders protested the infringement of "the inherent right to own and dispose of real property." An official in an East Toledo civic club contended that the ordinance in fact discriminated against the white race. A local businessman who claimed to be "the individual who slowed the drive in Little Rock and slowed the drive in Montgomery," vowed that he would prevent Negroes from wrecking property values and white neighborhoods in Toledo. The NAACP, he said, was trying to force the unfounded idea of equality on whites whether they liked it or not.[45]

Shortly after the first favorable vote, the real estate and home-building organizations threatened a city-wide referendum if city council should pass the ordinance.[46] Nevertheless, the second reading of the ordinance on August 23 produced another five-to-four decision to approve. Officials in the Board of Realtors and the Toledo Association of Home Builders were soon at work gathering the 14,600 signatures (15 per cent of those voting in the last council election) necessary to place the fair housing ordinance on the ballot in the November election. Realtors and homebuilders argued that advocates of fair housing in city council and the BCR had failed to inform the public and were attempting to "railroad through" a "hurry-up" ordinance.[47]

The day before the third and final vote on the ordinance, *The Blade* played its hand. Fearful of a divisive, damaging referendum battle, *The Blade* urged postponement and renegotiation of the issue. The threat of a referendum, said *The Blade*, "is a possibility so disruptive and potentially harmful to community relations that Toledo cannot afford to take it." *The Blade* continued:

[44] See the *Toledo City Journal*, August 12, 1961, p. 1031.
[45] *Toledo City Journal*, August 23, 1961, pp. 1095–1096.
[46] *The Blade*, August 9, 1961, p. 25.
[47] *Ibid.*

It would be particularly unwise, it seems to us, to risk a devastating campaign on an emotional issue that is bound to be misinterpreted through the nation and the world as a nose count on prejudice.[48]

After criticizing the Board of Community Relations for failing to work with realtors and home builders before presenting its recommendations to city council, *The Blade* urged the proponents of fair housing to seek a compromise. In the event that this failed, city council was advised to refer the ordinance back to committee to prevent a few individuals and groups from "saddling Toledo with an inflammatory campaign in the name of 'community relations.' "[49]

The day after *The Blade's* editorial appeared, city council voted (6–3) to delay its third and final vote on the fair housing ordinance to permit amendments to be offered.[50] Several councilmen were quick to echo *The Blade's* complaint that the BCR had failed to work with the realtors and home builders in "laying the groundwork for the legislation." One councilman recommended that the Board of Community Relations be reorganized to include representatives from the Toledo Board of Realtors, Association of Home Builders, Savings and Loan Associations and additional members from the Chamber of Commerce.[51] The home builders and realtors, pleased at the turn of events, protested that they were invited to appear at council hearings only once and were not asked to participate in drafting the ordinance.[52]

The voices of fair housing proponents were scarcely heard in the clamor. John Yager, chairman of city council's committee on fair housing, vainly argued that an ordinance which has had six hearings and three readings "is not being rammed down anyone's throat."[53] The executive secretary of the Board of Community

---

[48] *The Blade*, September 10, 1961, Section II, p. 4 (© Toledo Blade Co.).

[49] *Ibid.*

[50] *The Blade*, September 11, 1961, p. 1.

[51] The composition of the Board of Community Relations, defined by a 1951 ordinance, is: Chamber of Commerce, 6; AFL, 3; Council of Churches, 2; Catholic Church, 2; Jewish Welfare Federation, 2; and Interdenominational Ministerial Alliance, 2. In 1965 there were several suggestions that these categories be revised or eliminated, but no changes were made. There are 5 "public" members.

[52] *The Blade*, September 12, 1961, p. 17.

[53] *Ibid.*

Relations recalled that of hundreds of organizations contacted by the BCR, only the realtors and home builders refused to endorse the suggestions for a fair housing ordinance. Leaders of the NAACP and the IMA appealed for passage of the ordinance. One NAACP official argued that "inasmuch as the Emancipation Proclamation freed Negroes from slavery, council should not hesitate to pass legislation which would embody those principles."[54] Vice-Mayor Simmons, after reiterating his belief that such a controversial issue should not have been raised at election time, suggested that it was time to see if Toledo was a Little Rock.[55]

The protests of fair housing advocates were to no avail. City councilmen met with representatives of the Board of Community Relations, Board of Realtors, and Association of Home Builders to negotiate a compromise ordinance, which was passed (6–3) on September 25, 1961.[56] The compromise ordinance extended the coverage of the law to include private persons selling their homes without a real estate agent. In addition, it provided for a Fair Housing Board with "the power to engage in conciliation efforts and determine facts." The penalty clause was omitted, however.

Spokesmen for all groups attempted to find cause for satisfaction in the new ordinance, with varying degrees of success. Vice-Mayor Simmons and leaders in the NAACP and the IMA expressed gratitude for the realtors' and home builders' "willingness to compromise" and for the declarations of good intent by these groups.[57] But several officials in the Board of Realtors and the Home Builders' Association remained openly intransigent, indicating their continued opposition to a fair housing ordinance in any form.[58] Within a month of its passage, the ordinance was challenged in the courts, where it remained until March 1965, when the Ohio Supreme Court ruled it unconstitutional for lack of a penalty provision.

In the spring of 1965, several councilmen were apprehensive that the unconstitutionality of the 1961 ordinance and the possible defeat of a state fair housing bill might again raise the specter of fair housing in city politics. City councilmen voted unanimously to

[54] *Ibid.*

[55] *Ibid.* Simmons' comments produced a disapproving editorial in *The Blade*, September 13, 1961, p. 13.

[56] *The Blade*, September 25, 1961, p. 13.

[57] *The Blade*, September 20, 1961, p. 1.

[58] *Ibid.*

endorse a state fair housing law, which passed, to the relief of city politicians.[59]

City Officials and Civil Rights

Although Negro leaders are confident of their bargaining position with city officials, past experiences, such as the events of 1961, do not always justify this faith. Among the city officials of the mid-1960s, few share Mayor Potter's commitment to civil rights. In the opinion of one councilman:

> The methods used by Negro leaders here have been cold, hard pressure tactics, with veiled innuendos and threats, finally retreating to a more moderate tone through committee action. Seldom have their [Negroes'] demands been refused. The [Negro] leaders have been effective, because on a number of occasions they have dealt with people with no guts. But we've gone as far as we can go and we must remember that the majority has rights also.

In another judgment:

> The Negroes would like to be in power. In the meantime they want political appointments, fair employment, fair housing, and other pieces of so-called antidiscrimination or favoritism legislation, depending on your point of view. Any time they don't get their way, they'll threaten a demonstration. And the more success there is, the more extreme they become.

Nor are leaders in other community organizations as accessible and understanding as Negro leaders describe them. The business executive who has to ask his secretary's assistance or refer to files to produce the names of more than one or two Negro leaders is not greatly concerned with civil rights problems in Toledo. Some labor leaders who support civil rights legislation in national and state politics privately say that "every man's home is his castle" when a local fair housing issue arises. *The Blade,* a strong advocate of civil rights measures in state and national politics, is fearful of the

[59] For an account of the Ohio Supreme Court ruling on Toledo's 1961 fair housing ordinance, see *The Blade,* March 10, 1965, p. 1. In the late summer and fall of 1966, there were new moves for another try at a local fair housing ordinance.

inflammatory, disruptive effects of local action.[60] The local Democratic Party has made only a feeble effort to recruit Negro candidates or develop an organization in the 6th and 8th wards, where it is content to benefit from the party loyalties of national politics. Mayor Potter and Governor Rhodes, rather than the local Republican organization, have taken the initiative in seeking Negro support. The city government and major community groups are less than responsive to civil rights.

Yet there is little obvious impatience or frustration among Negro leaders; they are not seriously dissatisfied with their role in the city. They represent what James Q. Wilson has called the old order of Negro leadership.[61] In the old order, a Negro community was represented by a group of accepted leaders, who were men of prestige, of social position, and of personal achievement. Ministers, and to a lesser extent doctors, lawyers, businessmen, and politicians, were prominent in the old order. Action on behalf of civil rights goals was sporadic and poorly organized; little was attempted and little was accomplished. "Ends were typically sought by a deputation of leading Negroes paying a call on a public official or by the formation of a committee."[62] Under the old order, contacts with the white community were relatively infrequent and ritualistic, and the goals were merely token. In some cities the old order is giving way to more specialized, professional leadership drawn from renewed civic and political organizations. But the old order is still dominant in Toledo.[63] The Negroes in public positions and the offices of civil rights organizations are (with few exceptions) prestige leaders. They are "good" Negroes who wish to preserve and protect the pleasure of representing the Negro community.

[60] *The Blade* aroused the ire of various religious organizations when it declined to publish a full-page ad with the names of those signing a freedom of residence pledge in a campaign for fair housing conducted by the Interfaith Conference on Religion and Race. The Interfaith Conference campaign was supported by the five member organizations, the Council of Churches, Jewish Welfare Federation, First Unitarian Church, Roman Catholic Diocese of Toledo, and Bahai World Faith. *The Blade* feared that signatures might not be authentic, thus opening the possibility of libel charges.

[61] Wilson, *Negro Politics*, pp. 295–298.

[62] Wilson, p. 296.

[63] See Lewis Bowman, "Racial Discrimination and Negro Leadership Problems: The Case of 'Northern City,' " *Social Forces*, XLIV (December 1965), 173–186. The period following the Watts upheaval in Los Angeles and the disturbances in other cities has not produced a noticeable change in the composition, approach, or tenor of Negro leadership in Toledo.

Negroes and Reform Institutions

Few Negro leaders are eager to alter the political system in which they have gained a certain status and recognition. A majority of Negroes in positions of leadership support reform institutions. In fact, some of the strongest exponents of reform in the city are Negroes. Lincoln Republicans in the NAACP and the IMA argue that the council-manager form of government can be responsive to all groups, while holding the good of the city above any particular interest. They defend the ideal of the nonpolitical government and the public official elected for merit rather than party. One minister argued:

> The nonpartisan ballot means that no one party can come up and monopolize the situation. It makes elected officials responsible to everyone and under pressure to nobody. The city manager form sees to the execution of the laws without undue political influence from the outside. It's a form of government which does not have to yield too much to political pressure.

The professional men in the Federated Council also find the manager form appealing:

> The city manager plan allows the greatest possibility for competent, professional handling of complex problems. There are still political overtones in Toledo, but there has been an evolutionary progress toward more efficient methods over the years. I hope that the direct election of the mayor won't be a step toward more political government and away from competent administration. Government's much too important to leave it to amateurs.

The scarcity of Negro politicians has not produced significant dissatisfaction with the political system. James B. Simmons, Jr., the one successful Negro politician, was a good government Democrat, a strong advocate of nonpartisanship, at-large elections, and the council-manager plan. One Negro Democrat commented:

> I've always opposed the ward system. Negroes ought to be elected by the people as a whole. Electing Negroes and others from wards means alley-paving and deals. Under the city manager plan it is possible to take a city-wide point of view, to consider

things without seeing the party boss, and to keep politics at a minimum. That's good for Negroes and for the community.

Several leaders argued that it is more desirable for Negroes to elect men acceptable to the whole city than to achieve political influence on the basis of numbers and residential segregation.

Not all Negro leaders are active advocates of municipal reform, however. Some are indifferent to the issue. This middle group contends that the form of government is inconsequential for Negroes and for the city. Yet when pressed these leaders favor reform in much the same way that business executives do: If the form of government makes no difference, there is little justification for changing it, especially when the existing situation is satisfactory.

A minority of Negro leaders in the ministry, civil rights organizations, and other positions of leadership support the strong mayor form of government. This, they argue, could give the city greater leadership and more aggressive action on programs such as urban renewal. In the minority view, an openly political system under executive direction would also be more responsive to Negroes and other lower-income groups than the distinctly middle-class government existing under reform institutions.

Summary

Prominent Negroes, like the key officials in labor and industry, have a satisfying degree of community recognition. Although business executives, labor officials, and Negro leaders represent groups which are relatively uninvolved in the community, they are consulted, appointed to committees, and invited to public ceremonies. They can achieve goals on specific problems without undertaking a major role in the community. Negro leaders, as well as labor and business officials, enjoy the prestige of community leadership without responsibility.

The civic and political weakness of Negroes is part of the disorganization and lethargy prevailing in the city as a whole. These conditions are particularly costly for Negroes, however. Negroes are more isolated and more impoverished than other groups. Without organization, they receive less consideration than powerful labor unions and national corporations and they need more. Schools, streets, recreation, law enforcement, and housing cannot be written off as irrelevant, in the manner of the corporation executive considering the community where his firm or branch now happens to be located. Business and labor leaders can afford to accept reform institutions because they have been safe and comfortable. Negro leaders support reform despite its repressive effect on the political influence of the group which they "lead." In an odd turn of events, Negro leaders are the keepers of the middle-class, white, Anglo-Saxon political ethos.

12 THE PRESS AND THE LOCAL COMMUNITY

In addition to reporting the activities of labor and business, political parties, city council, and civil rights organizations, the press is itself a participant in the local political system. In its news coverage, feature stories, and editorial positions, a newspaper is both chronicle and protagonist; it records the events of the local community, but it is not a neutral or inert medium; it provides organization and interpretation as well as information. Publishers and editors have considerable freedom in selecting issues for attention, so that editorials, feature stories, and the number and location of news articles all reflect an assessment of a given question. The press, in short, has an important role in determining both the issues before the community and what people know and think about these issues.[1]

Newspapers no longer hold a monopoly in news reporting and analysis, however; the rapid growth and multiplication of television and radio stations has challenged the primacy of the press. Nevertheless, newspapers retain an advantage in local news coverage and comment. As Banfield and Wilson point out, the local newspaper is often rooted in the com-

---

[1] For a discussion of the relationship of news reporting and public issues and decisions, see Douglass Cater, *The Fourth Branch of Government* (Boston, Mass.: Houghton Mifflin Co., 1959), pp. 1–22.

munity in a way that the broadcasting station is not.[2] A broadcaster depends on his network affiliation and revenues from national advertisers, while a newspaper is more oriented to the community and to advertising revenues from local department and grocery stores.

The Blade—Its History

In Toledo the paramount news source is *The Blade,* an evening paper with a daily circulation of 180,833. The morning *Times,* also owned by *Blade* publisher Paul Block, Jr., provides no real competition for *The Blade,* although the editorial positions of the two papers differ.[3] Of the television and radio stations in the Toledo area, only WSPD has made a notable effort to compete with *The Blade* in reporting and interpreting local news.[4] Despite WSPD's introduction of nightly radio and television editorials in 1961, *The Blade* remains supreme in detailed local news coverage and wide-ranging, biting editorial comment.

The Blade began publication in 1835, more than a year before the incorporation of Toledo.[5] The paper was founded by a group of Whig leaders to advance the cause of their party and community. After the demise of the Whigs, *The Blade* became an unswerving proponent of the Republican Party. The paper early established a tradition of strong editorial positions, advocating the abolition of slavery and later the radical Republican program of reconstruction. National and local Republican candidates could expect regular support from *The Blade,* which fulminated in vain against Golden Rule Jones and the independent movement.

In the early decades of the twentieth century, *The Blade's* Re-

---

[2] Edward C. Banfield and James Q. Wilson, *City Politics* (Cambridge, Mass.: Harvard University Press and M.I.T. Press, 1963), p. 314. Also see Leo Bogart, "Newspapers in the Age of Television," *Daedalus,* XCII (Winter 1963), 116–121.

[3] *The Blade* has a Sunday circulation of 186,074. *The Times,* which is not published on Sunday, has a daily circulation of 30,956. Circulation figures are from *N. W. Ayer and Son's Directory of Newspapers and Periodicals, 1966,* William F. McCallister, ed. (Philadelphia: N. W. Ayer and Son, 1966), p. 863.

[4] WSPD-TV is affiliated with ABC; WSPD-radio is an NBC affiliate.

[5] For an account of *The Blade's* history, see William Howard Taft, "The 'Toledo Blade': Its First One Hundred Years, 1835–1935" (unpublished Ph.D. dissertation, Studies in American Culture, Western Reserve University, 1950). Toledo received its charter by an act of the Ohio legislature passed on January 7, 1837.

publicanism continued as its strength grew. Its circulation surpassed that of its nearest rival in 1919.[6] In 1912 the paper briefly violated its party loyalty to support Theodore Roosevelt for the presidency on the Progressive ticket. *The Blade* gave its blessing to Warren Harding, Calvin Coolidge, and Herbert Hoover as well as to local and state Republican stalwarts; Woodrow Wilson, Franklin D. Roosevelt, and the anemic Toledo Democrats were frequently criticized, cautioned, and admonished.

With the death in 1941 of Paul Block, Sr., publisher since 1926, *The Blade* entered a new era. Paul Block, Jr., assumed control in 1942, and the paper gradually shifted to a more independent course.[7] In the 1950s and 1960s *The Blade* has endorsed candidates of both parties for national, state, and local offices. Although the preponderance of endorsements, particularly for state offices, continues to be with the Republicans, the position of *The Blade* can no longer be predicted by party loyalty.[8]

The Quality of The Blade

The Blade of the 1960s is an excellent paper. The publisher, far from being the absentee-executive increasingly characteristic of the American press, takes a deep interest in the operation of his paper.[9]

---

[6] For a discussion of *The Blade's* political and circulation battle with the *News-Bee*, a paper defunct since 1938, see Taft, ''The Toledo Blade,'' p. 525.

[7] Paul Block, Jr., and his brother, William Block, were elected copublishers of *The Blade* on September 29, 1942. Since that time Paul Block, Jr., has devoted his activities to *The Blade*, while William Block has directed the *Pittsburgh Post-Gazette*, purchased by his father in 1930. Taft, p. 533.

[8] *The Blade* is listed in *N. W. Ayer and Son's Directory* as an independent paper. *The Blade* endorsed its first Democratic presidential candidate in 1956, when it supported Adlai E. Stevenson. It also supported John F. Kennedy in 1960 and Lyndon B. Johnson in 1964. In its endorsements for all major partisan offices between 1952 and 1964, *The Blade* supported 56 Republicans and 40 Democrats. These figures do not include endorsements for county officials other than commissioners. When the elections for state secretary of state, auditor, attorney general, and treasurer are excluded, the balance of endorsements is 42 for Republicans and 38 for Democrats. *Blade* endorsements for 1966 were interrupted by a strike. Endorsements for city council will be considered later in this chapter.

[9] For a discussion of trends in newspaper ownership and management, see Raymond B. Nixon and Jean Ward, ''Trends in Newspaper Ownership,'' *Journalism Quarterly*, XXXVIII (Winter 1961), 3–12. Also of interest is Louis M. Lyons, ''Chain-Store Journalism,'' *The Reporter*, XXIII (December 1960), 60–63.

The character of *The Blade* reflects the publisher's standards. The staff, including the editor, associate editors, and reporters, is able, experienced, and varied, with a fair degree of specialization for a paper of its size. In addition to having its own foreign and Washington correspondents, *The Blade* has excellent writers specializing in science, education, labor, politics, and state government. While one reporter covers city hall, several writers report political, economic, and social developments within the local community. Whether the subject be NATO, medicare, reapportionment, or garbage incinerators, *The Blade* has a good record for first-hand reporting.

The depth and scope of *The Blade* are also evident in its editorial page, which is notable for its verve and originality. Instead of merely enunciating long-familiar clichés in the manner of many American newspapers, *The Blade* offers its own distinctive appraisal of international and domestic problems. *The Blade* editorial position lacks the predictable consistency of the *Detroit Free Press,* the *Oakland Tribune,* the *St. Louis Globe-Democrat,* or the *New York Times.* In taking either a liberal or a conservative position, *The Blade* hews its own course. The paper seldom resorts to such comfortable topics as the need for improved pest-control or the wonder of the changing seasons. Controversial questions are considered in a lively style that includes humor, irony, satire, and varying degrees of subtle and barbed criticism.

The Blade's local interests, as seen in news columns, feature stories, and editorials, cover the spectrum of community issues. Unlike other community organizations, *The Blade* has followed Toledo's urban renewal program with interest, as was evident in Chapter 9. The paper and its publisher provided crucial support and assistance in the development of the Toledo-Lucas County Port Authority and the creation of the Toledo State College of Medicine. *The Blade* has repeatedly indicated its concern for public education in the elementary and secondary schools, at Toledo University, and at Toledo University's community and technical college. Downtown redevelopment, industrial expansion, and civil liberties have long received its attention. The activities and vagaries of city council and other municipal agencies rarely escape scrutiny.[10]

[10] *The Blade's* local interests in the late 1950s are discussed by Reo M. Christenson, a former *Blade* editorial writer, in ''The Power of the Press: The Case of 'The Toledo Blade,' '' *Midwest Journal of Political Science,* III (August 1959), 227–240.

Criticism of The Blade's Policies

The Blade's local interests and the sharp edge of its editorials have not won universal appreciation from the community and its residents. *The Blade* is often depicted, by Toledo residents and leaders alike, as a capricious institution whose officials operate in a conspiratorial, vindictive manner. Leaders in every segment of the city voice resentment at *The Blade's* power and decry what they consider the destructive effects of its editorial comment and criticism. A business leader expressed a common opinion: *"The Blade* is more of a detriment than a help in local government and building up our city. It doesn't take strong stands, except to attack something. It's always tearing somebody down when it should be building them up."

Community leaders see *The Blade* as a powerful influence pervading the city. In the judgment of many officials, it seeks to obstruct and defy other organizations rather than to lead the community itself. One Negro leader commented: *"The Blade* doesn't control Toledo in a positive way, but it prevents others from doing so. It can block decisions and groups it doesn't like." Furthermore, some leaders complain that *The Blade's* disfavor is arbitrary. In the opinion of one business executive:

> Business seems to have a good relationship with *The Blade* sometimes, but it's peculiar. *The Blade* is like someone who gives you candy and quits . . . Or you could say *The Blade* is like someone who pats you on the head sometimes and hits you over the head other times. You remember the times he hits you over the head.

Nevertheless, the authority and impact of *Blade* judgments are widely respected; officials in all organizations feel compelled to harken to the editorial page. *Blade* officials are also believed to employ methods of persuasion more subtle than the editorial. One city councilman contended: "Paul Block wields great power. Once they have a decision at *The Blade* he will do anything for it—talk to anyone and everyone in the top circles of the city." The publisher and other *Blade* officials are sometimes depicted as moving stealthily behind the scenes, speaking softly but wielding the threat of future animosity on the editorial page or the denial of a valuable endorsement in the next election. Occasional politicians, Negro leaders, and union and business officials claim to have been drawn into star-chamber sessions at *The Blade*, where they say they have been asked to sacrifice principles for *Blade* sufferance in the future.

Some leaders believe that *The Blade* has succeeded in draining their organizations of integrity and independence. Thus one party official lamented the way some candidates covet, protect, and display a *Blade* endorsement at the expense of party identification and loyalty. A union spokesman argued:

> *The Blade* has the power to undercut its opposition. It has incurred the favor of both parties. Neither will risk its displeasure. In the last years Paul Block and Richard [Gosser, the former UAW leader] had gotten a good relationship, checking things out together. There was little chance that we [UAW] could move independently of *The Blade*.

Those who censure the power of *The Blade* and the press monopoly it holds usually place their hopes on WSPD rather than on the development of stronger community organizations. One Republican councilman envisioned the development of a "power play between *The Blade* and WSPD." A labor official described WSPD as "the only institution of any power that takes on *The Blade*." Others noted, however, that while WSPD has disavowed *Blade* positions on such questions as the location of a new Masonic dining and convention complex and the site of Toledo University's technical and community college, it has usually not offered a strong position of its own. WSPD's advocates admit that for every television and radio editorial questioning *The Blade*, there are many in behalf of tax breaks for the elderly, sobriety for teenagers, regulation of junk automobiles, and pigeon-control. Despite the hopes of some local leaders, WSPD's brief, ephemeral, and often innocuous editorials make it a weak counter to *The Blade*.

Although *The Blade's* predominance is universally recognized, it is received with differing degrees of emotion. Most leaders deplore the paper's critical bent, but only those who have felt the editorial lash express bitterness. One defeated candidate said:

> —————— [a *Blade* official] is an s.o.b., if I ever saw one. I couldn't count the number of editorials they've run against me in the last year or two. I've got a file full of them. Believe me, I'd sue for libel if I wanted to take the trouble.

Others are more philosophical, believing that they will regain the
paper's support in the future. Dissatisfaction is, in many cases,
balanced with a recognition that *The Blade* is a good paper, whose
officials are concerned with the future of Toledo. One Democratic
councilman concluded: *"The Blade* is often critical, but I think
Paul Block wants and tries to build up the community."

Views of Blade Officials on the Newspaper's Civic Role

Blade officials view the paper's role in the community more
cautiously than do leaders in other organizations. Their editorial
support, they point out, has not produced the election of favored
candidates such as Ned Skeldon; other candidates have repeatedly
gained election to city council with little or no assistance from the
paper. Nor do *Blade* officials find community organizations and
elected officials the obsequious creatures often described. Leaders in
major firms, labor unions, political parties, and Negro organizations
have often taken actions contrary to *The Blade's* preference. City
councilmen, despite their alleged deference to *The Blade,* have
remained remarkably resistant to editorial warnings on subjects
such as urban renewal. In the judgment of one *Blade* official:

> City councilmen are not always on the phone clearing actions
> with *The Blade,* as some people claim. On major disputes they are
> interested in *The Blade's* position. Some are more attuned to it
> than others, and some would like to use *The Blade* for their own
> purposes.

Blade leaders also note limits on the editorial comment considered
so potent by many community figures. Although editorials affect
decisions in some cases, they frequently go unheeded if the subject
touches a matter of community interest. The paper is often unsuccessful in gaining support for changes or innovations. One official
commented:

> *The Blade* is more successful at persuading those already pre-
> disposed to *The Blade* position. In changing opinions, *The
> Blade* is less successful. *The Blade* can't change fundamental
> convictions to any great extent. It works within existing pre-

dispositions. If *The Blade's* position fits with leaders' and voters' feelings, then it may work.

Blade officials agree with community leaders that criticism and opposition are the paper's most effective medium, but they are quick to deny that the paper has abused the function of criticism. A newspaper's responsibility, they argue, requires that it expose issues and call attention to local problems. Yet the impact of criticism alone provides an inadequate measure of *The Blade's* interests. In one opinion: "We have more success with negative positions than with putting a policy across. But this is always true. Negative positions are easier for politicians, too." The complaint that *The Blade* has tried to disparage the local community is dismissed: "*The Blade* has been critical, but it hasn't tried to tear down Toledo. After all, the interest of the community and the newspaper are tied together." If editorial controversies occasionally develop into vendettas, as one reporter suggested, they are for a worthy purpose which would otherwise go unrecognized.

Influence of The Blade in City Council Elections

The electoral influence of *The Blade* is less pervasive than its critics claim and wider than its officials suggest. Although *The Blade* has suffered some reverses at the polls, it has seen the election of many endorsed city council candidates. The precise effect of press endorsements on political attitudes and voting behavior is difficult to measure, however.[11] At times press endorsements may coincide with or reinforce larger influences or political trends. Nevertheless, an examination of city council election results reveals that *The Blade* is a significant consideration.

In the seven council elections between 1953 and 1965, more than three out of every four *Blade*-endorsed candidates were victorious.[12]

---

[11] One of the earliest of the few studies that have been concerned with the influence of the press on voting behavior is Harold Gosnell, *Machine Politics: Chicago Model* (Chicago: University of Chicago Press, 1937), pp. 156–183.

[12] In an examination of a number of California newspapers, James E. Gregg found a consistent and even higher percentage in the election of endorsed local candidates. Gregg also noted that nonpartisanship contributed to the power of

All *Blade*-endorsed incumbents gained reelection to city council, and more than two of every three *Blade*-endorsed nonincumbents were successful. *Blade*-endorsed councilmen have held a majority in all the councils elected since 1953, although established politicians opposed by *The Blade* have also been elected.

A closer analysis of the election results indicates some interesting patterns within *The Blade's* overall success. Charles E. Gilbert has noted the security of incumbent councilmen in nonpartisan electoral systems.[13] This pattern holds in Toledo, where five out of every seven incumbent councilmen achieved reelection in the period under consideration. Thus *The Blade* endorsement appears only slightly more significant than the influence of incumbency. The lack of a *Blade* endorsement, however, has a greater effect on Republican incumbents than on their Democratic counterparts. Only slightly more than one out of five Republican incumbents achieved reelection without *The Blade* endorsement, while more than half of the nonendorsed Democratic incumbents did so. The figures in Table 12.1 and Table 12.2 suggest that Republican voters are more attentive to *Blade* endorsements than are Democrats.

Voting behavior in Democratic and Republican wards generally, although not invariably, confirms this pattern. In the 1961 election, for example, voters in the four top Republican wards consistently favored endorsed Republican incumbents over their nonendorsed party colleagues. About 75 per cent of the voters in each of the wards supported the endorsed Republican incumbents, while only 45 per cent voted for the nonendorsed Republican incumbents. The same pattern held in the Republican wards for the 1963 election. In 1959, however, when *The Blade* supported the strong mayor plan and endorsed only one Republican incumbent, voters in Republican wards strongly supported the nonendorsed Republican incumbents.

Voters in areas of Democratic strength, on the other hand, have rarely favored endorsed Democratic incumbents over nonendorsed party officeholders. With the exception of 1959, when both *The Blade* and the Democratic Party advocated the strong mayor plan, the trend in the four top Democratic wards is in the opposite

---

the press in local elections. See his "Newspaper Editorial Endorsements and California Elections, 1948–1962," *Journalism Quarterly*, XLII (Autumn 1965), 532–538.

[13] Charles E. Gilbert and Christopher Clague, "Electoral Competition and Electoral Systems in Large Cities," *Journal of Politics*, XXIV (May 1962), 338–347.

TABLE 12.1
Blade Endorsements for Council, 1953–1965

	Number	Victorious	Percentage of Victories
Blade endorsement for incumbents:			
Democrats	8	8	100
Republicans	19	19	100
Total	27	27	100
Blade endorsement for nonincumbents:			
Democrats	20	10	50
Republicans	12	11	91.7
Total	32	21	65.6
Total *Blade* endorsements:			
Democrats	28	18	64.3
Republicans	31	30	96.8
Total	59	46	78.0

TABLE 12.2
Council Candidates Running without *Blade* Endorsement, 1953–1965

	Number	Victorious	Percentage of Victories
Incumbents without *Blade* endorsement:			
Democrats	11	6	54.5
Republicans	9	2	22.2
Total	20	8	40
Nonincumbents without *Blade* endorsement:			
Democrats	17	1	5.9
Republicans	29	4	13.8
Total	46	5	10.9
Total candidates without *Blade* endorsement:			
Democrats	28	7	25
Republicans	38	6	15.8
Total	66	13	19.7

direction. From 1953 through 1965 *The Blade* endorsed less than half as many Democratic as Republican incumbents, as is seen in Tables 12.1 and 12.2. In the relatively few instances when *The Blade* endorsed Democratic officeholders, party candidates seeking reelection without *The Blade's* blessing usually drew equal, if not greater, support.

In other respects, the effect of a *Blade* endorsement is more difficult to discern. An endorsement produces no clear or consistent advantage for incumbents of the opposite party in either Democratic or Republican wards. Voters in wards midway between Republican and Democratic strongholds sometimes, but not always, give *Blade*-endorsed candidates a small advantage useful in compiling a victory total. Although the pattern is not consistent at the ward level, *Blade*-endorsed novice candidates have a far better record of success than nonendorsed newcomers.[14] Fledgling Republican politicians aided by *The Blade* are notably more successful than their Democratic counterparts; and nonendorsed Republican novices, although facing poor odds, are more likely to reach city council than nonendorsed Democratic novices.

The Blade can find some satisfaction in the local election results of the 1950s and 1960s. It is doubtful, however, that its slate completely represents the newspaper's ideal or even its preferences. *The Blade* would be unlikely to sacrifice *realpolitik* for futile idealism; it would not jeopardize its future influence by endorsing a slate of probable losers. Indeed, *The Blade* has demonstrated an aptitude for practical politics and the balanced ticket in its endorsements. Whenever possible it has advocated the election of a Negro candidate and a representative of organized labor.[15] It has acquiesced in the predictable victories of popular, but distasteful candidates of both parties; an impressive primary showing has sometimes produced an endorsement for candidates spurned in previous elections and scorned on the editorial page. While gener-

---

[14] A *Blade* endorsement can give a new and inexperienced politician a boost. In 1965, for example, Clayton Umbles, a Democrat making his first try for office, rose from 14th in the primary election to 11th in the general election after a strong *Blade* endorsement. He still failed to win election to council, however.

[15] *The Blade* supported a Negro candidate for council in 1953, 1955, 1957, 1963, and 1965. *The Blade* abandoned Negro councilman James B. Simmons only after the strong mayor issue, the election for mayor and vice-mayor in 1961, and the difficulties of the 1959–1961 council term. Union officials seeking election to council received *Blade* endorsements in 1959, 1961, and 1963.

ally including a moderate quota of incumbents, particularly Republicans, *The Blade* rounds out its slate with an occasional Democratic or Republican unknown.

The Blade's electoral influence can best be understood in the context in which it operates. As previous chapters have indicated, many facets of Toledo's nonpartisan, at-large electoral system militate to the advantage of Republicans. The strength of *The Blade* does not alter or challenge the Republican advantages of the system. Instead, as might be expected, the press has its greatest effect on Republican candidates and voters. Many studies have reported that the upper- and middle-income voters largely found in the Republican Party are far more attentive to newspapers and their editorial pages than the lower-income voters constituting the mainstay of the Democratic Party.[16] *The Blade,* by supporting many Republican incumbents, has sharpened the Republican focus of its influence in local elections.

The Blade and Community Issues

Outside the electoral arena, *The Blade* has registered both success and failure in community issues. *Blade* support for the school system, economic growth, fair police practices, and cooperation between the county and city are to its credit and to the benefit of the community. In these and other areas *The Blade* has worked persistently, with varying degrees of frustration and accomplishment, to push Toledo toward community improvement.[17] City councilmen have been responsive to *The Blade,* sometimes reversing themselves after an editorial, as in the fair housing controversy of 1961. And although community leaders often go their own way, they, too, have modified decisions in order to satisfy *The Blade.*[18]

[16] See V. O. Key, *Public Opinion and American Democracy* (New York: Alfred A. Knopf, 1961), pp. 344–370.

[17] Reo M. Christenson presents a detailed account of *The Blade's* role and influence in various local issues: "The Power of the Press," pp. 227–240.

[18] There are various examples which can be cited. When Toledo's largest bank revealed that it wished to violate building regulations in an urban renewal district, *The Blade* ran a critical editorial. City councilmen and bank

On the other hand, *Blade* editorials lambasting and mocking local figures and their decisions usually have only limited effect. City managers, municipal administrators, school officials, business leaders, and others selected for venomous editorial treatment either become inured to *Blade* attacks or more convinced of their own rectitude and eventual triumph. Instead of displacing or changing the officials (or decisions) in question, *Blade* editorials and the response to them may, on occasion, take the form of a holy war increasingly irrelevant to the actual issue.

On money questions, *The Blade* has suffered some significant reverses. The electorate has not shown itself to be particularly entranced with *The Blade* vision of tomorrow's Toledo and its needs, especially when this has meant more taxes. *Blade* endorsements for municipal capital improvements programs and tax increases in 1956, 1958, 1959, 1961, and 1962 proved futile; pleas for the county levy in November 1965 also went unheeded.[19]

The Blade, like other local organizations, has reservations about controversial issues and startling changes in the community. It has advocated certain innovations itself, but it is more cautious about changes originating without its guidance or approval. Programs and organizations which might threaten or alter the existing distribution of influence are likely to receive limited support.

One *Blade* official explained: "We don't urge drastic changes. I'm an antirevolutionist. I want the city to adjust gradually to demands." *The Blade* wants controlled community change, without the risk of conflicts that would endanger the existing system.

The Blade has been particularly sensitive to the possibility of inflammatory issues in race relations. It wants to advance civil rights, but not if this advancement would cause disruptive conflict.[20]

---

officials soon responded to *The Blade* viewpoint, and the bank's original plans were changed. For the critical editorial, see *The Blade*, December 19, 1965, Section B, p. 4.

[19] In November 1966, however, when *The Blade* was on strike and made no endorsement, Toledo voters passed a .5 per cent increase in the payroll income tax by a comfortable margin.

[20] *The Blade's* position in the fair housing issue of 1961 is a case in point. Its fear of civil rights controversies which could "get out of hand" is usually not evident in its consideration of civil rights issues in places other than Toledo.

The Blade and Reform Government

The reform tradition has given *The Blade* its most difficult community issue. In this instance, *The Blade* has encountered, as one reporter observed, a community predisposition apparently impervious to the press. *The Blade* itself originally contributed to this predisposition, since it urged and aided the adoption of the council-manager plan. Yet the initial enthusiasm for the new form of government gradually faded. One *Blade* official commented:

> *The Blade* at first supported the manager form of government as a means to competent municipal government. But then we came to see that it was working against the adoption of public projects. We felt it weakened the two parties and caused a fragmentation which made it difficult to get action.

In another recollection:

> After watching it awhile, I felt that the manager form was a buck-passing contest between city council and the manager. Neither was willing to act. Then *The Blade* grew tired of being the sustaining force behind the city manager form of government. *The Blade* was being used as the political party sponsoring the manager form of government. The managers acted as if *The Blade* had hired them. They just opened their files to us.

The Blade's advocacy of a change in the form of government met with failure in the late 1950s, as recounted in Chapter 7. In 1957, although *The Blade* favored the strong mayor plan, it protected its flank carefully. Accurately sensing community feeling, *The Blade* endorsed five candidates also supported by the City Manager League; a strong mayor endorsement did not lead *The Blade* to disavow popular incumbent councilmen committed to and campaigning for the existing system. Editorial appeals represented, in one opinion, only a "feeble pitch" for the strong mayor proposal.[21] Although critical of the ineffectual Democratic campaign for the charter amendment, *The Blade* also revealed some of the hesitation and caution which afflicted the Democratic Party in advancing a controversial issue.

In 1959 *The Blade* resumed its editorial campaign with increased

[21] Christenson, "The Power of the Press," p. 239.

vigor, endorsing only candidates pledged to the strong mayor charter proposal. Despite the repeated admonitions appearing on the editorial page, Toledo voters again reaffirmed their satisfaction with the council-manager plan, although by a narrower margin than in 1957.

After the 1957 and 1959 defeats, *The Blade* abandoned its strong mayor hopes and turned its attention to aiding the passage of the more limited 1963 amendment providing for direct election of the mayor. One *Blade* official commented:

> We were discouraged by our previous failures. It seemed that Toledo people did not and would not want to change the manager form. The effect of strong bosses and corruption in the old days carries over. People are suspicious of proposals to change the manager plan of government. So in 1963 we helped promote a broad coalition in which all groups supported a smaller change.

Another official expressed a similar opinion:

> We concluded that the Democratic proposal [strong mayor plan] had attempted too much at once. The 1963 amendment was a way of putting an end to some of the more shocking problems without another divisive campaign. We decided that *The Blade* could be more effective assisting minor changes and adjustments dictated by the situation.

The Blade, while changing its strategy, continued to note the shortcomings of city government under the reform tradition. "Vigorous leadership is what Toledo sorely needs," *The Blade* contended in an editorial during the 1965 mayoralty campaign.[22] The failings of city councilmen and administrators regularly provide material for acerbic editorial comment. Whether reminding councilmen that Chase Park "won't go away" or asking "What is Mr. Backstrom [the city manager] for?" *The Blade* gives notice that city government lacks clear, forceful direction.[23]

Yet its advocacy of strong political leadership is somewhat inconsistent, which suggests that the paper is not totally dissatisfied with the reform tradition and the conditions it has produced. For example, after urging the election of Democratic mayoralty candidate Ned Skeldon, *The Blade* endorsed five incumbent Republicans who

[22] *The Blade*, October 23, 1965, p. 8.
[23] *The Blade*, September 14, 1966, p. 14, and October 21, 1966, p. 14.

would have been less than enthusiastic about aiding the leadership of an ambitious, partisan Democrat. It is unlikely that such a situation would have produced decisive city leadership and action.

Although *The Blade* is anxious to see improved public leadership, it appears uncertain about the role of power, parties, and political considerations. In 1965, *The Blade* chastised Mayor Potter for obtaining the election of a loyal ally as vice-mayor instead of allowing the position to go to one of his rivals in the Republican Party. The mayor's action, which was advisable for party harmony and for his position in council and in the community, was described by *The Blade* as "unity—with a price."[24] Similarly, when Mayor Potter tried to tighten the lines of city government by suggesting that councilmen direct information requests to the city manager's office rather than to municipal departments and their officials, *The Blade* indicated its displeasure.[25]

The Blade is resolved to avoid divisive charter battles like those of 1957 and 1959; it now hopes that improved public leadership will evolve on its own rather than as a consequence of charter revisions. The local political system, although unsatisfactory to *The Blade* in some respects, is closely related to the paper's distinctive role in the community, as *Blade* officials well realize. The fragmented power and apathetic community organizations fostered by the reform tradition have redounded to the paper's advantage. *The Blade* has weak competition from labor, business, party, and civil rights organizations bent on influencing local decisions and elections.[26] In Toledo, *The Blade* alone has allocated substantial resources to studying local issues and influencing their outcome. The comparative weakness of city council and other organizations accentuates the role of the press.[27] As one *Blade* reporter expressed it: "There's a wonderful vacuum here." In another opinion:

> Our influence is probably enhanced by the power situation in Toledo. *The Blade* doesn't face a strong taxpayers' league, Urban League, Municipal League, or anything else. Other organizations

[24] *The Blade*, December 9, 1965, p. 14.

[25] *The Blade*, January 10, 1966, p. 16.

[26] This conclusion is also advanced by Christenson, "The Power of the Press," p. 229.

[27] For a comparison, consider the influence of newspapers in Chicago, where there is a strong Democratic organization. For comments on the relative weakness of the press in Chicago, see Banfield and Wilson, *City Politics*, p. 325, and Edward C. Banfield, *Political Influence* (New York: The Free Press, 1961), especially pp. 47, 86, 95, 182, and 193.

don't speak with *The Blade's* consistency and force. The newspaper is more important in Toledo than some cities, because there are no effective organizations taking up causes and other positions differing from *The Blade's*.

Summary

In community issues and decisions, *The Blade,* unlike other local organizations, regularly demands and receives consideration. The feeble state of the party organizations and the half-hearted political efforts of other groups have undoubtedly increased the impact of the press on voting behavior. The reform tradition has also strengthened *The Blade's* hand in electoral politics: The nonpartisan ballot and independent voting have boosted the value of a *Blade* endorsement in local elections.

Nevertheless, *The Blade* is far from invincible in community elections and decisions. Individuals and organizations and inertia and tradition have combined to thwart *The Blade* on many occasions. *The Blade* has consistently advanced its opinion of what would be good for Toledo, but its suggestions have met with repudiation as well as acceptance.

The Blade does not rule Toledo, even in the negative sense described by its critics. Instead, the paper has taken a prominent, but not controlling, role in the local community. It has hoped to improve, not denigrate, Toledo, as some local leaders allege. *The Blade* has long advocated increased job and educational opportunities, improved municipal programs and services, expanded recreational and medical facilities, and other efforts to better the community. It has criticized, but the performance of city government and private organizations has often warranted criticism. In its editorials on urban renewal, industrial development, and educational needs, the paper has tried to stimulate rather than obstruct local action. Over the years *The Blade* has exhorted Toledo, while exercising and protecting its own ability to influence men and decisions.[28]

---

[28] *The Blade*, it should be noted, also exempts itself from some of the editorial recommendations extended to the community. For example, *The Blade* has often called upon labor and management to avoid prolonged strikes, described as ''unedifying spectacles'' damaging to the public interest and convenience. The paper has also noted the failure of local business and union leaders to refer disputes to the Labor-Management-Citizens Commission, a mediation agency. Yet protracted (and unmediated) strikes at *The Blade*, as in the fall of 1963 and 1966, have left Toledo without a paper for extended periods.

The Blade has both reflected and foundered on the political tradition of the local community. The paper has not aligned itself with any group, program, or philosophy.[29] Despite its strong interests in the community, *The Blade* has maintained its independence as well as the hauteur so distasteful to some community leaders. One official explained the paper's policy:

> *The Blade* tries to refuse political leadership. Leadership should come from a public source. If *The Blade* acts as a civic leader, it limits its freedom. *The Blade* has the interest, ability, and talent in its staff to advance policies—to act as a civic leader. But this would hurt its journalistic standards. The press must be free to be critical.

With the exception of its efforts in behalf of the port and the medical school, *The Blade* has avoided overt leadership in community issues.

In sum, even a strong newspaper like *The Blade* is an inadequate antidote for weak public leadership and community organizations. As Norton Long points out, a newspaper is a specialized game even when its reporters and officials are deeply concerned with their community. "The paper," Long writes, "does not accept the responsibility of a governing role in its territory. It is a power but only a partially responsible one."[30]

[29] For a statement of *The Blade's* philosophy of independence, see Paul Block, Jr., "Facing up to the 'Monopoly' Charge," *Nieman Reports*, IX (July 1955), 3–7.

[30] Norton E. Long, "The Local Community as an Ecology of Games," *American Journal of Sociology*, LXIV (November 1958), p. 260.

13 CONCLUSIONS: THE 1965 ELECTION AND THE IMPACT OF THE REFORM TRADITION

The Mayoralty Campaign of 1965

Toledo's first mayoralty election in 30 years presented voters with an opportunity to challenge established political practices and institutions. Democratic candidate Ned Skeldon, convinced that the voters were ready for a change, had seized the offensive early in a long campaign. He repeatedly charged Republican incumbent John Potter with giving Toledo stodgy, conservative, and unimaginative direction.[1] The Republican administration was declared guilty of ineptitude, bungling, disorganization, and failure to exploit opportunities for federal aid. Toledo, according to Skeldon, had fallen behind other cities because of its ineffectual political leadership and incompetent administration. Deficiencies in urban renewal, recreation, incineration facilities, expressways, and parking provisions were cited to illustrate the Democratic contention.[2]

To remedy these ills, Skeldon proposed a 21-point program calling for full utilization of all federal and state

[1] *The Blade,* October 14, 1965, p. 3.
[2] *The Blade,* October 12, 1965, p. 3.

223

programs; municipally operated downtown parking facilities; more imaginative, fast-moving urban renewal; qualified hometown administrators to replace ineffective, imported officials; a program to beautify the city's streets and neighborhoods; throughway construction; and other programs encompassing virtually every facet of urban life.[3] Furthermore, these goals were to be accomplished with no additional taxes. If elected, Skeldon promised to bring new vigor, verve, and boldness to Toledo. City Manager Backstrom, who failed to be "even a good municipal housekeeper," and other lackluster Republican retainers would be dismissed.[4]

Mayor Potter's campaign warmed under the Democratic attacks. The mayor defended his administration as one which had set the conditions for industrial expansion and increased jobs: "I offer as my chief claim for reelection, this time by the people of Toledo: progress, prosperity, and payrolls."[5] In defending his administration, Potter pointed to four years of steady, solid progress in urban renewal and other programs; advances in annexation and capital improvements; efficient municipal services; and sound fiscal practices. Furthermore, the Republican administration, which had inspired the confidence of industrialists and contributed to labor-management harmony, operated within the limits defined by the city charter. Skeldon, on the other hand, was pictured as a man whose ambitions could be contained by neither law nor personal scruples.

Potter warned Toledo voters of the dangerous implications of Skeldon's pledge to fire the city manager.[6] Such a step, he said, would indicate a return to the spoils system, which would inevitably bring industrial expansion "to a screeching halt," while "industrialists stop to reappraise the situation in Toledo."[7] Republicans saw Skeldon's avowed interest in electing Democratic councilmen and appointing new administrators as a frightening omen of a possible return to political bossism and "rubber-stamp" government. The blatant partisanship of the Democrats was contrasted with the

[3] For other points in Skeldon's program, see *The Blade*, September 11, 1965, p. 1.

[4] *The Blade*, September 10, 1965, p. 3.

[5] Address to the Teamsters, *Team and Wheel*, August 31, 1965, p. 16.

[6] Shortly after the election there was open discussion among Republicans about replacing the city manager. See *The Blade*, December 15, 1965, p. 1. See *The Blade*, December 20, 1965, Section 2, p. 1, for formal denials.

[7] *The Blade*, September 10, 1965, p. 3.

Republican concern for the good of the city. Mayor Potter described his administration as nonpartisan, earnest, prudent, and frugal. By contrast, the Skeldon administration in the county was character- ized as a bankrupt, boss-ridden political fief seeking a tax increase. Potter commented:

> It's inconceivable as to why Mr. Skeldon has to ask for an additional tax increase when, with Toledo and other municipalities expanding, the county should have need for less, not more. . . . I can't help but wonder what would happen to Toledo's taxes if my rival was elected mayor.[8]

Analysis of the Election Results

In November 1965, the Toledo electorate reaffirmed their adher- ence to the distinctive political tradition of their city. John Potter's comfortable victory confirmed the continuing ramifications of the reform tradition in Toledo.[9] Skeldon, the Democratic candidate in a city regarded as a Democratic stronghold in national and state politics, drew only 42 per cent of the vote. Potter cut significantly into areas of Democratic strength and received overwhelming sup- port elsewhere. Skeldon had campaigned forthrightly as a party man and a Democrat "proud of John Kennedy, Lyndon Johnson, and the Democratic mayors of our great cities."[10] He believed that sharpening party lines in the campaign would bring out the city's many Democratic voters in his behalf. "We've gotten this identified as a partisan election," Skeldon remarked in an optimistic comment a week before the election.[11] Mayor Potter continually tried to obscure party lines with speeches invoking the reform ethos, with Democrats-for-Potter meetings, and with strenuous efforts to gain the support of traditionally Democratic Negro voters and union members.

Potter's effort to break Democratic strength was greatly aided by his success in identifying Skeldon as a spender. Skeldon's attempt

---

[8] *Ibid.* The county government was seeking a renewal of its operating levy (defeated the previous May) and a 0.4 mill increase.

[9] Potter received 65,615 votes to 47,556 for Skeldon.

[10] Televised debate, WTOL, October 31, 1965.

[11] *The New York Times*, October 30, 1965, p. 21.

to develop progressive programs at the local level actually worked to his disadvantage. Republican oratory transformed Skeldon's achievements in developing a county recreation center and introducing many innovations in county government into a record of spendthrift irresponsibility.[12] Furthermore, Skeldon's insistence on the need for greater energy and action in city government and his proposed 21-point program seemed to suggest increased spending and taxation in the city, despite the candidate's denials. Democratic voters who support the social and economic responsibilities of the national and state governments prefer "sensible," frugal government at home.[13] Through his interest in clearly defined party responsibility in city government, open and organized party competition in local elections, strong political leadership, and an expanding, more vigorous city government, Skeldon had broken with the accepted political customs of Toledo. He did not have the personal appeal, campaign strategy and technique, or powerful organized support necessary to make such a change acceptable.

John Potter was a minority party candidate, endorsed by neither *The Blade* nor the United Labor Committee. Nevertheless, he had certain less obvious assets. The alternative to Potter raised the possibility of change and conflict, which most community leaders and voters feared. The mayor represented an acceptable form of government and style of politics. He had done a conscientious, if cautious, job, unmarred by scandals; he was safe, honest, and respectable. *The Blade* had commented before the election:

> Ned Skeldon would drive a bulldozer himself if necessary to begin changing the face of Toledo, while John Potter would continue to plow behind the steady clomping of mules.[14]

In Toledo the clomping of mules is considered preferable to unsettling ventures into change and the unknown.

---

[12] For a favorable interpretation of Skeldon's contributions to county government, see *The Blade,* October 23, 1965, p. 8.

[13] Studies indicate that upper- and lower-income groups may have a greater preference for local expenditures than middle-range groups, such as the industrial workers in the UAW. See, for example, Oliver P. Williams and Charles R. Adrian, *Four Cities* (Philadelphia: University of Pennsylvania Press, 1963), pp. 105–121. Also see James Q. Wilson and Edward C. Banfield, "Public-Regardingness as a Value Premise in Voting Behavior," *American Political Science Review,* LVIII (December 1964), 876–888.

[14] *The Blade,* October 31, 1965, Section B, p. 4 (© Toledo Blade Co.).

Furthermore, the organizations supporting Skeldon did not carry a significant impact. The Democratic Party was still divided between the Skeldon faction and the older leaders who were reluctant to exert themselves for the election of their opponent. Although the United Labor Committee endorsed and supported Skeldon, it failed to make a major effort on his behalf in the plants or on election day.[15] *The Blade's* endorsement was ineffective, probably because Skeldon was familiar to the electorate; newspaper endorsements are often more important in races involving relatively new and unknown candidates. While Skeldon hoped to benefit from the political influence of *The Blade,* the United Labor Committee, and the Democratic Party, Mayor Potter, true to the local tradition, built the political alliances and personal support which brought him victory.

Toledo's Preference for "Caretaker Government"

In 1965, as in previous years, Toledo voters expressed satisfaction with their local political system. This political system has produced what Oliver Williams and Charles Adrian have termed "caretaker government," or the maintenance of traditional services.[16] In a caretaker government, such as that in Toledo, there is little experimentation or expansion in city activities. Local governmental institutions have produced a diffusion of power which has made change difficult and infrequent. With power divided among nine councilmen, it is easier to obstruct or delay a decision than to make and implement one. The absence of direction in city council has fostered a corresponding timidity among city managers. Toledo city managers, with one exception, have been preoccupied with satisfying city councilmen.[17] City councilmen and managers have generally been more concerned with retaining local office than with using it to advance their careers. The retention of local office in Toledo has

15 *The Blade,* November 28, 1965, Section A, p. 2.

16 Williams and Adrian, *Four Cities,* pp. 27–29.

17 Williams and Adrian point out that caretaker government conflicts with the professional values of city management. The profession-oriented manager is interested in achievements which will help him to "move up" to more desirable cities. See Williams and Adrian, pp. 283–284.

neither required nor stimulated initiative and achievement by city officials.

The caution of elected and appointed officeholders and the prolonged, uncertain process of decision-making have undoubtedly contributed to the negativism of the electorate. City voters have frequently rejected referenda issues providing for municipal innovations and improvements. Tax increases encounter strong resistance, as is seen in the defeat of property tax increases for capital improvements in 1956, 1958, and 1959, the defeat of the 1961 and 1962 payroll tax increases, and the rejection of the county operating levy in May and November of 1965.[18] It seems unlikely that Toledo voters reject money issues because they regard the city's tax rate as excessive.[19] Rather, local officials have failed to counter reservations about tax increases by creating confidence in city government.

The vacillations and fractious divisions characteristic of many city councils have not enhanced the public regard for local government. There is a widespread disposition to keep city government activities to a minimum. This arrangement has seemed a satisfactory solution to Toledo voters, who have rejected the admonitions of *The Blade*, several strong mayor proposals, and Skeldon's appeal for more vigorous city leadership and government. The weakness of city leadership and the negativism of the voters have reinforced each other, creating a political pattern highly resistant to change.

In Toledo's version of caretaker government, city councilmen have often attempted to defer to other organizations for guidance. City council, lacking internal direction and public confidence, has grasped for leadership from other sources. Urban renewal consultants, planning firms, and public relations agencies are hired to facilitate programs and decisions.[20] City councilmen are usually responsive to the suggestions of recognized leaders from business, labor and Negro organizations. Yet they have found most organizations to be relatively uninterested in the election and responsibilities of city councilmen.

[18] In 1966, however, Toledo voters broke with long-established precedents by passing a 0.5 per cent increase in the payroll income tax. Several days before the election, an editorial on WSPD-TV noted that Toledo voters had not approved one new additional tax for the city since 1946, when the payroll income tax was passed. WSPD, November 4, 1966, mimeographed editorial.

[19] Toledo ranks seventh among the eight largest Ohio cities in property tax rates; it ranks sixth in taxes paid on both property and income. These calculations do not consider the 1966 tax increase.

[20] *The Blade*, December 7, 1965, p. 22.

The Effects of Reform Institutions

The conditions which contribute to the lack of decisive action in the city government have also affected the interest and influence of major organizations in the community. Reform institutions have had particularly debilitating effects on local party organization and activity, as this research hypothesized. The tradition of independent voting and maverick politicians, rooted in the era of Golden Rule Jones, has weakened political parties as a community force. The political parties play a secondary role in the campaign efforts of local candidates and have an even more negligible role in policy questions, as many councilmen have been disappointed to learn. The party system, which in other cities (e.g., Chicago, New Haven) has furnished an important source of public leadership and political cohesion, is atrophied.

Reform institutions have accentuated the disunity and detachment of community organizations. Personal organization rather than an alliance or coalition of groups has been characteristic. Many self-styled politicians have by-passed any or all of the key community organizations in seeking elective office. Once elected, city officials have found that they lack the powers (such as those available to Mayor Lee in New Haven) or the organization (e.g., the Daley organization in Chicago) to involve these groups in community problems.

An initial hypothesis of this research stated that the compatibility of reform institutions with middle-class civic ideals would encourage participation by business leaders. This research refutes the hypothesis and its underlying assumptions. The inactivity and respectability of city government under the council-manager plan have lulled business leaders into indifference. The community participation of executives is confined to good works and isolated issues of direct concern to business.

In the case of labor, nonpartisanship, at-large elections, and the council-manager plan have blunted the impact of union political activity, as hypothesized. But labor leaders have made no consistent, organized effort to attain a controlling or decisive political position in the city or to influence community decisions which do not directly impinge upon labor. The restrictive effects of reform institutions on minority and lower-income groups are more striking in regard to Negroes. The hypothesis that large electoral districts and a weak party system retard and inhibit the political influence of Negroes was confirmed in Toledo. Nevertheless, Negro leaders, like labor and business leaders, are relatively unconcerned with city government and politics.

There have been few dramatic issues to compel the attention of leaders in business, labor, Negro organizations, and the political parties. Most leaders have a complacent feeling that "not too much is happening" and "everything is going pretty well." The absence of community controversies has allowed leaders of various groups to concentrate on the concerns of their own sector.

The Blade, although less content with the local political system, has been neither consistent nor successful in challenging the reform tradition. It has not shown a single-minded determination to alter a political system which has given the press wide range. Despite its interest and influence in Toledo, *The Blade* has not assumed functions abdicated by the city government and community organizations.

In summary, the power structure of Toledo is amorphous. There is no dominant elite of decision-makers drawn from economic dominants or from public leaders. Community organizations rarely initiate policy proposals or precipitate local controversies. Nor is there a coalition of actors, organizations, and institutions which tends to prevail in most community issues. A new convergence of business, administrative, and political executives has not emerged to reshape the local scene.

Toledo has an extreme case of what Robert Dahl has described as "slack in the system."[21] Power is dispersed; political resources are not fully mobilized by any organization or combination of organizations. In Chicago and New Haven, the slack was taken up by political entrepreneurs who could pyramid resources or buy and sell influence to construct an informal structure of control. The slack in Toledo's political system is less mutable. It has ossified under the impact of governmental institutions, long-established political practices, and the reform ethos.

Thus Toledo has had neither a ruling economic elite nor an executive-centered political system. The extreme decentralization of power resulting from reform has produced a governmental break-

---

[21] Robert A. Dahl, *Who Governs?* (New Haven, Conn.: Yale University Press, 1961), p. 305.

down rather than a local democracy in which all groups and individuals are actively engaged in seeking the community good. The local political system is poorly suited for considering and resolving community problems. The diffusion of power in city government and in the community and the parsimony of the electorate present almost insurmountable obstacles to decisive, concerted action.

One hypothesis of this research proposed that the reform movement enhances the influence and interests of business and middle-class groups at the expense of lower-income and minority groups. This hypothesis is not completely true. Although the role of lower-income groups has been restricted, the participation of other groups has not increased. Lower-income groups in need of municipal services (such as recreational facilities, for example) have suffered from the inadequacies of the local government. But business interests and middle-class residents have garnered few positive benefits from a political system in which little progress results for anyone.

In 1966, 69 years after the first election of Golden Rule Jones, the ethos and institutions of reform are still widely accepted. Any changes in the political system and the pattern of community influence are likely to come through gradual modifications rather than full-scale charter revisions or startling changes in administration. The major possibility for greater direction in city government and increased participation by community organizations lies in the gradual development of vigorous leadership by a directly elected mayor. Such an official could begin to provide the stimulus and cohesion needed in community decision-making. An elected mayor untainted with partisanship, avowed political ambition, or other violations of the reform ethos would be most likely to accomplish such modifications. Any abrupt break with caretaker government and reform politics would be virtually certain to founder on a deeply rooted local political tradition.

In conclusion, the political ideals and institutions embedded in the community are inadequate and inappropriate for Toledo's needs. The values of reform are in fact antithetical to the character of the large industrial city. Municipal reformers aspired to an idealized preurban society without interest groups, centralized authority, professional politicians, and political organizations. Reform efforts to restrain these features of modern life failed to yield adequate substitutes in complex, variegated cities.

Part-time officeholders, public-spirited organizations, and citizen participation, even at their best, are not sufficient to govern a large city. The administration of a vast array of municipal services and the mobilization of community action in programs such as urban renewal cannot be accomplished without a degree of professional leadership, centralized authority, organized support, and interest group participation unanticipated in reform doctrine. To the extent that governmental institutions inhibit these influences they complicate the task of meeting the problems of urban areas. Both local efforts and federal legislation may be blunted or nullified in communities in which governmental institutions are associated with an amorphous power structure. The diffusion of power, pervasive disinterest, and governmental paralysis seen in Toledo are more threatening to local self-government than the forces feared by reformers.

Yet cities face a critical period. Urban problems first noted at the turn of the century have multiplied. Progress in combating poverty, racial discrimination, delinquency, slums, and blight requires local initiative and responsibility. In an urban society it is important that cities have political systems which are responsive to the diverse groups within them, yet capable of decisive action. This study suggests that reform institutions, when used in a large city, facilitate neither of these conditions. The lower-income and minority groups whose fate is crucial to the future of American cities are likely to find political access difficult under reform institutions. Nor are the skills of business and administrative officials readily available for the service of the community.

Furthermore, abstract reform ideals such as public virtue and the general interest have limited utility in making decisions on urban renewal objectives, educational facilities, or expressway locations. The reform inclination for what has been called an apolitical, partyless, and problemless politics may stifle or inhibit the consideration and resolution of difficult issues, as in the area of racial discrimination in education, housing, and employment.[22]

Reform politics in Los Angeles, Cincinnati, Boston, or Toledo do not reveal the fully nonpartisan, democratic, and effective local government envisioned by reformers.[23] Nor do such cities have the

---

[22] The tendency toward an apolitical, problemless politics is discussed by Benjamin DeMott, ''Party Apolitics,'' *The American Scholar*, XXXI (Autumn 1962), 595–602. Also see Banfield and Wilson, *City Politics*, pp. 329–332.

[23] For a discussion of reform politics in various large cities, see the following studies: Charles G. Mayo, ''The 1961 Mayoralty Election in Los Angeles: The

professional politicians, political cohesion, and responsiveness which a machine can supply.[24] A city such as Toledo does not have an old-style boss and machine system. Nor does it have effective political leadership. Wide-scale municipal corruption is missing, but so is good government. Politics and partisanship survive, without the benefits of leadership and organization. Toledo's experience suggests that the ethos and institutions of reform can have debilitating consequences in populous, industrial cities.

Political Party in a Nonpartisan Election," *Western Political Quarterly*, XVII (June 1964), 325–337; Leonard E. Goodall, "Reform Politics in the Big City: The Phoenix Experience," *Western Political Quarterly*, XVI (September 1963), 20–22; Edward C. Banfield and Martha Derthick, *A Report on Politics in Boston* (Cambridge, Mass.: Joint Center for Urban Studies, 1960); A. Theodore Brown, *The Politics of Reform: Kansas City's Municipal Government* (Kansas City, Mo.: Community Studies, 1958); and Ralph A. Straetz, *PR Politics in Cincinnati* (New York: New York University Press, 1958).

[24] On the merits of the machine in achieving unity in city government and a degree of accommodation among competing claims before they reach the policy agenda, see Theodore J. Lowi, *At the Pleasure of the Mayor* (New York: The Free Press, 1964), pp. 215–226. Martin Meyerson and Edward C. Banfield discuss the responsiveness of the machine to divergent interests in *Politics, Planning, and the Public Interest* (New York: The Free Press, 1955). Also see Robert K. Merton, *Social Theory and Social Structure* (New York: The Free Press, 1957), pp. 71–81 ("The Latent Functions of the Machine").

BIBLIOGRAPHY

Books

Banfield, Edward C., and James Q. Wilson. *City Politics*. Cambridge, Mass.: Harvard University Press and M.I.T. Press, 1963.

Banfield, Edward C. *Political Influence*. New York: The Free Press, 1961.

——————, ed. *Urban Government*. New York: The Free Press, 1961.

Bentley, Arthur. *The Process of Government*. San Antonio, Tex.: Principia Press of Trinity University, 1949.

Blalock, Hubert M. *Social Statistics*. New York: McGraw-Hill Book Co., 1960.

Bromage, Arthur W. *On the City Council*. Ann Arbor: The George Wahr Publishing Company, 1950.

——————. *Introduction to Municipal Government and Administration*. New York: Appleton-Century-Crofts, 1957.

Brooks, Robert C. *Political Parties and Electoral Problems*. New York: Harper & Row, 1923.

Brown, A. Theodore. *The Politics of Reform: Kansas City's Municipal Government*. Kansas City, Mo.: Community Studies, Inc., 1958.

Burgess, M. Elaine. *Negro Leadership in a Southern City*. Chapel Hill: University of North Carolina Press, 1960.

Cater, Douglass. *The Fourth Branch of Government*. Boston: Houghton Mifflin Co., 1959.

Childs, Richard S. *Civic Victories*. New York: Harper & Row, 1952.

Dahl, Robert A. *Who Governs?* New Haven, Conn.: Yale University Press, 1961.

Daland, Robert T. *Dixie City: A Portrait of Political Leadership*. Tusca-

234

loosa: University of Alabama Bureau of Public Administration, 1956.

Drake, St. Clair, and Horace R. Cayton. *Black Metropolis*. New York: Harper & Row, 1945.

Eldersveld, Samuel J. *Political Parties*. Chicago: Rand McNally & Co., 1964.

Fine, Sidney. *The Origins of the United Automobile Workers*. Ann Arbor: The Institute of Labor and Industrial Relations of the University of Michigan and Wayne State University, 1960.

Fleming, George James. *An All-Negro Ticket in Baltimore*. (Eagleton Institute Cases in Practical Politics, Case 10.) New York: Holt, Rinehart and Winston, 1960.

Form, William H., and Delbert C. Miller. *Industry, Labor and Community*. New York: Harper & Row, 1960.

Frazier, E. Franklin. *Black Bourgeoisie*. New York: The Free Press, 1957.

Gerth, H. H., and C. Wright Mills, eds. *From Max Weber: Essays in Sociology*. New York: Oxford University Press, 1959.

Glazer, Nathan, and Daniel Patrick Moynihan. *Beyond the Melting Pot*. Cambridge, Mass.: Harvard University Press and M.I.T. Press, 1963.

Gosnell, Harold. *Machine Politics: Chicago Model*. Chicago: University of Chicago Press, 1937.

——————. *Negro Politicians: The Rise of Negro Politics in Chicago*. Chicago: University of Chicago Press, 1935.

Gross, Bertram. *The Legislative Process: A Study in Social Combat*. New York: Thomas Y. Crowell Co., 1953.

Hofstadter, Richard. *The Age of Reform*. New York: Vintage Books, 1960.

Hunter, Floyd. *Community Power Structure*. Chapel Hill: University of North Carolina Press, 1953.

International City Managers' Association. *Recent Council-Manager Developments and Directory of Council-Manager Cities*. Chicago: ICMA, 1961.

James, Ralph, and Estelle James. *Hoffa and the Teamsters*. Princeton, N.J.: D. Van Nostrand Co., 1965.

Janowitz, Morris, ed. *Community Political Systems.* New York: The Free Press, 1961.

Jennings, M. Kent. *Community Influentials: The Elites of Atlanta.* New York: The Free Press, 1964.

—————, and Harmon Zeigler, eds. *The Electoral Process.* Englewood Cliffs, N.J.: Prentice-Hall, 1966.

Johnson, Wendell F. *Toledo's Nonpartisan Movement.* Toledo, Ohio: H. J. Chittenden Company Press, 1922.

Kammerer, Gladys M., *et al. City Managers in Politics.* Gainesville: University of Florida Press, 1962.

Kaplan, Harold. *Urban Renewal Politics.* New York: Columbia University Press, 1963.

Key, V. O. *Public Opinion and American Democracy.* New York: Alfred A. Knopf, 1961.

Kneier, C. M. *City Government in the United States.* New York: Appleton-Century-Crofts, 1947.

Kornhauser, Arthur, *et al. When Labor Votes.* New York: University Books, 1956.

Lane, Robert. *Political Life.* New York: The Free Press, 1959.

Lee, Eugene C. *The Politics of Nonpartisanship.* Berkeley: University of California Press, 1960.

Lewis, Anthony, and *The New York Times. Portrait of a Decade: The Second American Revolution.* New York: Random House, 1964.

Lockard, Duane. *The Politics of State and Local Government.* New York: Macmillan Co., 1963.

Long, Norton E. *The Polity.* Chicago: Rand McNally & Co., 1962.

Lowi, Theodore J. *At the Pleasure of the Mayor.* New York: The Free Press, 1964.

MacAllister, William F., ed. *N. W. Ayer and Son's Directory of Newspapers and Periodicals, 1966.* Philadelphia: N. W. Ayer and Son, Inc., 1966.

McKean, David Dayton. *The Boss.* Boston: Houghton Mifflin Co., 1940.

Mason, Edward S. *The Corporation in Modern Society.* Cambridge, Mass.: Harvard University Press, 1959.

Merton, Robert K. *Social Theory and Social Structure.* New York: The Free Press, 1957.

Meyerson, Martin, and Edward C. Banfield. *Politics, Planning, and the Public Interest*. New York: The Free Press, 1955.

Mowry, George E. *The Era of Theodore Roosevelt and the Birth of Modern America*. New York: Harper & Row, 1958.

Nye, Russell. *Midwestern Progressive Politics*. East Lansing: Michigan State College Press, 1951.

Osofsky, Gilbert. *Harlem: The Making of a Ghetto*. New York: Harper & Row, 1966.

Presthus, Robert. *Men at the Top*. New York: Oxford University Press, 1964.

Romer, Sam. *The International Brotherhood of Teamsters*. New York: John Wiley, 1962.

Rossi, Peter H., and Robert A. Dentler. *The Politics of Urban Renewal*. New York: The Free Press, 1961.

Sayre, Wallace S., and Herbert Kaufman. *Governing New York City*. New York: Russell Sage Foundation, 1960.

Seidman, Joel, *et al. The Worker Views His Union*. Chicago: University of Chicago Press, 1958.

Steffens, Lincoln. *Autobiography*. New York: Harcourt, Brace & World, 1958.

Stewart, Frank Mann. *A Half Century of Reform: A History of the National Municipal League*. Berkeley: University of California Press, 1950.

Stieber, Jack. *Governing the UAW*. New York: John Wiley, 1962.

Straetz, Ralph A. *PR Politics in Cincinnati*. New York: New York University Press, 1958.

Thompson, Daniel C. *The Negro Leadership Class*. Englewood Cliffs, N.J.: Prentice-Hall, 1963.

Truman, David. *The Governmental Process*. New York: Alfred A. Knopf, 1951.

Warren, Robert Penn. *Who Speaks for the Negro?* New York: Random House, 1965.

White, Leonard D. *The City Manager*. Chicago: University of Chicago Press, 1927.

Whitlock, Brand. *Forty Years of It*. New York: Appleton-Century-Crofts, 1925.

Williams, Oliver P., and Charles R. Adrian. *Four Cities*. Philadelphia: University of Pennsylvania Press, 1963.

——————, and Charles Press, eds. *Democracy in Urban America*. Chicago: Rand McNally & Co., 1961.

Wilson, James Q. *Negro Politics*. New York: The Free Press, 1960.

——————. *The Amateur Democrat*. Chicago: University of Chicago Press, 1962.

Wright, William E. *Memphis Politics: A Study in Racial Bloc Voting*. New York: McGraw-Hill Book Co., 1962.

Zink, Howard. *City Bosses in the United States*. Durham, N.C.: Duke University Press, 1930.

Articles and Essays

Adrian, Charles R. "A Typology for Nonpartisan Elections," *Western Political Quarterly*, XII (June 1959), 449–548.

——————. "Leadership and Decision-Making in Manager Cities: A Study of Three Communities," *Public Administration Review*, XVIII (Summer 1958), 208–218.

——————. "Some General Characteristics of Nonpartisan Elections," *American Political Science Review*, XLVI (September 1952), 766–776.

Anton, Thomas. "Power, Pluralism, and Local Politics," *Administrative Science Quarterly*, VII (March 1963), 425–458.

Bachrach, Peter, and Morton Baratz. "The Two Faces of Power," *American Political Science Review*, LVI (September 1962), 947–953.

Bates, Frank G. "Nonpartisan Government," *American Political Science Review*, IX (May 1915), 313–315.

Block, Paul, Jr. "Facing up to the 'Monopoly' Charge," *Nieman Reports*, IX (July 1955), 3–7.

Bogart, Leo. "Newspapers in the Age of Television," *Daedalus*, XCII (Winter 1963), 116–128.

Bowman, Lewis. "Racial Discrimination and Negro Leadership Problems: The Case of 'Northern City,'" *Social Forces*, XLIV (December 1965), 173–186.

Bremner, Robert H. "Civic Revival in Ohio: Samuel M. Jones," *The American Journal of Economics and Sociology*, XIII (January 1949), 151–162.

Calloway, Ernest. "A Reform Period Closes," *Focus Midwest*, III (Nos. 10 and 11 [1965]), 14–15.

Christenson, Reo M. "The Power of the Press: The Case of 'The Toledo Blade,'" *Midwest Journal of Political Science*, III (November 1959), 227–240.

Cutright, Phillips. "Activities of Precinct Committeemen in Partisan and Nonpartisan Communities," *Western Political Quarterly*, XVII (March 1964), 93–108.

D'Antonio, William V., and Eugene C. Erickson. "The Reputational Technique as a Measure of Community Power," *American Sociological Review*, XXVII (June 1962), 362–376.

DeMott, Benjamin. "Party Apolitics," *The American Scholar*, XXXI (Autumn 1962), 595–602.

Downes, Randolph C. "The Toledo Political-Religious Municipal Election of 1913 and the Death of the Independent Party," *Northwest Ohio Quarterly*, XXX (Summer 1958), 137–163.

——————. "Jones and Whitlock and the Promotion of Urban Democracy," *Northwest Ohio Quarterly*, XXVIII (Winter 1955–1956), 26–37.

Duggar, George S. "The Relation of Local Government Structure to Urban Renewal," *Law and Contemporary Problems*, XXVI (1961), 46–69.

Ellis, Ellen D. "National Parties and Local Politics," *American Political Science Review*, XXIX (February 1935), 60–67.

Flinn, Thomas A. "Continuity and Change in Ohio Politics," *Journal of Politics*, XXIV (August 1962), 521–544.

Ford, Harvey S. "Walter Folger Brown," *Northwest Ohio Quarterly*, XXVI (Summer 1954), 200–210.

Form, William H. "Organized Labor's Place in the Community Power Structure," *Industrial and Labor Relations Review*, XII (July 1959), 526–539.

——————, and Warren L. Sauer. "Organized Labor's Image of Community Power Structure," *Social Forces*, XXVIII (May 1960), 331–341.

Freeman, J. Leiper. "Local Party Systems: Theoretical Considerations and a Case Analysis," *American Journal of Sociology*, LXIV (November 1958), 282–289.

Freeman, Linton, *et al.* "Locating Leaders in Local Communities," *American Sociological Review*, XXVIII (October 1963), 791–798.

Gamson, William A. "Rancorous Conflict in Community Politics," *American Sociological Review*, XXXI (February 1966), 71–81.

————. "Reputation and Resources in Community Politics," *American Journal of Sociology*, LXXII (September 1966), 121–131.

Gilbert, Charles E. "National Political Alignments and the Politics of Large Cities," *Political Science Quarterly*, LXXIX (March 1964), 25–51.

————. "Some Aspects of Nonpartisan Elections in Large Cities," *Midwest Journal of Political Science*, VI (November 1962), 345–362.

————, and Christopher Clague. "Electoral Competition and Electoral Systems in Large Cities," *Journal of Politics*, XXIV (May 1962), 323–347.

Goodall, Leonard E. "Reform Politics in the Big City: The Phoenix Experience," *Western Political Quarterly*, XVI (September 1963), 20–22.

Gray, Kenneth E., and David Greenstone. "Organized Labor in City Politics," *Urban Government*, ed. Edward C. Banfield. (New York: The Free Press, 1961), pp. 368–379.

Greenstone, J. David. "Party Pressure on Organized Labor in Three Cities," *The Electoral Process*, ed. M. Kent Jennings and Harmon Zeigler. (Englewood Cliffs, N.J.: Prentice-Hall, 1966), pp. 55–81.

Gregg, James E. "Newspaper Editorial Endorsements and California Elections, 1948–1962," *Journalism Quarterly*, XLII (Autumn 1965), 532–538.

Hart, C. M. M. "Industrial Relations Research and Social Theory," *Canadian Journal of Economics and Political Science*, XV (February 1949), 53–87.

Hawley, Amos. "Community Power and Urban Renewal Success," *American Journal of Sociology*, LXVIII (January 1963), 422–431.

Hays, Samuel P. "The Politics of Reform in Municipal Government in the Progressive Era," *Pacific Northwest Quarterly*, LV (October 1964), 157–169.

Herson, Lawrence J. R. "The Lost World of Municipal Government," *American Political Science Review*, LI (June 1957), 330–345.

Jacob, Herbert. "Initial Recruitment of Elected Officials in the United States: A Model," *Journal of Politics*, XXIV (November 1962), 703–716.

Jennings, M. Kent, and Harmon Zeigler. "Class, Party, and Race in Four Types of Elections: The Case of Atlanta," *Journal of Politics*, XXVIII (June 1966), 391–407.

Jones, Samuel M., III. "Brand Whitlock and the Independent Party," *Northwest Ohio Quarterly*, XXXI (Winter 1959), 94–112.

Kammerer, Gladys. "Role Diversity in City Managers," *Administrative Science Quarterly*, VIII (March 1964), 421–442.

Kaufman, Herbert, and Victor Jones. "The Mystery of Power," *Public Administration Review*, XIV (Summer 1954), 205–212.

Kessel, John H. "Governmental Structure and Political Environment: A Statistical Note about American Cities," *American Political Science Review*, LVI (September 1962), 615–620.

Long, Norton E. "The Corporation, Its Satellites, and the Local Community," *The Corporation in Modern Society*, ed. Edward S. Mason. (Cambridge, Mass.: Harvard University Press, 1959), 202–217.

————. "The Local Community as an Ecology of Games," *American Journal of Sociology*, LXIV (November 1958), 251–261.

Lyons, Louis M. "Chain-Store Journalism," *The Reporter*, XXIII (December 1960), 60–63.

Martin, John Bartlow. "The Town that Tried 'Good Government,'" *Urban Government*, ed. Edward C. Banfield. (New York: The Free Press, 1961), pp. 276–284.

Masters, Nicholas A. "The Politics of Union Endorsement of Candidates in the Detroit Area," *Midwest Journal of Political Science*, I (August 1957), 136–151.

Mayo, Charles G. "The 1961 Mayoralty Election in Los Angeles: The Political Party in a Nonpartisan Election," *Western Political Quarterly*, XVII (June 1964), 325–337.

McKee, James. "Status and Power in the Industrial Community: A Comment on Drucker's Thesis," *American Journal of Sociology*, LVIII (January 1953), 364–370.

McKenna, William J. "The Negro Vote in Philadelphia Elections," *Pennsylvania History*, XXXII (October 1965), 407–415.

Miller, Delbert C. "Decision-Making Cliques in Community Power Structures: A Comparative Study of an American and an English City," *American Journal of Sociology*, LIV (November 1958), 229–310.

————. "The Seattle Business Leader," *Pacific Northwest Business*, XV (February 1956), 5–12.

Morlan, Robert L. "The Unorganized Politics of Minneapolis," *National Municipal Review* (November 1949), pp. 485–490.

Nixon, Raymond B., and Jean Ward. "Trends in Newspaper Ownership," *Journalism Quarterly*, XXXVIII (Winter 1961), 3–12.

Norton, James A. "Referenda Voting in a Metropolitan Area," *Western Political Quarterly*, XVI (March 1963), 195–212.

Olmsted, Donald W. "Organizational Leadership and Social Structure in a Small City," *American Sociological Review*, XIX (June 1954), 273–281.

O'Shea, John. "Newark's Negroes Move toward Power," *Atlantic*, XXVI (November 1965), 90–98.

Otten, Allen L., and Charles B. Seib. "The Minor Masterpiece of Ray C. Bliss," *The Reporter*, XXXIV (February 10, 1966), 35–38.

Pellegrin, Roland J., and Charles Coates. "Absentee-Owned Corporations and Community Power Structure," *American Journal of Sociology*, LI (March 1956), 413–419.

Polsby, Nelson. "The Sociology of Community Power: A Reassessment," *Social Forces*, XXXVII (March 1959), 232–236.

Price, Don K. "The Promotion of the City Manager Plan," *Public Opinion Quarterly*, V (Winter 1941), 563–578.

Price, Hugh Douglas. "Review of *Who Governs?*", *Yale Law Review*, LXXI (July 1962), 1589–1596.

Rodalbaugh, James H. "Samuel Jones, Evangel of Equality," *Quarterly Bulletin of the Historical Society of Northwest Ohio*, XXVIII (Winter 1943), 10–18.

Rossi, Peter H. "Community Decision-Making, *"Administrative Science Quarterly*, I (March 1957), 415–443.

Salisbury, Robert H. "Dateline: St. Louis," *Focus Midwest*, III (Nos. 10 and 12), 17.

————. "St. Louis Politics: Relationships Among Interests, Parties, and Governmental Structure," *Western Political Quarterly*, XIII (June 1960), 498–507.

————. "Urban Politics: The New Convergence of Power," *Journal of Politics*, XXVI (November 1964), 775–797.

————, and Gordon Black. "Class and Party in Partisan and Nonpartisan Elections: The Case of Des Moines," *American Political Science Review*, LVII (September 1963), 584–592.

Schulze, Robert. "The Bifurcation of Power in a Satellite City," *Community Political Systems*, ed. Morris Janowitz. (New York: The Free Press, 1961), pp. 19–81.

Seligman, Lester. "Political Recruitment and Party Structure," *American Political Science Review*, LV (March 1961), 77–86.

Sharpe, Carleton F. "Teamwork in Urban Renewal," *Public Management*, XLIV (September 1962), 198–202.

Sheppard, Harold L., and Nicholas A. Masters. "The Political Attitudes and Preferences of Union Members: The Case of the Detroit Auto Workers," *American Political Science Review*, LIII (June 1959), 440–443.

Sherbenou, Edgar L. "Class, Participation, and the Council-Manager Plan," *Public Administration Review*, XXI (Summer 1961), 131–135.

Smith, Lincoln. "Political Leadership in a New England Community," *Review of Politics*, XVII (July 1955), 392–409.

Snowiss, Leo M. "Congressional Recruitment and Representation," *American Political Science Review*, LX (September 1966), 627–640.

Streck, Phillip (pseud.). "The New Negro and A. J. Cervantes," *Focus Midwest*, III (Nos. 10 and 12), 11–13.

Walker, Jack L. "Protest and Negotiation: A Case Study of Negro Leadership in Atlanta, Georgia," *Midwest Journal of Political Science*, VII (May 1964), 99–124.

Whitlock, Brand. "As to Grafters," *Cosmopolitan*, XLIX (July 1910), 142–145.

Williams, Oliver P., and Charles R. Adrian. "The Insulation of Local Politics under the Nonpartisan Ballot," *American Political Science Review*, LIII (December 1959), 1052–1063.

Wilson, James Q. "The Flamboyant Mr. Powell," *Commentary*, XLI (January 1966), 31–36.

————. "The Strategy of Protest: Problems of Negro Civic Action," *Journal of Conflict Resolution* (September 1961), pp. 291–303.

————. "Two Negro Politicians: An Interpretation," *Midwest Journal of Political Science*, IV (November 1960), 346–369.

——————, and Edward C. Banfield. "Public-Regardingness as a Value Premise in Voting Behavior," *American Political Science Review,* LVIII (December 1964), 876–888.

Wolfinger, Raymond. "Reputation and Reality in the Study of Community Power," *American Sociological Review,* XXV (October 1960), 636–644.

——————. "Some Consequences of Ethnic Politics," *The Electoral Process,* ed. M. Kent Jennings and Harmon Zeigler. (Englewood Cliffs, N.J.: Prentice-Hall, 1966), pp. 42–55.

——————. "The Development and Persistence of Ethnic Voting," *American Political Science Review,* LIX (December 1965), 896–909.

Reports, Pamphlets, and Unpublished Material

Alford, Robert R. "Governmental Units Analysis." Codes for IBM Decks. Survey of Governmental, Economic, and Social Characteristics of American Cities. 1965. (Mimeographed.)

Baisden, Richard. "Labor Unions in Los Angeles Politics." Unpublished Ph.D. dissertation, University of Chicago, 1958.

Banfield, Edward C., and Martha Derthick. *A Report on Politics in Boston.* Cambridge: Joint Center for Urban Studies of the Massachusetts Institute of Technology and Harvard University, 1960. (Mimeographed.)

Department of Political Science, University of Toledo. *The Background of City Government and Politics in Toledo.* Toledo, Ohio: University of Toledo, 1955. (Mimeographed.)

Emch, Donovan. "The City Manager Government of Toledo, Ohio." Unpublished manuscript prepared for the Committee on Public Administration, Social Science Research Council, 1938.

Ford, Harvey S. "The Life and Times of Golden Rule Jones." Unpublished Ph.D. dissertation, University of Michigan, 1953.

Gray, Kenneth E. *A Report on Politics in Kansas City, Missouri.* Cambridge, Mass.: Joint Center for Urban Studies, 1959.

Greenstone, David. *A Report on the Politics of Detroit.* Cambridge, Mass.: Joint Center for Urban Studies, 1960.

Jones, Samuel M. *Annual Statement of the Finances of Toledo Together with the Mayor's Message for the Year Ending April 1, 1900.* Toledo, Ohio: City of Toledo Publication, 1900.

National Council of Churches. *Churches and Church Membership in the United States: An Enumeration and Analysis by Counties, States, and Regions.* Washington, D.C.: National Council of Churches, 1957.

National Municipal League. *A Guide for Charter Commissions.* New York: National Municipal League, 3rd ed., 1957.

—————. *Getting the National Parties out of Municipal Elections.* New York: National Municipal League, 1953.

Rossi, Peter H. *Industry and Community,* Report No. 64. Chicago: National Opinion Research Center, 1957.

Taft, William Howard. "The 'Toledo Blade': Its First One-Hundred Years, 1835–1935." Unpublished Ph.D. dissertation, Western Reserve University, 1950.

Toledo Area Chamber of Commerce. *Directory of Manufacturers in the Toledo Area.* Toledo, Ohio: Toledo Area Chamber of Commerce, 1964.

—————. *This Is Toledo.* Toledo, Ohio: Toledo Area Chamber of Commerce, 1964.

Toledo Council of Social Agencies. *Report of Urban Planning Committee: The Older City Area.* Toledo, Ohio: Toledo Council of Social Agencies, 1963.

Toledo-Lucas County Port Authority. *Port Newsletter, March–April 1965.* Toledo, Ohio: Toledo-Lucas County Port Authority, 1965.

United States Bureau of the Census. *U.S. Censuses of Population and Housing: 1960, Final Report PHC (1)–158.* Washington, D.C.: U.S. Bureau of the Census, 1960.

U.S. Housing and Home Finance Agency. Urban Renewal Administration, *Urban Renewal Project Directory.* Washington, D.C.: March 31, 1965.

Newspapers

Team and Wheel.

The Blade.

The Bronze Raven.

The New York Times.

The Times (Toledo).

Toledo City Journal.

Toledo Municipal News.

Toledo Union Journal.

INDEX